Cruelty to Animals

The Moral Debt

Les Brown

formerly Professor of Education
University of New South Wales

MACMILLAN
PRESS

First published 1988

Published by
THE MACMILLAN PRESS LTD
Houndmills, Basingstoke, Hampshire RG21 2XS
and London
Companies and representatives
throughout the world

Printed in Hong Kong

British Library Cataloguing in Publication Data
Brown, Les
Cruelty to animals: the moral debt.
1. Animals, Treatment of
I. Title
179'.3   HV4708
ISBN 0–333–45806–0 ✓
ISBN 0–333–45807–9 Pbk

PAN

A significant part of the Greek vision was of the shepherd-god Pan, befriender and protector of animals. Implicit in this vision was the need for a moral transformation of human attitudes towards animals, from cruelty and unconcern to compassion and care, informed by an understanding of man – with all his presumption – as part of the animal world. Pan was himself half human, half animal.

Contents

Preface

The general purpose of this book is to expose and explain unfavourable attitudes to animals from as detached a moral standpoint as possible; to help others in a sense to step outside their humanness, to assume a degree of impartiality that is not typical of humans. Practical morality will not be strengthened by moralising, especially by denouncing *others* for acts of cruelty. For we are all guilty, from the boy mischievously pulling wings from flies or tying crackers to a dog's tail, to the most mature adult who closes his eyes and sums it all up with the judgement, 'What can you expect? People have always been cruel to animals.' If practical morality requires action, it must be action which stems first from understanding, and second from a moral impulse to improve the situation as we find it. The assumption of improvability is fundamental.

Thus we begin with evidence of cruelty to animals, so that the facts leap forth as inescapable, boldly confronting the sympathetic and the unsympathetic alike, the indifferent as well as the thoughtlessly heartless. Then in Chapter 2 we block the route of the would-be evader still further by bringing these facts into conjunction with an understanding of the meaning of morality and of moral principles, and of how it is that vertebrate animals generally and mammals in particular form part of our moral world. Chapter 3 strengthens the moral case by showing that animals do not need to be like humans to be considered moral objects, that the next important step is to understand their natures *as* animals and to give them a moral respect for what they are. Chapter 4 puts our impartiality to the test more than any other, for who of us can totally and willingly give up the benefits from animal experimentation, including immense relief from as well as prevention of suffering, for humans as well as for animals? To help overcome the difficulty and as an explanatory tool to subdue the almost general propensity to see animal life through the refracted and exalted eyes of humanity, there is an imaginative appeal to ideal theory, to the perspective of a totally uninvolved being who views the habitation of the earth externally. Partiality is the great handicap from which we

ix

suffer, along with presumption, and the central theme of this book is the limited human capacity for impartiality in giving consideration to the interests of animals. As we see in Chapter 5, education too is needed, one of whose many possible avenues is an understanding of the law; while recent legislation on cruelty to animals, with its increasing specificity in some states, is a response to powerful human inclinations towards evasiveness.

The fact that we too are animals is common knowledge in our times, and is therefore assumed to need no explanation: the term 'animals' implies 'other animals'. Our main focus is on the sentience of vertebrates and the wider interests of mammals. There are nonetheless linguistic confusions or vaguenesses in some other aspects of the study, so that certain expressions call for clarification, such as 'cruelty', 'pain', 'distress' and so forth. First 'pain': some philosophers (under the influence of utilitarians) use the term to apply to all suffering; its opposite is 'pleasure'. To physiologists sometimes 'distress' is the inclusive term, with pain and psychological stress included under it. Given these terminological differences it has been considered less ambiguous to remain closer to ordinary language than to technical distinctions. 'Pain' is used to refer to the sensation derived from the physical nerve endings which transmit messages to the brain; in that sense it is 'physical', with a common capacity in all vertebrate animals. 'Distress' is used to refer to psychological suffering: fear, anxiety or conflict. Distinctions between 'distress' and 'stress' tend to be arbitrary, though at times 'stress' is used to apply rather to milder forms of anxiety, as when an animal is faced with a sudden increase in numbers of its kind, without an opportunity to relate to them in a hierarchical order to which it is accustomed. Where there is still likely to be ambiguity, 'suffering' is used, for 'pain', 'distress' and 'stress' are all included within it, and from the standpoint of practical morality it is animal *suffering* that is relevant, whatever form it takes.

'Cruelty' is ambiguous chiefly when ordinary language and legal interpretations are confused. While there is much in common between the two, the law of the UK, for instance, leaves many gaps in its stipulations which ordinary language interpretations broadly cover. While there are penalties in law for brutally treating a dog, such as striking it repeatedly with a heavy weapon, onlookers who find delight in the spectacle of suffering as the dog jumps and yelps are not considered cruel in law. It would be considered cruel in the ordinary language sense to allow a sheep that has been burnt severely in a bushfire to continue to suffer rather than ending its suffering swiftly by shooting it, but that omission is not cruel in law. A hunter who shoots a deer, injuring it but not killing it, is not considered cruel in law; nor is a farm slaughterer whose lack of skill causes prolonged suffering, or who uses methods which themselves exacerbate the suffering. A person who knowingly causes an animal to suffer fear or anxiety is cruel in the ordinary language sense, but not in law. An act of cruelty is one knowingly committed (that is, with awareness of the guilt involved) or is a clear case, based on factual evidence, of an omission to act when an appropriate act would have prevented an animal's suffering. Understandably the emphasis in law is on acts which '*cause* unnecessary suffering': for example, 'cruelly ill-treating an animal' in various ways stipulated in the *Protection of Animals Act 1911*, such as overloading horses (c.27, s.1). But the same Act also covers *protection* of animals, and a person is cruel in law, and has committed an offence under this Act, 'if he shall have failed to exercise reasonable care and supervision in respect of the protection of the animal therefrom' (s.1(2)). Ordinary language senses of cruelty also include omissions to act, amounting to indifference to animal suffering.

To avoid further confusion and misunderstanding of the law it must be explained that the abbreviation 'UK' is used for England and Wales, Scotland and Northern Ireland in ways which need qualification. Legislation emanating from West-minster sometimes does not apply to Scotland or Ireland without (usually minor) modifications which are given in Halsbury's *Statutes of England* or the previously published *Public Acts*; in a relatively few cases the legislation does not apply beyond England and Wales. Since it was enacted before the separation of Northern Ireland, the *Protection of Animals Act 1911* was relevant to Ireland, with certain modifications (s.17); but Scotland legislated its own separate Act in 1912. Other variations are given in the notes to Chapter 5 (see notes 35 and 37). These do not affect in any significant way the generalisa-tions referring to 'the UK', which at times would be equally inaccurate if England alone were mentioned.

The foregoing difficulties refer to ambiguities and disagreements in terminology. There are other sources of muddle-headedness which lie in our own natures, simply in the way we perceive animals. The tendency is to see animals not as they are in nature, but as we *want* to see them for our own advantage, notably as objects of use to us. To see them as closely as humanly possible to what they are is not only to have relevant knowledge of their animal characters, but also to understand the bias of our perceptions: to recognise, that is, that often we are not viewing them *impartially*. As an illustration, in the last decade capuchin monkeys have been trained to serve the needs of quadriplegics. By means of a laser pointer held in the handicapped person's mouth, the animal is directed to turn lights off and on, close or open doors, bring food, snacks or drinks, bring books, even to insert an audio tape into a cassette player. Leaving aside the facts that the animals have all their teeth drawn for safety and are given electric shocks if they do not perform as expected, those with compassion for quadriplegics see them as a great boon. Those with compassion for animals as well, and with more impartiality, see them as obedient merely for the sake of survival, for the monkeys depend on 'rewards' of food. As conditioned slaves, deprived of the company of others of their kind, they are degraded to mechanical operators or living robots. In time that is seen as their nature: in some perceptions there is nothing more to them than that. Those with higher impartiality still may change the roles, imagining a situation of a human, instead of a monkey, obliged to live out his life as a slave to another human, performing unvaried menial tasks for him in return for minimal sustenance. How is the slave seen by the tyrant and by unperceptive spectators? Again, as being able to do nothing else: as a creature who does only as directed, without thoughts of his own, without imagination, sensitivity or emotions, degraded by despotic self-interest. So it is that from the standpoint of practical morality self-deception leads to false perceptions, with a trail of rationalisations and fundamental misunderstandings of animals. Humans too are severely limited. Perhaps it was an advantage to Pan to be half animal.

The philosopher's normal approach is an attempt at non-involvement, exercising the highest degree of impartiality of which he is capable. But beyond rational clarification lies an even more important field where decisions have to be taken on moral action, sometimes on behalf of entire societies. Philosophers cannot presume to be the chosen ones for this most responsible of all functions in the state, though that was Plato's solution. It is still his fundamental thought which leads to the suggestion with which the book ends.

L.M.B.

Acknowledgements

The following organisations have been generous in their response to requests for information on local activities: the Royal Society for the Prevention of Cruelty to Animals, Horsham, West Sussex; Compassion in World Farming, Hampshire; British Union for the Abolition of Vivisection, Islington, London; the American Anti-Vivisection Society, Jenkintown, Pa; Scientists Center for Animal Welfare, Bethesda, Md; the National Anti-Vivisection Society, Chicago; the American Fund for Alternatives to Animal Research, New York; Psychologists for the Ethical Treatment of Animals (through Dr Kenneth J. Shapiro); the Animal Protection Institute of America, Sacramento, Ca; the Animal Welfare Institute, Washington, DC; People for the Ethical Treatment of Animals, Washington, DC; the Humane Society of the United States, Washington, DC; Society for Animal Protective Legislation, Washington, DC; International Society for Animal Rights, Inc., Clarks Summit, Pa; Friends of Animals, Neptune, NJ; Beauty without Cruelty, New York.

Selected reports of these organisations have been invaluable for up-to-date information, and so too have been some of the collected data on relevant matters such as recent statutes, current bills and research. Biases have been taken into account and the accuracy of the documentation confirmed.

1 Cruelty: Historical and Contemporary

INTRODUCTORY

In this chapter the facts will serve tacitly as both commentary and explanation. Neither expressions of horror nor of repugnance are needed to give weight to the facts, and there is no need for moralistic reprobation. Instead it is enough initially for reader reaction to remain individual, everyone imposing his own pauses as the need arises so that what is presented has an opportunity to work on the mind: at times to evoke graphic images, at others to engage reflection and self-criticism, in order to modify any vague or inaccurate impressions by means of a stronger, clearer and more resolute organisation. The first moral probings at the end of the chapter may serve as a sensitivity test for some, but only for some; for others they may be largely superfluous.

The instances that follow are not selected from abnormal times. They are not products of wars or of traumatic social upheavals of any kind. They are selected from the actions of persons who, though they may have been excited or frustrated in some situations, were not as far as we know pathological killers or torturers, or handicapped intellectually, but individuals going about their lives in a normal way, freely making their own decisions on their actions. In a few cases, such as the first, the actions may have been considered beyond the pale by magistrates even for their times, but in fact the culprits were given a mild penalty. Most of the other cases were in no way abnormal in either historical or contemporary context. Further, they are reports of *known* instances: what happened in secret places, or under cover of spontaneous shame or guilt, may in some cases have been worse.

Does anyone mistake the face of cruelty in these preliminary unsorted instances? Towards the end of the eighteenth century, when Australia was beginning two hundred years of history and America had recently won its independence, a small number of

1

sheep owned by a butcher in Manchester had their feet cut off:
they were then driven along a street on the stumps of their legs.[1]
In the first half of the last century calves were sometimes bled,
and killed without stunning, with one end of an iron rod driven
from beneath the tail until it emerged at the other end through
the nose.[2] At this stage some were still conscious. In the hunt, on
occasion a fox or a stag had one leg cut off and was forced to
continue the sport on the remaining three.[3] In both England
and the United States the tongues of horses have been torn out
by frustrated drivers; indeed in England a tongue was torn out
with the left hand, while with the right the horse was beaten
mercilessly over the head for ten minutes longer, the driver
using the handle of his whip.[4] Another driver burnt his horse's
belly with a fire lit under it, annoyed with the horse for failing to
pull a loaded cart out of the mud.[5] Skinning cats or badgers alive,
cutting otters into slices, roasting live hares over slow kitchen
fires – these were not uncommon practices in the first half of the
last century.[6]

Today animals are still killed in the gin trap (so called in the
UK, but outlawed there) or steel-jaw leghold trap (as it is called
in the USA). The vice-like grip of the steel-jaw trap (as we shall
call it) leaves the animal to gnaw off a limb as the only means of
escape.[7] Young seals are still clubbed to death, sometimes within
sight of their mothers. Karakul lambs may be skinned alive, also
within sight of their mothers.[8] Shortly after World War II
millions of rabbits were destroyed by the virus myxomatosis,
ending their days often blinded, with tumours causing gross
malformations of the head, unable to eat and helpless prey to
predators. More recently scientists have contrived ways of
clamping live rabbits in position for two or three days while they
force chemicals into their eyes or onto their skins, knowing that
if they suffer painful irritations, as they sometimes do, and even
blindness, the substances will be unsuitable for human use (such
as for cosmetics, or for eye or skin complaints). In remote
villages in the Philippines live pigs are prepared for festivals with
stakes driven into their lungs and rotated. The animals scream
in pain until they die, perhaps half an hour later.[9] Animals are
used in war to terrorise an enemy. The Mau Mau in Kenya cut
out the entrails of cows owned by the British settlers and
suspended disembowelled cats above their doors.

These are all *strong* examples, but not unusual. There are

certainly milder forms of cruelty, and to differentiate each of these from acts that are not cruel at all a working definition of 'cruelty' is needed. 'Cruelty' will be applied to unnecessary suffering knowingly inflicted on a sentient being (animal or human), though as will become evident in Chapter 4 what is to count as 'necessary' suffering in experimental situations is a matter of some contention. The suffering may be a sensation of pain induced by physical means, or it may be distress resulting from acts of enforced confinement, for instance, or of maternal deprivation. Cruelty to animals has both positive and negative forms, the first referring to an act committed against an animal, the second to omission or failure to act, as in neglecting to provide adequate food, water or shelter. To recognise cruelty it is not necessary to grade the suffering according to principles of intensity or duration. There are obviously on the one hand borderline cases, and on the other cases so severe that they amount to *torture*. An animal suffers regardless of whether it is subjected to physical pain or to distress.[10] Animal sentience will be explained in Chapter 2, and also in Chapter 4 in connection with pain in experimental animals.

To demonstrate the continuity of cruelty to animals, the following pages give further instances from historical situations in the nineteenth century, and then from contemporary situations, using the end of the nineteenth century as an arbitrary division between the two.

HISTORICAL PERSPECTIVES

Acts of cruelty are here considered in the following contexts: sports and amusements; slaughtering for food; killing for fashion; animals for commercial gain; and cruelty from belief or habitual practices, where the impact of superstitions, religious beliefs and unexamined ways of life have contributed to suffering. Islands of compassion are noted before the general evidence is briefly reviewed.

Sports and amusements

Domestic birds such as fowls, turkeys and pigeons have been used frequently in competitive games, and for centuries fighting cocks were kept, usually associated with gambling. One of the earliest sports was to tie a fowl to a post or tree and see who could kill it by throwing sticks at it from a prescribed distance. This game was kept going for as long as possible by various means, such as greasing the feathers so that some of the sticks would glance off.[11] Cockfighting in the UK revived in popularity under the Tudors. In the USA it was widespread in the first half of the nineteenth century and practised in many remote areas subsequently.[12] Much the same occurred in the UK, with Devonshire and Cheshire named as areas of illegal cockfighting towards the end of the century. There 'the efforts of the police are severely taxed to circumvent offenders', it was said, 'who are cunning as well as cruel'.[13]

The baiting of animals by dogs – usually bears, bulls or badgers – was both more brutal and more bloody, and commensurably, it seemed, more enjoyable. English bulldogs proved most suitable for worrying and baiting chained bulls or bears. It was recommended in one publication that the lower jaw of a badger should be sawn off so that the younger dogs could bait it without being injured or discouraged.[14] In bull-baiting the main source of amusement was the spectacle of the battle between bulldog and bull, in which the bull tried to toss the dog as the dog tried to bite its nose. If the dog succeeded in gripping its teeth into the soft flesh of the bull's nose and hanging on, it was deemed to have 'pinned the bull' and to have won the engagement.[15] Bears and badgers were even more vulnerable and often suffered more. Bear-*beating* (in addition to bear-*baiting*) was popular in Tudor times, when bear gardens were common. Between episodes of bear-baiting ladies were said to have found great entertainment in seeing the bears laid upon with sticks.[16] Bears continued to suffer in the UK until the sport was outlawed in 1835. In the USA it was reported to be very common in some centres much later.[17] In badger-baiting spectators found it amusing to see the badger retreat into a hole dug especially for the encounter, with bulldogs competing to see which one of them could bring the badger out. Eventually, whichever dog and gambler won, the badger was set upon by all the dogs and killed. Towards the end of the century in the USA one traveller reported a fight between dogs and a badger which continued for two hours before the badger was killed *with clubs*. Over that time it had fought off 'successive relays of dogs'.[18]

Endless variations of cruelty were contrived in the fox hunt, using hounds working in packs. The odds against the fox were overwhelming. Exhausted, and in great distress, it was usually caught by the hounds and killed. Wild animals in captivity were exhibited in a variety of travelling shows. Partly to excite the spectators, lion tamers used instruments which threatened pain or injury: steel whips, pitchforks and hot irons. Animal cages were cramped and unclean, food and water often inadequate. Towards the end of the last century one social critic wrote of a polar bear that was being taken through Europe for exhibition in a caravan: 'He is kept in a cage in which he cannot turn; he has a pan of water two inches deep, and a few ounces of bread'.[19]

Slaughtering for food

In 1829 calves were described as bundled into carts with their legs tied together, before they were muzzled to stifle their moans and taken to an underground slaughterhouse. There they were slowly bled to produce white veal, sometimes killed first with a blow to the head, but sometimes bled before killing.[20] Later in the century they were often killed by knife alone, as were sheep and pigs. Pigs were often found difficult to kill as they were not easily stunned, and consciousness could last for three or four minutes of bleeding as they faced 'a mental terror of death'.[21]

At the turn of the twentieth century a parliamentary committee was set up to report on the humane slaughtering of animals. From the minutes of the evidence it is clear that the current practices were those which had pertained also in the previous century and before. To a question asked of one witness, 'Do you give two blows for every animal?' the answer was, 'With English cattle I have never seen them killed with one blow. I have always seen them felled first with a blow on the poll and afterwards struck on the forehead.' To the question, 'Do you find that cattle particularly show signs of fear on being taken into the slaughterhouse either from the smell or sight of blood?' the answer came, 'Some do; bulls do occasionally, but others do not; . . . some are very nervous.' Other witnesses testified to animals being terrified by the smell of blood.[22]

Nineteenth-century accounts show that methods of slaughtering varied from place to place, and the extent of animal suffering was related to local slaughtering practices, the skill of the slaughterer and whether the killing was on a farmer's private property or on a butcher's premises. In 1878 it was complained that what really occurred in slaughterhouses was extremely difficult to ascertain, because master butchers regarded their premises as private property, not open to inspection.[23] Pigs were described variously as killed by stunning, followed by cutting the throat, and in some country areas as by the knife only; in London they were stunned, then immediately 'stuck', so dying before consciousness returned. Sheep were placed on their sides, stuck in the neck, and generally cut to break the spine between vertebral bones. Ritual killing of oxen by Jews was by cutting the throat.

The killing of sheep and pigs on farmsteads and in small towns was usually by the knife only. Pigs squealed for sometimes five to ten minutes before falling. Sheep died rather more quickly, but again raced about the yard for two or three minutes before dropping. The skill of the slaughterer was vital when sheep were killed using the method of severing the spinal chord between the vertebral bones of the neck, thereby cutting off sensation in the brain after the throat had been cut. One account stated that an expert requires only *twenty to thirty seconds* to perform this operation, whereas 'a bungler or a young hand requires two or three minutes'. In such circumstances of inexperience the killer cut the sheep's throat, and then attempted to break the neck of the sheep by exerting pressure with his knee.[24]

The poleaxe was the common instrument used by butchers in killing oxen.[25] The poleaxe with its heavy cutting head was wielded against the head of the ox, using a shaft about four feet long. Skill was needed, and many a mishit left the animal painfully injured. In the hands of a bungler it was described as a 'terrible instrument of torture. We have seen a countryman of enormous strength strike a poor bullock thirteen times with it, the last blow being the only effective one ... The twelve preceding blows caused the poor beast to moan with indescribable agony.'

Killing for fashion

In the last century millions of animals perished for their furs in the steel-jaw trap. A hierarchy of fashion was established to strengthen class divisions. Leopard skins from Africa were made into garments or expensive rugs for floors. Tiger skins from India made fashionable trophies. Animals snared in Africa by methods more primitive than the steel-jaw trap were often left to perish in the sun.

For a time towards the end of the last century feathers were even more fashionable than furs. Sometimes the two were worn together, when a lady used an aigrette of osprey feathers as well as a jacket lined with astrakhan fur taken from an unborn lamb with the appealing curl and kink of its fleece. Osprey feathers were sometimes seen as for princesses; ladies of society were quick to follow their example. Ordinary people had to be content with swallows and warblers, and the working classes correspondingly with dyed sparrows and finches.[26] Birds were sold by their thousands in London slums, and thousands were suffocated as they were crammed into small boxes or crates.[27]

Animals for gain

Killing of animals and birds for fashion was only one way of profiting by them. Horse traders had no scruples. A lame horse might give a prospective buyer the impression that it had a high-stepping gait, when in fact its feet were made tender by beans that had been put under its shoes.[28] By 1882 the Society for the Prevention of Cruelty to Animals in New York was able to exhibit, among the stock of cruel inventions, 'sets of leather burrs, filled with tacks, to be attached to the bits, the points of the tacks being turned inward to prick the horses' mouths when the reins were drawn'. That was another way to make horses appear spirited.[29] In the UK in the middle of the century those who traded in stolen horses sometimes disposed of them in knackers' yards. A knacker's method of dealing with an impending police search for a missing horse was to break the animal's leg. He could then claim that it had been taken to his yard to be killed.[30]

The suffering of horses as beasts of burden in the UK and the USA in the last century and before is well documented. Carts and wagons were frequently overloaded. It was not unusual for horses to be driven to the point of exhaustion, goaded by desperate drivers. Flesh wounds were a daily sight, inflicted by whips with gutta-percha thongs or with wire ends, or even by bludgeons and heavy sticks.[31] The cheapest horses were used for night cabs in London, since the business was not lucrative. Horses which had been condemned as suitable only for the knackery were sometimes sold by knackers to do this menial cab work, not unusually dropping dead at their work.[32] In the USA wire whips and twisted strands of cable wire were sometimes used as goads, capable of cutting into the flesh. One exhibit by the SPCA in New York in 1882 was a bit two inches in diameter which was fixed to a long iron rod in such a way as to yoke the horse, preventing it from moving its head up or down; other exhibits were clubs, hammers, axes and knives used by drivers to 'punish' their horses.[33]

In 1878 the RSPCA explained that there was much abuse of horses, ponies and donkeys in places away from public view – places such as canal banks and tow paths closed to all except those on business. Deep suspicions were expressed about cruelty to horses and other animals used in mines. About 200 000 of them spent their lives underground once they had descended. Some were injured in low cuttings or galled under harness.[34]

Dogs were used as draught animals until about the middle of the last century. In compensation for their relative disadvantage in strength, they were cheaper than horses to keep alive. Records show that they were often ill-fed and forced to pull loads much in excess of their capacities. They too were whipped incessantly and sometimes dropped from exhaustion.[35] Earlier in the century, as well as in the eighteenth century, dogs were used in kitchens as turnspits. The wheel was by a fireside, so that in summer they toiled under continually oppressive conditions. Sometimes, if whipping or beating was unsuccessful, a hot coal was put into the wheel to stimulate activity, so it was said in 1822, and as a 'method of teaching them originally their business'.[36]

Indifference to animal suffering had a variety of expressions. From time to time the RSPCA's attention was drawn to the exposure of newly-shorn sheep to bitterly cold weather, without any attempt to cover them.[37] Animals regarded as pests or suspected predators on sheep or cattle were often left to die in steel-jaw traps which were inspected most irregularly. Such was the fate of dingoes in Australia.[38]

Ignorance, superstitions, habitual practices

In the nineteenth century owls were still killed in hundreds in farmstead barns in the UK without thought of their value to the farmer. In pre-Elizabethan times they had been feared as messengers of death, with their eerie nocturnal hoots or hisses, shrieks or screams – a tradition to which Shakespeare referred more than once. When Macbeth announced to Lady Macbeth that he 'had done the deed' in murdering Duncan she replied that she had 'heard the owl scream' (II. ii. 17) with a foreboding of the act:

> It was the owl that shriek'd, the fatal bellman,
> Which gives the stern'st good-night.
>
> (II. ii. 3–4)

It was the combination of ignorance and superstition which led to the religious attribution of magical powers or evil spirits to particular animals, along with the conviction that if they were not killed, or severely punished, they might bring disaster.[39]

For over six centuries animals' evil spirits were acknowledged by the Roman Catholic Church as it brought animals to trial in ecclesiastical or lay courts. Animals could be hanged, beheaded or executed in other ways. A cow was executed in France as late as 1740. Sometimes the punishment was to be beaten to death.[40]

In anti-popery demonstrations in the seventeenth and eighteenth centuries a popular amusement was to put cats inside an effigy of the Pope, then to set it on fire. The suffering animals gave out piercing cries that appeared to come from the Pope's mouth.[41]

In the early nineteenth century so much was the 'unceasing sound of the lash' heard in London streets and elsewhere that it became a social norm to whip animals, if not in punishment for failing to meet every expectation, at least with some contempt for their inferior status. Pigs were whipped to death without reason. The cropping of dogs' ears caused suffering for weeks. Dogs could be kept chained for life without adequate food or exercise.[42]

Islands of compassion

Like cruelty, compassion has been historically continuous. But unlike cruelty, it has lacked social diffusion. In the early fifth century BC Empedocles taught the kinship of all living things. Pythagoras taught not only the immortality of the soul but also its transmigration into various animal bodies, views which had become tenable within the wider and more general belief in the

kinship of all living things.[43] Though denying souls to animals,
leaders of the Christian Church in the UK sometimes taught and
practised humanity to animals.

Humphry Primatt wrote *A Dissertation on the Duty of Mercy and
Sin of Cruelty to Brute Animals* in 1776. This work is significant as
the first in English devoted entirely to humanity towards
animals, for the emphasis it placed on animal suffering, and
through that for its probable influence four years later on
Jeremy Bentham.[44] Like Pythagoras, Primatt saw a unity in all
life: all creatures – man included – as 'a wheel in the great
machinery of nature' (p. 3). He gave a physiological reason for
his assertion that 'a brute is an animal no less sensible of pain
than a man' (p. 10). He was sensitive to man's presumption, his
pride in 'the superior powers of the mind' (p. 14), the 'fond
conceit of our own dignity and merit' that makes it appear
absurd for us even to compare the brutes with ourselves.
Strongly didactic, Primatt attacked the brutality of 'sportive
cruelty' which he found practised daily by people of all classes,
including persons otherwise 'truly amiable and respectable'
(p. 15). Contrasting with these cruelties were the 'shocking
barbarities, . . . the brutal rage, exercised by the most worthless
of men, without controul of law', and the 'many barbarous
practices' which men in high public positions 'connived at' if they
did not countenance them (ibid.). To him members of the
'higher orders' of society who did nothing to change the
situation of widespread cruelty to animals were as reprehensible
as the 'lower orders' who were 'cruel from mere insensibility'. He
pointed trenchantly to butchers and drovers as 'an inhuman set;
cattle are slaughtered with the greatest barbarity'.

Anticipating Jeremy Bentham's 'the question is not, Can they
reason: nor, Can they talk? But, Can they *suffer*?'[45] Primatt had
already written: 'in the case of cruelty to any of our own kind, the
oppressed has a tongue that can plead his own cause, and a
finger to point out the aggressor' (p. 18). But suffering brutes,
unable to speak for themselves, have no such redress in the
courts (p. 19). He particularised some of the sports which gave
pleasure to the common people, such as cockfighting with
artificial spurs; the distress of deer and hare, flying for hours
until 'sinking from despair', only to be 'devoured by their
merciless pursuers'; the cruelty of men overworking animals in
their service (p. 80).

Animal suffering was exposed further by Thomas Young in *An Essay on Humanity to Animals*. Practices abhorrent to him included throwing at cocks, cutting live fish into pieces for frying (the 'crimping' of fish) and nailing fowls by their feet to cram them in for the market.[46]

Review of historical evidence

It was clear at least to a compassionate few that one source of cruelty to animals was *thoughtlessness*, a simple failure of imagination and reason to weigh the consequences of actions. Another was seen as *ignorance*, particularly ignorance of the nature of animals. It was argued that in the eighteenth century children were punished regularly because it seemed the only way to train them. So it was claimed to be with workhorses. Their drivers saw punishment as the only way to get them to do what was expected of them. A third source of cruelty was held to be *avarice*, making money at the expense of the animals, especially horses, which were overworked, underfed and tortured in the process. Such was a summing-up of the position in 1874.[47]

Historical analysis for its own sake is not relevant to this study. It is sufficient to note that cruelty is given continuity into our own times partly by common social conditions, such as inequalities in educational opportunity, poverty and underprivilege, and even fashions in furs, which are related to social distinctions or pretentions.

CONTEMPORARY PERSPECTIVES

Continuities are evident in some of our sports and amusements, such as the recreational hunt. We still kill animals for food, and animal distress remains in our slaughtering practices. Trapping animals for furs continues, with techniques and methods hardly changed at all. There are twentieth-century forms of cruelty exceeding the thoughtlessness of our forefathers, while in avarice and commercial competitiveness we have become more efficient. The grossest cruelties to animals cannot be held to be representative now, any more than they were in the eighteenth and nineteenth centuries; but they do occur. Matching the Manchester incident, a man has been prosecuted recently for building a bonfire and throwing his own dog into the flames. He too was given a light penalty.[48]

Sports and amusements

Cockfighting and dogfighting continue even in countries which have banned them.[49] In other countries, as in parts of Asia, cockfighting is both culturally and legally confirmed. In some countries, such as Spain and parts of Latin America, bullfighting continues unabated.[50]

A little more than a decade ago the rodeo was described as America's 'distinctive contribution to the harassment of large domestic animals' and 'the fastest growing form of recreational abuse' in the country.[51] Horses, bulls, steers and calves are all subjected to distress and physical injury. Horses may suffer abrasions while rearing in the chute before entering the arena, or muscle and tendon injuries while bucking, or spur injuries from their riders. While waiting nervously in the chute they are usually shocked with an electric prod. When they surge into the arena the flank strap which is tightened around the sensitive groin area causes further writhing and bucking: the animal's suffering is misunderstood as spirit, with a fair contest of wills. In steer roping the animal is tripped and thrown violently to the ground. Then, when sometimes unconscious and seriously bruised, three of its legs are quickly tied. The cruelty of calf roping leads to common injuries to larynx and trachea when the lasso jerks tightly around the calf's throat. The rider pulls his horse up suddenly, flinging the calf to the ground, when again three legs are quickly tied. There are variations, such as the rider leaping from a horse, twisting the calf's neck and forcing it to the ground.

Birds are still attractive to recreational shooters as live targets, whether they are moving or not. In some of the regular turkey shoots held by certain clubs in the USA the birds may be confined in stalls, with only the head protruding. Live pigeon shoots are also held, offering moving targets.[52] Earlier in the century in the UK live pigeon shooting was popular among ladies, who clapped excitedly as birds fell.[53] Open seasons on wild game birds such as ducks are proclaimed in a number of countries. Birds are protected through a breeding season, unprotected in the shooting season. The shooters are conservationists in the breeding season, even erecting nestboxes in some wetlands to increase the birds' numbers.

Open seasons are proclaimed in some countries for the hunting of wild animals also, quite distinct from the culling by skilled marksmen which is sometimes considered necessary to check population pressures. Pressure groups in the USA have persuaded the authority which administers the nation's Wildlife Refuges to open up all of them for hunting, 'as long as it is compatible with refuge purposes'.[54]

Some countries encourage hunting to attract tourists, as China does to attract hunters from the USA.[55] Similarly big-game fishing along the Great Barrier Reef attracts international tourists: the excitement that draws many tourists to centres such as Lizard Island is the excitement not merely of hooking a marlin, but also of trying to win a supposed contest with it. The fish may endure distress and pain for hours, with a large hook caught in its jaw.[56]

In the UK the *Report of the Committee on Cruelty to Wild Animals*, presented to Parliament in 1951, reflects both pressure-group influence and the force of habit in traditional attitudes to animals.[57] Field sports are strongly defended: there are 'not many complaints about cruelty' in them (para. 129, p. 36). Hunts help to control the numbers of wild animals, it is claimed (para. 139). Moreover appreciable economic loss is caused by foxes killing poultry. The committee concluded that 'any sport that has a reasonable measure of support and is a traditional activity of the countryside, and which has some utilitarian value (either by making a useful contribution to the control of some wild animals or by providing recreation for an appreciable number of people) should not be interfered with except for some very good reason'. Little concern was expressed for animal suffering: 'a certain amount of suffering is inevitable in all field sports'. Moreover the committee was confident that animal suffering was slight only: 'interference would be justified if there were more than a slight degree of suffering'.[58]

Killing for food and for fashion

At the beginning of this century the *Report of the Committee on Humane Slaughtering of Animals*[59] in the UK recommended that 'all animals, without exception, should be stunned, or otherwise rendered unconscious, before blood is drawn' (6a, p. 220). Further, 'animals awaiting slaughter should be spared as far as possible from any contact with the sights or smells of the slaughterhouse itself' (8a, p. 221), and 'cattle should, when possible, be slaughtered screened off from their fellows' (8d, p. 221). Although either stunning or instant killing is now widely practised in larger slaughterhouses, there are still exceptions in smaller slaughterhouses and on private farms; moreover the problem of animal distress prior to slaughter has not been solved. A common practice is for one after another to be electrocuted within sight of those following after[60] – a distress sometimes aggravated by previous long periods of waiting without food or water, as well as by long transport to the holding yards.

Another major failure to meet the humane recommendations of the UK report is in the continued political concessions to religious pressure groups. Because Jews and Moslems believe that animals should be killed while conscious, even large animals continue to be killed by having their throats cut. Various mechanised procedures, such as devices for firmly securing the animals, seem only to increase their distress.

In both the UK and the USA the large-scale killing of birds for fashion and for food continued into the early part of this century.[61] Though the large-scale demand for feathers has ended, in some other countries the trapping of migratory birds for food as they fly over the Mediterranean persists, despite legal prohibitions, either by liming with heavily-glued sticks placed in bushes or on tree branches, or by using mist nets which are invisible to birds.

In the trapping of animals for furs some countries such as the USA still have not banned the steel-jaw trap. In some cases untoothed and even padded jaws have been used under pressure from humane organisations, but suffering is still inflicted. From the trapper's standpoint the unmodified steel-jaw trap is a requirement, to make sure of the catch.[62]

Animals for gain

In graziers' attempts to protect animals from predators their use of the steel-jaw trap has changed little in over a century. Trap lines are still inspected most infrequently in some cases, so that trapped dingoes in Australia, for instance, and many other species not classified as pests die slowly.[63] Until the second half of this century, or until the acceptance of mechanisation, pit ponies continued to be used in mines, with conditions much as they were in the nineteenth century.[64]

Indifference to the suffering of domestic animals has not abated significantly. Until recently it was not uncommon for calves to be transported from farm to city with legs tied together and even, in some cases, for mouths to be bound also so that calves could not feed from their mothers. Cows brought a higher price in the cities if their udders were full.[65] Newly-shorn sheep continue to suffer when measures are not taken to blanket them in winter. In some countries where there are no legal prohibitions farmers still shear in winter and leave sheep uncovered.[66] As late as a decade ago the practice of 'soring' horses was reported in the USA. To circumvent the slow procedure of training a horse to lift its front feet high, quicker results have been sought by applying chemicals to the feet with irritating and blistering effects.[67]

In developing countries the more advanced clock of the developed countries may be turned back by as much as a century: the suffering of draught animals through overuse, overloading or abandonment when usefulness is over appears unchanged.[68] One of the products of the technological revolution is vastly improved mechanised transport: long road-trains may be seen crammed with cattle or sheep, continuing with inadequate rests for food and water. Swift air transport has meant that animals captured for the world's zoos can be delivered from Africa and elsewhere within a day or so of leaving agents' holding centres. But this haste makes also for cruelty to animals. Almost makeshift packing has been confirmed on a number of occasions: monkeys have been despatched in overcrowded wire and hessian crates; tigers have perished in crates too small for them; birds with long necks have had them broken when extending them through cracks in their boxes or crates.[69]

Intensive farming

In various ways animals are used for gain in farming, nowhere more single-mindedly than on the factory farm, which warrants special attention as a phenomenon of our times. Cruelties on the factory farm have been exposed for more than twenty years.[70] Its name derives from the closely confined, mechanised conditions in which animals are forced to live in factory-like, enclosed buildings. It knows no sentiment except the sentiment of gain: indeed if animals show any sign of weakness they are killed and replaced with healthier stock. The confinement of veal calves, pigs, battery hens and broilers described here will illustrate the suffering inflicted by factory techniques. Because the factory farm is usually inaccessible to the public, the facts need to be presented in some detail in order to leave graphic visual impressions.

In the standard situation as it was first developed, veal calves live out their lives in pens two feet wide (or less) and no more than five feet in depth, giving them standing space, but space for lying down in a cramped posture only. The floor is not earth but wooden slats. At times the calves are prevented from moving their heads sideways by two fixed vertical members which allow them to slide down to a position of rest, but with their heads still yoked in the original position, their collars tied to the vertical members.[71] With this degree of immobility the calves require little attention. The feeding buckets contain only a milk diet (without roughage), suitable for producing white meat: that can be done only by making the calf so deficient in iron as to leave it anaemic. The calves remain in darkness most of the time, without exercise. It is significant that white veal has no special food value. The calves' suffering is similar in unnecessariness to the forced feeding of geese to produce pâté de foie gras.

At least in the UK the factory farming of veal calves is slowly changing: fewer than ten producers continue with the individual crate or stall. The Brambell Committee of 1965[72] recommended against all three of its basic characteristics. First, on the question of adequate space for the calf's movement, it stated that 'calves should have sufficient room to be able to turn around, to groom themselves, and to move without discomfort', specifying that pens for calves of 200–300 lbs liveweight should measure at least five feet by three feet six inches. That gave the calf an additional twenty inches in the width of its pen over the normal twenty-two inch pen, sufficient for it to turn around and to lie down. But the committee fell short of recommending against factory farming entirely, though observing that 'calves are normally active, playful animals. They lick and groom themselves, show curiosity about their environment and are sociable' (para. 147). Indeed 'the objectionable habits associated with close confinement', it is admitted, are seldom found in the natural state of freedom. Second, on the question of an adequate diet for veal calves, the committee recommended that iron be added to their diet and that 'all calves be provided with palatable roughage daily at all ages from a week after birth' (para. 145). This followed from the observations that in the natural state of rearing the calf 'begins to nibble grass or other roughage . . . probably when it is not much more than a fortnight old', and that when it is fed on an exclusively liquid diet 'it cannot ruminate because it has no roughage'. But beyond that it made observations which, if followed through, would have led to an inference that veal calves should not be subjected to factory farming (economic and political considerations aside): first, that since calves are ruminants, part of the satisfaction of feeding must be in ruminating; second, that young calves derive satisfaction from suckling; third, that 'the yoking or close tethering of calves, except for short periods and for specific purposes (e.g. feeding or veterinary treatment) should be prohibited' (para. 149).

To the factory farmer in the USA veal is necessarily white, so neither iron nor roughage is added to the skim milk diet.[73] Experts from veterinary departments of universities or from government agencies, as well as those writing in a variety of farming journals or magazines, continue to explain the undeviating economic purposes and methods that must be pursued if the veal producer is to enlarge his profits.

In the UK the Brambell Committee included all farm animals in its disapproval of any confinement 'which necessarily frustrates most of the major activities' natural to the respective animals. The common principle was this: 'An animal should at least have sufficient freedom of movement to be able without difficulty to turn around, groom itself, get up, lie down and stretch its limbs' (para. 37). In one respect factory-farmed pigs are even more vulnerable than veal calves: physiologically they are unable to insulate themselves adequately against the heat that is generated under factory conditions. Despite improvements in the ventilation of some factories, conditions are fetid and unhealthy, with inadequate dung disposal a major contributor to disease.[74] The effect of long confinement on the pig – an active, exploratory, and in many ways resourceful, hardy and persistent animal – is observable in signs of physical discomfort and the stress of unrelieved boredom. Mechanised factory farming aims to get by with as little attention to animals as possible, a similar attitude to the pride with which the monitor system of teaching was promoted in the UK, one teacher allegedly coping with even five hundred pupils.[75]

In the USA the factory farm has agricultural engineers to design efficient systems that will reduce labour costs and animal scientists to explore equally efficient cost-benefit feeding systems. Veterinarians are also caught up with the economics of pig farming. Organisation is leading to increasing specialisation: farrowing may be left to particular corporations, with young pigs supplied to the factory farmer whose function is then to 'grow' them for the market. Marketing itself may become a separate corporate specialisation. The social dislocation of agribusinesses taking over from independent farming communities produces both human and animal suffering.

Confinement stalls for pigs in factory farms are made usually of tubular steel for easy assembly, though sometimes of strong steel wire mesh. They are large enough for pigs to lie down. Sometimes they are two-tiered or even three-tiered, the excrement from animals in the higher tier falling down on to the others. Floors are usually of wooden or metal slats, or of concrete, though sometimes of strong wire mesh.[76] The physiology of pigs' feet and legs is no more suited to such floors than is that of veal calves. Under natural conditions much of a pig's life is spent exploring and rooting in relatively soft earth. Constant exercise among feral pigs keeps them lean, their legs easily supporting their weight. In unnatural conditions of completely rigid floors animals develop strains to muscles and joints; sometimes these extend to the back. Sores may develop on their feet. The suffering of pigs is aggravated as their body weight increases; permanent and painful lameness may continue until they are slaughtered.[77] Since, like veal calves, they are generally kept in total darkness except at feeding times (or for occasional inspections), a misplaced step on a slatted or meshed floor may lead to a painful jar or an aggravated injury.

Young pigs are taken from the sows when two or three weeks old and spend the rest of their lives in the growing section of the factory, normally about five months. Stress symptoms develop early. Since there is no relief from boredom except when the lights are switched on, stress is not always containable. Fighting breaks out whenever pigs are being moved from their pens; some are killed in the fighting, some badly mauled, despite the precautions taken soon after birth of cutting piglets' tails, clipping sharp teeth and castrating the males. Aggression may lead even to cannibalism, beginning with the biting of any remaining tail and progressing into the animal's rump. The not unusual phenomenon of pigs dropping dead when they are moved to novel situations, such as larger pens, is itself an effect of stress.

The life of breeding sows in the factory farm is manipulated more than that of the growing male pigs. The farmer who prefers to be self-contained confines his breeding sows in individual stalls (or sometimes in stalls with several others) for four months, kept dark except at feeding time. Their weight is not significant to the farmer, so regular feeding is replaced by what is necessary: feeding on alternate days or even once in every three. Near the end of the gestation period the sow is individually stalled, if she was not before, with sufficient room to stand for feeding and to lie down to feed her piglets, but with insufficient room to exercise or to turn around. When she has fed her piglets for two to three weeks they are taken from her and put into the growing factory, while she returns to the breeding area to repeat her reproductive functions.

Animal scientists strive to improve upon nature in the sow's breeding capacity. Large litters are promoted by using progestins or steroids. But perhaps the least fortunate sow is the one selected to become a donor of embryos (the eggs previously fertilised by artificial insemination) to other sows, since she may be operated on every two months or so each year until her usefulness as a donor is over. Animal scientists no less than the agribusiness company executives are intent on cost reduction, both in the endless drive to streamline mechanised processes, and in the provision of animal food. The limits to which they are prepared to go involve waste recycling: even raw manure is mixed with food in some cases.[78]

It is difficult to assess the degree of animal suffering, though physical suffering in the factory farm is probably similar regardless of species. Distress may vary considerably: if boredom is related to mental capacity, it may be assumed that confinement causes greater distress to pigs than it does to poultry. But hens too suffer when denied an existence natural to them. This is evident from the need to 'debeak' chickens in order to prevent them attacking and mutilating each other: cannibalism is a problem in poultry as well as in pigs. It is even more unnatural for a chicken to be debeaked than for a piglet to be de-tailed, for the beak is used for feeding, not merely as an instrument of protection or of aggression when aroused. Mechanical debeaking machines use hot blades to cut through a very sensitive area of tissue. The behaviour of birds during and after debeaking leaves no doubt that they suffer.[79] Various devices for burning off the beaks are still used in the USA: burning was the first method used, probably inflicting as much pain as the hot blade technique. For egg-layers (but not for broilers) the torture is repeated after three or four months, and then the suffering may be more acute and more prolonged than when the birds were only six or seven days old. Like bungling in the slaughter of cattle, inefficient debeaking has serious consequences: tongues may be severed, the beak may not be cut completely through, a blade too hot may cause blisters in the mouth, a growth may develop which becomes tender when the stump of the beak is used for feeding or grooming. To add to their discomfort, sometimes toes are clipped to prevent fighting.

Broiler chickens in the UK, the USA and elsewhere may be kept on large floors each accommodating as many as 90 000 birds. The impression is of a restless sea of birds with standing room only, though there are opportunities to turn around, to jostle for new positions, and sometimes to attempt to peck and fight. Because of the hysteria that spreads quickly among such large flocks at any unusual situation, such as an outbreak of fighting, and the ease with which disease can spread among the birds, the broilers usually have a short life of two months only from the time they arrive at two weeks old. That has proved to be the optimum economic point for killing them.

Apart from the congestion, the system of lighting adds to the birds' distress. Long rows of lights dissect the spacious floor of the broiler factory or run along the sides. The lights go on for eighteen to twenty-three hours each day to encourage feeding from the hoppers. In the short period of darkness the birds may

sleep – a pattern very different from their normally uninter-
rupted rest in roosting. Even the almost constant incentive to eat
makes for restlessness. Under such conditions stress kills a
proportion of the birds, as do disease and sudden temperature
changes when temperature control is inadequate. Their frustration is the result of the factory farmer's denial of their instincts to
nest, roost and groom themselves, with the lack of adequate
space for these basic comforts.[80]

Battery hens kept for egg production are even more strictly
confined. Their lives are spent in wire cages about twelve by
eighteen inches, each cage normally taking four or five birds.
Again they jostle for position, or simply for standing room, and
peck at each other when stresses increase. Artificial lighting is on
for most of the day to encourage egg-laying. To add to the
discomfort of congestion, hens stand insecurely on wire mesh
floors and, like pigs provided with flooring unsuitable for their
feet and legs, suffer similarly from stresses and strains to muscles
or to ligaments and tendons that normally cushion the weight of
the body when they stand. Deformities may develop from the
awkward postures the birds are sometimes forced to adopt.
Mechanisation in the battery farm is similar to that in the broiler
farm: artificial heating is installed when needed in winter and
automatic watering is provided. Battery hens may continue
laying for one or two years; at the end of their usefulness they
are killed for the broiler market if in sufficiently good condition,
or otherwise killed and converted into chicken soup. Under
present conditions birds from both battery farms and broiler
farms have a number of vitamin deficiencies seldom encountered in free-ranging birds. Some factory birds suffer from
anaemia, some from blindness, some from swollen joints, some
from structural bone deformities attributable in part to factory
feeding.

Factory farming methods in the UK and the USA have
extended to the farming of mink in wire mesh cages (the floor
also of wire), each cage normally no more than twenty-four by
twelve by ten inches. The cages are stacked in sheds. Generally
the animals are born and die in captivity. In this environment
they too are prone to a variety of diseases and deformities. Their
killing is sometimes by crude methods of inexpert electrocution
or by poisoning.[81]

Traditional farming practices

It is not only in the factory farm that domestic animals continue to suffer. For instance, in high-risk farming sheep or cattle are grazed on marginal lands with a low annual rainfall and subject to droughts that may last as long as several years. The gamble is always on a few good years of adequate rains for pastures, then the marketing of the stock and a quick profit. When no rains come the stock slowly perishes.

Inexpert operations are sometimes performed by farmers without veterinary guidance. One of the most painful of these is the practice of 'mulesing' sheep to prevent blow-fly strike. A large area of skin is cut, then sliced away from around the tail parts. Unskilled operators, slicing the skin away with shears, may cause serious injury by cutting into muscle. Under good conditions the sheep suffer for three to five weeks while the mulesing wound heals.[82] In some countries, including Australia and recently the UK, the teeth of ageing sheep are ground down with an electric grinder disc, often by farmers themselves. Bleeding and exposure of the tooth pulp may occur, when pain is inflicted on the sheep not only from the grinding, but also from exposure of the pulp, leading to the condition of pulpitis. The painful castration of young male lambs with a knife is still practised, although alternatives of chemical castration are available.

Unskilled dehorning (or dishorning) of calves or cattle has caused unnecessary suffering. One witness before the Committee on Humane Slaughtering of Animals in the UK in the early part of this century was asked by the chairman if dishorning is a painful process. His reply was, 'Not very painful if done early in life; there is a certain amount of pain attached to it, but it is a very harmless operation if performed when the calf is a few weeks old.'[83] The docking of horses' tails persists in some countries, though prohibited in others. The operation of cutting through the bony part of the tail in order to shorten it is painful in itself, and leaves the horse more vulnerable to attacks by flies and other stinging insects, especially in warmer climates.

The farming of the seas and oceans for profit continually brings its own cruelty. Modern technology has simply increased efficiency in the killing of whales over the previous primitive method of harpooning. The giant mammals suffer similar distress to that of foxes, hares or deer in the hunt. Gillnets intended for salmon kill an estimated 50 000 fur seals off Alaska each year. Elsewhere they trap dolphins and many thousands of seabirds. Each net may extend for more than twelve miles.[84]

Miscellaneous cruelties

Other conditions and circumstances contributing to unnecessary animal suffering are: first, religions, superstitions and cultural habits; second, the needs of war; third, the needs of science and industry. Ideas about magic have long led to animal suffering: when an animal was attributed with a magical power or believed to have an evil spirit within it, it was thought to be better destroyed before it brought harm to people.[85] Today superstitions concerning animals are common in some developing countries. In parts of Malaysia cats are killed by any methods found convenient, such as scalding; then their eyes are gouged out and eaten raw in the belief that they will benefit human eyesight. Monkey brain is eaten as an aphrodisiac, the monkey suffering slow torture when, with a bowl fitted around its head above the ears and its body cramped in a box to prevent movement, the scalp is cut and the exposed brain spooned out or sucked out with a straw.[86]

Except in the case of certain forms of Buddhism, which have taught kindness to animals and sometimes their liberation, religions of the world have at times exacerbated cruelty. For centuries the literal interpretation of 'dominion over animals' was construed by many in Christian countries as giving man an unquestioned use of animals for his purposes, whatever they might be. The inhumane slaughtering practices of Jews and Moslems have been modified in some places but not universally. Animals have been sacrificed to many deities in the hope of favours to humans, and the killing has almost always been slow and painful. In parts of Indonesia, such as Java and Bali, sacrifices by practising Hindus take the form of pushing animals such as mules, donkeys or pigs over the knife-edges of volcano rims, to meet their end struggling in the loose ash below. Other religions still practise primitive sacrificial killings.[87]

As part of their total service to man, animals have almost always been used in war. From the time of Hannibal's use of elephants in crossing the Alps and throughout the various campaigns of history, animals such as mules and donkeys have been pressed to man's service. The historical cavalry charges may have brought terror to enemy infantry, but they brought distress to horses too, however well trained they were. Before veterinary hospitals were set up in the two world wars, animals wounded on the battlefield were mostly left to their fate. Animals have shared with man, because they have had no choice, the hazards of artillery shelling, air bombing and naval bombardments, as well as small-arms fire. They have hauled guns and ammunition over extremely heavy terrain. Dogs have been used not only in dangerous patrols, but also even as mine detectors.

The use of animals by man for experimental purposes is a large topic which will be deferred to Chapter 4. It includes experiments in biomedical research which aim to benefit man and other animals, as well as experiments for the cosmetic industry which have trivial value only, and animals in experimental psychology.

SUMMARY

The facts to be summarised are briefly these: first, cruelty to animals has a historical continuity to the present, though some of its forms have a contemporary flavour; second, there has been a continuity of compassion also, but without social diffusion; third, despite the influence of some Church leaders, religious beliefs, as well as superstitions and ignorance, have contributed to cruelties to animals; fourth, the conspicuous concentration of cruelties in factory farming is unique to the avarice and competitiveness of our own times; fifth, this clouding of sympathy by overriding economic self-interest is compounded by ignorance of animal natures, particularly of their sentience and – for mammals especially – of their capacity for pleasurable experiences.

Moral probings on the basis of the factual evidence will appear trite or unnecessary to some who have allowed themselves sufficient time for reflection and critical evaluation, for to most of these questions will already have been asked. As a bridge to the next chapter, we may wonder if we are not taking animals too much for granted. Do we consider enough what is good for *them*, apart from what is good for ourselves? Yet do we know what is good for them? Do we know, that is, enough about animal natures? When we talk about cruelty to animals, are we going too far in attributing distress to them, as though they were human? In fact, are we not showing a tendency to read into animals the kinds of mental reactions that we have ourselves? Is there not a possibility that they are almost mindless creatures? Is there any reason why we should not hunt them for sport, or slaughter them for food, or use their skins for warmth or for fashion, as long as we are not fiendish or vicious in killing them? Do we not elevate them beyond their true worth? In view of human population pressures, with populations continually increasing, why should we not use intensive or factory farming methods to help feed the hungry of the world? Do human needs not come first? And in view of the immense suffering of humans from disease, why should not lower-order creatures be used as experimental subjects in attempts to prevent or to reduce this suffering?

At this stage, like the facts preceding them, these questions may evoke variable responses. If the facts have not spoken clearly for themselves, the responsibilities of the following chapters will be all the more onerous in strengthening *understanding* – an understanding of what morality means in practice, which will be the central concern of Chapter 2; of the natures of sentient animals, which will be discussed in Chapter 3; of the extent and justification of animal experiments, which will be the subject of Chapter 4; of ways of relieving the moral debt through education and the law, which will be the focus of Chapter 5. Then, at the end, there may be benefit to some in rethinking the facts of this chapter and formulating an individual assessment of the moral debt as a basis for action.

2 Practical Morality and the Moral Debt

MORALITY OR THE MORAL POINT OF VIEW

What is it to be moral? In descriptive senses 'moral' is applied to character held to be good or bad, or to acts regarded as right or wrong. People are said to have moral scruples, moral convictions or moral attitudes and values – determined perhaps by home upbringing, religious instruction, the influence of particular teachers in the classroom or of peers or other associates, or by the literature they read and the films or plays they see. Some are said to make moral judgements in practical situations. It is easy to see that some dispositions and some performances are different from others; that some people are habitually guided by principles, having preferred some principles to others. But the crucial question is: What makes these dispositions, actions, principles, decisions or judgements *moral*, as distinct from being immoral or perhaps not a question of morality at all?

Various stances have been taken on this question, either separately or in combination. One is that in making moral judgements about people, or about situations involving people, it is important to be as *uninvolved* as humanly possible, and at the same time *benevolent* towards others: as one relates one's own wellbeing to that of others, one needs to be 'as strictly impartial', in Mill's words, 'as a disinterested and benevolent spectator' (*Utilitarianism*, p. 291).[1] This may be viewed as clearing the ground for a moral point of view, removing passions and prejudices so that ideally one perceives a human situation rationally, or with something of the bias-free perspective of a physical scientist (though philosophers and scientists alike acknowledge that perfect detachment is not humanly achievable). But one may be *disinterested*, and yet have no perception of what constitutes the specifically *moral* character of the situation. Is the addition of benevolence, without further understanding, enough to remove the difficulty?

A second stance is Kant's. One may feel impelled to act, as he himself felt, according to *imperatives of duty* as these are dictated by reason, or by a 'rational will'. Kant believed that by a rational intuition all men could make moral decisions or judgements about others and about themselves, so that they would act *morally* in the only way the rational will allowed them to act, if they obeyed it and were not distracted by desire or inclination. For instance, duty impelled them not to kill, never to break promises and so forth, and it is not difficult to see the strength of a rational case to be made (intuitively, where deliberate reasoning is not necessary) for obeying either of these imperatives. But there are conflicts in some situations which the inflexibility of the commands of duty does not allow for, and there are many less obvious cases which Kant did not consider but which fall within the province of moral decisions today, notably those which form the subject matter of this book and which relate to animals. It is not easy to imagine Kant saying that duty commands us not to experiment with animals under *any* conditions, or never to kill animals for food, or under no circumstances to hunt or to cage animals. Here some may find reasons for and against, and the moral situation may be so complex as to give rise to many dilemmas. In other words, duty may speak to different people, equally rational, with different voices, not with the univocal imperatives which he imagined. To Kant some dispositions were plainly good or bad, some acts categorically right or wrong. Duty is perfect and obligatory when subject to the rational will; each of its commands may be subsumed under this general rule: 'Act only on maxims in adopting which you can at the same time wish that they should become universal laws.'[2]

A third and very different stance is one with a social orientation, in which there is a perspective of benevolence being widely distributed among all individuals who may be affected by a particular act. From this viewpoint an act is determined to be right or wrong according to the *consequences* for the happiness (satisfaction or wellbeing) of everyone affected in any way by the act. The measure of its rightness or wrongness is the extent of the total happiness it produces by satisfying the *interests* of those involved. Thus Bentham expressed what he saw as the core of any practical morality: 'Ethics at large may be defined, [as] the art of directing man's actions to the production of the greatest possible quantity of happiness, on the part of those whose interest is in view.'[3] When Bentham wrote, against a background of human poverty and misery, this stance on morality had wide appeal – as it has to some today, including those who extend it to the wellbeing of animals. Human acts may be declared right or wrong according to the aggregates of satisfactions or sufferings which they produce for animals as well as for humans. Aggregates of satisfactions for humans, as for animals, present formidable difficulties in practice, though, because literal quantification of the satisfactions or sufferings of animals and humans affected by an act cannot be achieved except by making a very broad assessment of consequences. Preference Utilitarians amend the classical version of Bentham's stance by arguing that it is not simply *totals* of satisfactions that are to be weighed, but the desires or preferences of all persons involved in an act. Further, broad assessments of the consequences of acts are all that are required for practical judgements on whether acts are right or wrong. In this process of evaluation it has been said that we 'accommodate ourselves to the preferences of others'.[4]

The utilitarian stance has certain advantages over the preceding two, noticeable particularly in some situations: first, it focuses on social relations with others and on a practical morality as necessarily concerned with responsibilities to others about us; second, it draws attention to individual *interests*. The most general and comprehensive interest every individual has is his *wellbeing*. A prominent utilitarian in the early part of this century explained that 'the standard of right and wrong in conduct is its tendency to promote the interest of everybody'.[5] The most general human interest is derived simply from human nature. Every individual has certain needs, such as for health and security (including freedom from unnecessary suffering), for intellectual satisfaction according to variable human capacities, and for social relationships. Any act by another which interferes with any of these interests to such an extent as to lead to a loss diminishes to that extent the individual's wellbeing. Animals do not share all of these human interests, though they may share some. No animal shares our intellectual satisfactions, for instance. Some animals are solitary by nature and so do not share our need for social relationships; other animals such as mammals and certain birds do. It is a loss to human wellbeing to be kept in solitary confinement, for an infant to be separated from its mother. Why do we not see it as a loss to animal wellbeing in similar circumstances?

Each of these moral stances has its merits in enlightening or informing the practical morality by which we live. One may benefit from Mill's notion of benevolent impartiality in the approach to living with others. One may act intuitively out of a sense of moral *duty* in some cases, without any thought for the consequences of one's acts, for one may judge spontaneously that an act of cheating is wrong, or of rape, or of cruelty to animals. In other circumstances one may consider the consequences of acts before attempting to judge them morally right or wrong. There are situations in which one may combine all three approaches in one's judgements and justifications. We shall ignore other moral approaches such as the Contractarian, which are not relevant to the present argument, and return to the pressing question already foreshadowed: Why do we confine our practical morality to humans when animals have a wellbeing to be considered too, and are very much affected by human acts?

One answer was provided by Montaigne four centuries ago. It lies in *presumption*, the 'natural and original disease' of humankind,[6] a viewpoint which Primatt repeated in 1776. We are proud of our intellectual superiority over other animals, overlooking our own animality and failing to understand the nature of theirs and our oneness with them in the animal world. There is a need 'to bring us back and join us to the crowd: we are neither above nor below the rest'. For long the notion of animal inferiority has been common in references to the inferior beasts, brutes or automata driven by instincts. Some still see animals as unaware of what is happening to them, things born to be preyed upon and eaten, whose only justification for existence is to help man satisfy his various needs. Mill's spectator stance of benevolent detachment helps us to recognise our animality and to demolish the grounds for our human presumption.

Kant leads us to a second answer, that we have a moral duty not to be cruel to any creature – animal or human – capable of feeling pain, or of any kind of suffering. Intuitively we recognise that cruelty is wrong; that the infliction of unnecessary suffering is an evil. These are moral convictions which we need no consideration of consequences to justify, any more than we need such a consideration for judging that thieving is wrong or that sexual abuse of children is wrong. In other words it is a moral duty to prevent the infliction of pain or distress on humans or on animals alike.

Utilitarians – both Classical and Preference – lead us to a third answer: when we consider the consequences of particular acts we cannot, without contradiction, avoid considering animal wellbeing as well as human wellbeing. It is just as unreasonable to prevent or to inhibit the enjoyment of animals, according to their natures, as it is to prevent or to inhibit the enjoyment of humans, according to *their* natures. Each animal species, including the human, has its own potential for satisfaction. To restrict completely the liberty of free-ranging animals has consequences to be weighed in our moral considerations, as has a total restriction of human liberties. There are animal interests and human interests. As the nearest approach to a utilitarian ideal Mill considered that laws and social arrangements should place 'the interest of every individual as nearly as possible in harmony with the interest of the whole' (*Utilitarianism*, p. 292). But if animals have interests, why should they not form part of the larger interest, the interest of the whole?

From the second and third approaches to a moral point of view, there are two notions of primary significance to the argument: the first is *sentience*, the second *interests*, each of which requires further explanation.

Sentience

The realisation that animals are capable of suffering is one source of the compassion which some have for them, often in an untutored way in childhood. At a more sophisticated level of understanding an awareness of animal sentience comes from learning that vertebrate animals have a nervous system which sends messages to the brain, registered as sensations of pain in relevant circumstances. Even before Primatt's references to animal sentience, noted in Chapter 1, another clergyman in the eighteenth century had denounced the common view that animals are no more than 'stocks or stones, or things that cannot feel'.[7] Primatt himself reasoned that 'superiority of rank or status exempts no creature from the sensibility of pain, nor does inferiority render the feelings thereof the less exquisite. Pain is pain, whether it be inflicted on man, or on beast; and the creature that suffers it, whether man or beast, being sensible of the misery of it, whilst it lasts, suffers evil; and the sufferance of evil, unmeritedly, unprovokedly, where no offence has been given, and no good end can possibly be answered by it, but merely to exhibit power or gratify malice, is cruelty and injustice in him that occasions it.'[8] 'A brute', he explained, '. . . has similar nerves and organs of sensation; and his cries and groans, in case of violent impressions upon his body, though he cannot utter his complaints by speech or human voice, are as strong indications to us of his sensibility to pain, as the cries and groans of a human being, whose language we do not understand.'[9] As noted also in Chapter 1, Primatt made several pertinent references to the incapacity of animals to talk and to their consequent inability to plead their own cause.

Very soon after Primatt's work appeared, Bentham published his *Introduction to the Principles of Morals and Legislation*, in a footnote of which he asserted what has been repeated so often in recent years by animal sympathisers, that the real question is whether animals can suffer, rather than whether they can either reason or talk.[10] In an explanation preceding Bentham's correspondence, his editor alleged that Bentham considered animals to have claims to our humane duty to them 'only modified by the consideration, that the sum of pain and pleasure involved in the sufferings and enjoyments of brutes, is less in amount than that involved in the sufferings and enjoyments of human beings'.[11] Particularly with reference to suffering, Bentham had no evidence to support that judgement (if it was fairly attributed to him), yet throughout the nineteenth century there were those who made a similar inference from the intellectual inferiority of animals to their inferior sentience. One moral philosopher in 1817 explained that though the 'brute creation . . . have feeling as well as we', it is 'not in the same degree or kind'. [12] Another in 1872 conveyed the conventional view of lower animals as creatures merely of instinct, capable of experiencing pleasure only 'in accordance with the laws of their nature' over which they have no control. Unlike human sentience, with the power of intelligent self-direction, animal sentience is very limited.[13] In the previous century Rousseau had seen, more clearly than these moral philosophers, that there is no necessary connection between intellectual powers and sentience. Animals were to him fellow creatures because of a common sentience. He saw himself obliged not to cause them any hurt, 'less because they are rational than because they are sentient beings'.[14]

In leading to the notion of the moral debt to animals, there are several questions to ask on sentience. First, how does one know

that animals suffer pain? Second, if it is assumed that human
pain is of a different order from animal pain, is it appropriate to
consider Bentham's criteria of intensity and duration in order to
compare animal pain, in aggregate, with aggregates of human
pain? Third, does it matter morally if animal pain is not quite
like human pain? That is, is it enough simply to regard pain as
pain, as Primatt argued?

The standard and sufficient way of judging that animals are in
pain is by interpreting abnormal behaviour as we observe it with
our senses. That is no different from ascertaining that a human
is in pain. (We may observe pain in another human, as Primatt
had suggested, who does not speak our language.) To gain
empirical knowledge of animal suffering, as of human suffering, it is not normally necessary to use physiological measurements such as of temperature or pulse-rate: only humans can be
guilty of malingering, and if this is suspected we have the
opportunity to resort to more sophisticated techniques. A dog
hit by a car may yelp, writhe, bleed or froth at the mouth; a
human may groan, contort his body too, and similarly bleed or
froth at the mouth. Suffering is apparent in either case. Less
dramatically, a starving animal will be abnormally thin and will
walk, if at all, with effort. Similar behaviour is observable in
starving humans. To deny the evidence of our senses combined
with our evaluative intelligence would be contrary to reason.

We may claim empirical knowledge of others' suffering by
inferences from *changed* patterns of behaviour; in the case of
animals, from a basis of knowing what constitutes a normal
pattern of behaviour for that animal or species. Over lengthy
periods we may observe a deterioration in an animal's general
health; then veterinary examination may reveal signs of stress
symptomatic of disease.[15] In some cases, as when we recall the
effects of a blow to the head, we may infer that an animal suffers
similarly in similar circumstances, but in less obvious cases such
inferences are hazardous, either from humans to animals or vice
versa. True, there are borderline cases of slowly developing
illnesses where a minimal suffering is difficult to detect without
professional diagnosis. The general principle is that from the
observation of our senses in most cases, and otherwise from
professional physiological measurements or the more specialised techniques of neurologists, we infer the presence of
suffering – certainly something no one can see or hear or touch,

something recorded in the human or animal brain as a purely mental event. No one can infer that pain is an *identical* experience in humans and animals, though induced in similar circumstances, from the fact that humans and animals are alike in their physiological mechanisms of pain – each with a brain and a nervous system.[16] Neurologists have means of ascertaining that some humans experience pain more acutely and for longer than others, but individual differences do not affect an inference that pain is present. It is probable that warm-blooded vertebrates experience more pain than cold-blooded vertebrates, but again, we must ask if the degree of suffering has any moral significance.

In making our moral judgements we may adopt one or more of a variety of stances, as we have seen, and if we assume a Kantian viewpoint we may be satisfied with the intuitive judgement that any pain or suffering is an evil. But to a Classical Utilitarian such as Bentham who was concerned with the impact of a human act on all individuals affected by it, a value could be placed on any act according to certain criteria, which collectively would enable aggregates of pleasure and of pain to be determined. The two criteria which on first thoughts appear relevant to animal suffering are *intensity* and *duration*,[17] Bentham believing that in a general way it is possible to use a kind of arithmetic in totalling the pain or pleasure produced by a human act. But the further Bentham pushed the notion of calculation – broad as it was – the more his argument suffered. Duration may be more readily ascertainable than intensity of suffering, which appears relevant mainly to acute pathological conditions in humans, and even then it is beyond precise quantification. The prospect of an exact measurement of the *intensity* of animal suffering is still more impracticable.[18] There are cases in which the immorality of a particular act, such as an act of driving thousands of cattle into areas where their survival depends on unpredictable and purely fortuitous rains, is related, in a broad sense, to *total* suffering. The immorality of such an act does appear to be compounded by the numbers of the victims, but the animals suffer individually, not collectively.

The first two questions on sentience have raised considerations which lead to the third. Because of the difficulties inherent in any precise quantification of pain, human or animal, we may wonder whether, in moral terms of the rightness or wrongness

of a particular act, it makes any difference whether the suffering
inflicted on an animal is slight or severe, rare or frequent,
transient or indefinitely prolonged, in association with many
others or in isolation. This provisional conclusion will be
reviewed following a further consideration of the notion of
interests.

Interests

It has been suggested already that human interests and animal
interests are related to their respective *natures* and that, from a
utilitarian stance, the most comprehensive interest of each of the
various species is its many-sided *wellbeing*, dependent upon its
particular nature and the wide-ranging needs associated with it.
This utilitarian approach was explained by Bentham thus: 'A
thing is said to promote the interest, or to be *for* the interest, of
an individual, when it tends to add to the sum total of his
pleasures: or, what comes to the same thing, to diminish the sum
total of his pains.'[19] One common interest of animals and of
humans is health, though needs are different according to
natures, the needs of Eskimos clearly different from those of
caribou. Another common interest of humans and warm-
blooded vertebrates (mammals in particular) is the satisfaction
of curiosity, though again the particular needs depend upon
species differences. Humans may need intellectual satisfactions,
though within a wide range of varying capacities. Some animal
species may be much more exploratory than others, and again
there are intra-species differences. With the exception of certain
companion animals, total restriction of liberties may lead to
suffering rather than satisfaction. Another common interest
contributing to wellbeing (again considering mammals in particular) is social relationships. Human families and children need
the security of the home, parents need the satisfaction of
protective drives, wives normally benefit from the satisfaction of
mothering children; all normally benefit from contacts with
other families or other groups, with stimulation in individual
differences and challenges. Some animals benefit from raising
their young and protecting them, and some find satisfaction
from larger gregarious groupings. In other words, humans and
animals are similar in *having* interests, but different *according to
their respective natures* in the kinds of interests they have, and how

these interests may be either satisfied or frustrated to bring either pleasure or pain. Some of their interests are broadly common, but it is their natures that determine their needs and how their interests are to be fulfilled. This point is of central significance to the argument, and will be developed further in the next chapter.

The utilitarian stance of considering the *consequences* of human acts which contribute to or diminish others' wellbeing occupies a prominent place in any practical morality, since in our relations with others many of our acts do affect one or more of them. This position does not entail an exclusive dedication to either Classical or Preference Utilitarianism as a systematic philosophy. There are occasions, as we have noted, when duty demands no consideration of consequences in our moral judgements. Even though, after the judgement has been made, the consequences may be worked through, their understanding is not always necessary to the moral judgement and therefore not necessarily antecedent to it. The utilitarian stance is significant for its focus on *interests*, and one interest in common for humans and animals is freedom from suffering, for this is a contradiction of wellbeing. In practical terms neither humans nor animals can be expected to be totally free from suffering, but from the utilitarian stance any act is wrong which leads on either side to *unnecessary* suffering. (Humans face accidental and painful injury, so do animals; and each may suffer to some degree during medical or veterinary attention, despite pain-relieving drugs.)

Animal suffering does not always involve cruelty. In the previous chapter cruelty was explained as the conscious infliction of unnecessary suffering on another: that is, the imposition of suffering with some awareness by the agent of the consequences of his act or omission. It may take the form of a physical blow such as whipping, stoning, beating, or striking with an arrow or a bullet as in hunting; or of neglect of the basic needs of domestic or captive animals; or of deprivation of satisfactions, such as by isolating a gregarious animal or taking infants away from mothers soon after birth. The question of the agent's awareness is sometimes difficult to resolve, as is the question of responsibility. Very young children and the intellectually limited may be only vaguely aware of the suffering they are causing, but a similar principle applies to adult hunters. If their sensibilities are so dulled as to leave them unaware that their killing is cruel (recreational hunters are seldom so skilled in marksmanship as to cause instant death) they are as immature as young children in moral thinking. But if of normal intelligence, though perhaps poorly educated in humane values, their failure to take command of their self-interest and personal gratification does not absolve them from moral responsibility for their acts of cruelty, for a presumption is made that they have the capacity for sufficient understanding. On the other hand, a motorist who unavoidably hits an animal which has suddenly leapt onto a road cannot be said to have committed an act of cruelty. Only if he is negligent or reckless in such circumstances, and so indifferent to an animal's suffering which he might have prevented by responsible driving, can he be held morally culpable.

The torturing of animals is a severe form of cruelty – severe inasmuch as the suffering inflicted is itself severe, and the agent's mind is correspondingly more highly motivated to inflict the suffering with severity. He may be sadistic or in other ways mentally disturbed; or frustrated that an animal is not living up to his expectations, as in training, and therefore impelled to 'punish' it. (We shall return shortly to the moral implications of such 'punishment'.) Cruelty is in the human mind, not in the mind of the animal.

Legislation on cruelty to animals usually defines cruelty by example, but it is also required to specify its interpretation of 'animal'. Here there are wide variations. The *Cruelty to Animals Act 1876* in the UK included cold-blooded vertebrates (though in its original draft these were excluded). Some legislation includes *all* animals; some excludes fish and venomous reptiles.[20] From a moral standpoint, as we have stated, the animals we refer to are all sentient, all capable of feeling pain, including fish and reptiles.

To sum up the argument thus far, our moral intuitions point unequivocally to suffering as an evil when inflicted (with agent awareness) on another human or on a sentient animal. For moral justification we may turn to two different moral stances: first, the Kantian rational intuition that our duty is not to be cruel to another; second, the utilitarian stance in its attention to others' interests, for cruelty to animals fails to consider their interests, specifically avoidance of suffering. Humans and animals have often died in similar circumstances: from famine, for instance, or from toxic chemical inhalations as at Bhopal. Some may assume that their suffering is similar in such circumstances. In other situations, such as road accidents, it may be assumed that animals are quickly overcome by shock and suffer less acutely than humans. We may assume that animals are fortunate or unfortunate in comparison with ourselves: it is highly probable that mental suffering in humans exceeds that in animals, as the human brain exceeds the animal brain in complexity. But in the last resort the immorality of inflicted suffering which amounts to cruelty is unaffected by all such physiological and mental comparisons. Whether animal suffering is like or unlike human suffering is morally irrelevant. This supports the tentative conclusion reached in connection with sentience. Reflections on animal sentience and on their interests lead to the question of whether it is morally appropriate to speak of *respect* for animals.

Respect for animals

Is respect for animals analogous with respect for persons? When we respect persons we may be expected to have a sense of kinship, an understanding of others through self-understanding. We are aware of others' ambitions, for instance, as well as of their short-term objectives, of their emotions and the causes of their frustrations, of the things that bring satisfaction to them. We have a variable capacity to distinguish between desires which may contribute to their wellbeing and those which threaten danger. We appreciate the advantages of having a home and the benefits of nutritious food and suitable exercise. Others are not 'stocks and stones' when we respect them as persons, but human beings with similar interests and needs to our own. *Respect* then has a dual connotation when we respect persons: first, it refers to our understanding of others' common humanity; but second, and equally of importance, it refers to a degree of sympathy which gives us the impulse to wish them well, and in a practical way to support rather than frustrate their aspirations, in so far as we see them contributing to their wellbeing. (In practice few humans are able to live up to a consistent moral respect for persons. More usually there is interpersonal conflict as ambitions clash, and malevolence towards others who threaten personal objectives.)

For some, respect for persons may be a response to an imperative of duty, or it may be a rational position worked out by reflecting on others' interests, combined with humane attitudes and values. In either case there is an apprehension of others' wellbeing, a fundamental realisation that others have interests which ought to be considered by us, and that we ought not to be concerned exclusively with self-interest. What is meant by 'equal consideration of interests' is that we ought to adopt Mill's benevolent detachment, setting aside our passions and prejudices, regarding all persons' interests as deserving of equal consideration whether they are employers or employees, black or white, Christian or Moslem, literate or illiterate, male or female, political allies or political adversaries.

Part of the common human nature which helps us to respect others as persons is the capacity for rational foresight and planning which is not evident to us in the natures of animals. In the most general sense the capacity for rational thought does not attract respect in the sense of *admiration*, unless we adopt a biased anthropocentric standpoint and compare ourselves with animals not so fortunate in their genetic inheritance; or unless we reflect selectively on man's highest achievements, as Hamlet did in his famous soliloquy. Human rationality may be directed towards complete self-interest without regard for the interests of other humans or of animals; cruelty to animals does not contradict it in all cases; murder, indiscriminate killing, life-long captivity of others, including animals, may be the means to a perfectly rational end. In short, human rationality may lead to acts of which animals are incapable. For this reason respect for persons is not admiration for humanity, except in selective instances; and if we extend its reference to human capacities or potentialities, the long and unmitigated history of cruelty to animals insists that we be sufficiently impartial to put human capacity for good, through our benevolent and rational powers, against human capacity for evil. No moral 'oughts' have yet changed human nature on any grand scale, though they have sometimes modified attitudes and values affecting moral conduct. We are what we are: respect for persons is based on the simple fact of human nature. By analogy, and without any impulse to show that animals are *like* us in certain respects, is it possible to use a similar approach to respect for animals which is also moral to the extent of considering animal interests based on what *they* are, rather than anthropomorphising?

First, by using our rational powers and attempting to assume Mill's benevolent, impartial spectator stance, we find no difficulty in acknowledging that sentient animals have the interests we have already attributed to them. From this position it is not difficult to move to the view that all animal interests are to be considered equally, the interests of a mouse as equal to the interests of a lion; those of a rabbit or monkey as equal to those of any powerful predator – jaguar, tiger or eagle. Further, we can be sufficiently impartial in our deliberate disinterestedness to rid our minds of any prejudices and preconceptions, including antipathies towards particular species of animal. A dingo that has killed a sheep has interests to be considered no less than those of the sheep and its owner. The interests of an unfriendly neighbour's German shepherd are not to be disregarded because of our relations with the neighbour. The interests of cattle on common pastures are not affected by their owners' competition for limited resources. An impounded animal has interests, so has an unappealing animal suffering from mange, or one with three legs instead of four, or one that is timid by nature rather than daring.

Second, and more specifically, from the impartial and benevolent stance we are capable of appreciating that animals may suffer from cruelty no less than humans. It is by no means clear from past and contemporary history that *all* persons have the required self-mastery and understanding to assume such a disinterested and benevolent stance towards animals, but for present purposes we may assume that such a general human propensity is subsumed under human rationality, acknowledging the large degree of variability which this admits. Rational persons do understand that animals have interests which contribute to their satisfactions in living, or to their wellbeing, which if frustrated by either natural forces or human intervention lead to their suffering. For many humans this understanding of animal nature founded on their interests may need to be better informed by further education. If it is merely at the naive level of pity for all dumb creatures, it shows very little understanding of animal interests. The nature of animals will be considered further in the next chapter. In many instances it is necessary to understand the needs of particular species before their wellbeing can be comprehended fully, though common to all is the capacity to suffer, and that understanding is the crux of our moral respect for them according to Primatt, Bentham and contemporary utilitarians. It is in fact one arm only of considering animal interests through respect for their natures: the second arm concerns the consideration of interests which add to their satisfactions in living. In practical morality, which considers what is practicable, the second of these has its clearest application to mammals.

The three dimensions of our respect for animals, analogous to respect for persons, are benevolence, the utmost impartiality of which we are capable, and knowledge. It was the third that was deficient in Kant's perception of animals. His respect for humanity was vast through his belief in the human potential to combine reason and good will, but his knowledge and understanding of animals was limited. 'Animals are not self-conscious,' he said, 'and are there merely as a means to an end. That end is man . . .' Though he could see that 'animal nature has analogies to human nature', he spoke of 'doing our duties to animals in respect of manifestations which correspond to manifestations of human nature', in this way indirectly doing our duty to humanity.[21] There is little respect for animals in regarding them merely as means to human ends, or in perceiving no duties to them except in so far as our acts serve our fundamental duties to humanity. Even Kant's acknowledgement that we ought not to be cruel to animals was viewed as important to humans, for by forming habits of cruelty to animals we might more readily give way to cruelty to other humans. Kant had respect for *persons*[22] whose nature at its best he professed to understand; his understanding of animals was insufficient to give him an independent moral respect for them from an informed, benevolent and impartial standpoint.

Indeed, every perception of animals as merely serving man's purposes is partial and self-interested, missing the entire point of their unique natures. It is the perception of those who see animals merely for food, or for recreation or amusement, or for relieving man of incessant toil on the land. How can it be said that the wellbeing of any animal is seriously considered when it is fed, protected and eventually killed merely to be eaten, or when animals in the wild are killed indiscriminately as attractive moving targets for hunters? The failure to see the uniqueness of animal natures according to species, and the ready dismissal of everything that does not fit somehow into a loose analogy with humans, is a failure of impartiality as much as of knowledge. This is the 'vanity of imagination' of which Montaigne wrote, by which man 'equals himself to God' and 'withdraws and separates himself from the crowd of other creatures'. Man's presumption in his attitudes to animals is based on ignorance of their natures and capacities. 'How does he know, by the strength of his understanding, the secret and internal motions of animals?'[23] To take Mill's benevolent spectator viewpoint, with the added strength of appropriate knowledge which Montaigne lacked, is to understand that whether an animal bays or barks, howls, shrieks or hoots does not make it inferior to humans, but merely *different* in the way it communicates. If it is protected with thick fur against the cold, or shaggy hair, or a fleece of wool, it is not inferior to man in his nakedness, but merely *different*. To kill animals unnecessarily to supply warmth for our own bodies, now far removed as we are from our primitive past and with the capacity to use a variety of synthetic or natural materials which do not require killing of animals at all, is – from an external and impartial spectator standpoint – merely dull and insensate. Similarly, to think of animals as inferior because they find shelter in burrows or under rocks, or make nests in trees, instead of building houses of substantial and durable materials, is a failure to understand the differences between human and animal natures, to see animals *as they are*. It does not make them properly objects of contempt, or of amusement, to be fired on merely for sport. When draught animals submit to harness and yoke, heave and pull in obedience to drivers' commands, increase their efforts under the sting of a whip or the torture of barbed goads, they are not rightly understood as underlings for man's convenience. In fact their natures are little understood at all, or indeed their needs and their interests.

MORALITY AND DUTY

In respecting *persons*, as such, the disinterestedness of Mill's benevolent spectator does not require any special knowledge of human nature. Self-understanding and reflection on social relations with others is usually sufficient, as we have observed, for a recognition of others' interests and general wellbeing –

though certainly there are opportunities for improving the perception of common humanity, such as studies in the social sciences. But in respecting *animals* we need to adopt a more deliberate impartiality, to divest ourselves of all involvement with them, to learn as much as we can about their independent natures rather than resorting to broadly analogical approaches. Animals are different one from another and from humans, so that respect for them, as we have been suggesting, is dependent largely on an understanding of these differences.

Practical morality is a consideration of others' interests – the interests of sentient animals as well as the interests of other humans.[24] It is a practical consideration inasmuch as it is oriented *benevolently* towards helping others to satisfy *their* interests, rather than being indifferent to them or intentionally obstructing them. The consideration of others' interests is not total, for our own interests have to be considered too. The involvement in a moral situation with others is evident particularly when we experience a tension between self-interest and a perception of others' interests, which an act of ours can either advance or retard, the sense of the moral 'ought' coming to us when we experience an obligation to relax some of our self-interest to serve the interests of another. Such considerations may lead to conflict and a regular appraisal of our moral values, by this means keeping our readiness to act morally in better shape. It is not necessary for the consideration of interests to call for a cumulative weighing of the consequences of acts: sometimes, as in cases of cruelty to animals, the response of the moral agent is spontaneous or intuitive. Response to moral duty requires no deliberation.

In other situations a number of persons may be affected by an act, and it may be appropriate to make an appraisal of consequences with respect to each. Consideration of interests accommodates both the intuitive and the utilitarian stances. When we consider animals as having avoidance of suffering as a significant interest, we include all vertebrates, even reptiles, amphibians and fish; when we consider all the factors which may contribute positively to their wellbeing and which a human act may facilitate rather than frustrate, it is more appropriate, as already noted, to narrow our focus to mammals and certain social birds, because social relationship is a clear interest. But there are some interests common to the wellbeing of all other vertebrates: a suitable habitat with appropriate conditions for amphibians, for instance, or for birds, reptiles or fish. It is these wider interests which may become more evident as our knowledge increases of the natures of the various species.

Reference has been made to Kant in two contexts: first for his notion of the imperative character of moral duty; second for his idea that our duties to animals are no more than indirect duties to mankind. The notion of moral duty deserves closer attention for a possible bearing on our relations with sentient animals. Can it be shown that we have direct duties to animals, without any circumlocution about an ultimate duty to mankind? There were some in the nineteenth century who thought so, but until the end of the century most moral philosophers disagreed.[25] Then at least one moral philosopher was aware that an evolving morality began to acknowledge moral duties to animals. It was a rather reluctant admission, based largely on sympathy for their suffering without appreciation of the positive aspects of well-being according to animal nature, and still with an overriding impression of their inferiority: 'That the lower animals, as sentient beings, have a claim on our sympathies, and that consequently, we have duties in respect of them, I can no more doubt than that we have duties in respect to the inferior members of our own race.' But this 'progressive morality', as it was called, made no attempt to define the duties we have to animals; instead, it affirmed our 'right, within certain limits, to use them'.[26]

Compassion for animals has not always had a clear moral connection. It is probable that in medieval England Chaucer had pity for the victims of the hunt – the deer 'slayn with houndes', and others which 'with arwės blede of bittrė woundes'[27] – without adopting a moral stance at variance with the social values of the time. Shakespeare may have been in a similar position two centuries later. Philosophers have realised that the distinctions made by Kant between 'perfect' and 'imperfect' duties are difficult to sustain, with perfect duties pointing unequivocally to legislative imperatives and imperfect duties subject to inclination and therefore variable.[28] Have we an unconditional duty not to inflict suffering on animals, so that poverty-stricken people in Colombia, for instance, are duty bound not to satisfy their children's hunger by killing forest animals? In some situations such as this, duties conflict.[29]

In order to arrive at some solutions, rather than following an imperative call of duty alone, we may need to combine different moral approaches: to note the immediate promptings of moral intuitions, but at the same time to consider consequences, while adhering to the discipline of a benevolent impartiality. It needs to be noted further that moral duty is not always clearly distinguished from duty in legal, quasi-legal or official senses. 'It is the duty of citizens to report their finding of lost or abandoned animals' has a strong administrative flavour, serving mainly social purposes, though there may be a moral dimension to be clarified as well. Similarly, 'It is the duty of every owner of a female cat or dog to have it spayed' satisfies a *prima facie* social purpose, though there is a connection with animal wellbeing which again calls for explanation.

The moral resolution of difficult cases of conflict of duty is never reached by reason alone. To decide that X is the best course to be pursued in the circumstances is not necessarily to be left with a clear impression of the rightness of the course. In a tentative way, Hume was led to the view that '*reason* and *sentiment* concur in almost all moral determinations and conclusions'. The final judgement on the goodness of characters or the rightness of acts 'depends on some internal sense or feeling', even though much reasoning precedes this, with the making of 'nice distinctions', the drawing of conclusions and the making of comparisons, the examination of complicated relations and the accurate ascertaining of the relevant facts.[30] This 'internal sense or feeling' is more clearly described as a complex of feelings, opinions or viewpoints constituting a predisposition towards a decision, conclusion, judgement or act (if an act is relevant) which we have designated elsewhere as a disposition,[31] reason invariably interacting with it. Sometimes the two are in sympathy, at other times one exerts a contrary pull to the other. Dispositions include motives, and particularly attitudes and values because of their relative stubbornness and durability. These will be considered more fully in Chapter 3. In moral thinking reason is never alone; nor are dispositions.

That is a statement of the way things *are*, not a normative account of the way things ought to be. Our moral oughts are the products of these interacting forces whenever we are compelled to deliberate on a complex moral situation. In simple situations we may reach an intuitive judgement that an act is wrong based on the moral attitudes and values that comprise our moral convictions. Such is frequently the case with respect to acts of cruelty. Would we deliberate that poverty is a mitigating circumstance in India, for instance, if we were to encounter a performing Himalayan bear, with all its teeth drawn when young and a leading rope forced through a perforation made from the roof of the mouth into the nostril? Would we find amusement as it obeyed its master's signals on pain of further suffering?[32]

The moral debt to animals

Does humanity owe a long-standing debt to animals for the way they have been treated? If there is a debt, can it ever be repaid? Are domestic or captive animals indebted to us for their ironic security? The simplest and most naive views of our debt to animals are illustrated in the moral instruction of young children, sometimes extended in moralising to uncritical adults. *Angell's Lessons on Kindness to Animals* included, in the last century, a section on 'What We Owe to Animals', inviting children to reflect on the wretchedness that would be ours if there were no animals. What we owe to animals was sometimes confused with what we owe to God: we should all be grateful to these creatures 'which God has mercifully provided for our use'. Imagine our predicament if we had 'no horse to draw us, no ox to toil for us, no cow or goat to give us milk, no sheep to give us wool, no hens to give us eggs, no dog to be our companion and guard us at night'.[33] Does the means justify the end, an indoctrination of young children with false notions of animals *giving*, when in fact we take from them whatever we want for our use? Is the inference warranted that because they provide us with these things, we should therefore be kind to them? There must be better moral reasons for being kind to animals. 'The Farmer's Deep Debt to Animals' urged people similarly to be kind to animals. How could a farmer manage without a horse to plough his ground, it was asked. How could a shepherd do without his sheepdog? And then, 'The sportsman – what could he do without his dog?'[34]

These views were well grounded in fundamentalist religious beliefs stemming from Genesis, according to which animals were created for man's benefit. The more subtle point that man ought to treat animals in his care with responsibility was beyond the understanding and the interests of many professed Christians for centuries. In the instruction of young children at a pre-rational level (using the expression broadly, and allowing for exceptions) it is sometimes commented that such an approach still tends to complement the necessarily unreal world portrayed in picture books: animals on the farm or in the zoo, all contented, well-fed and sheltered, keeping their skins and their fleeces, their furs, feathers or scales, even keeping their young. In some religious instruction the irony of benign imagery such as of the Good Shepherd may be concealed as children grow older, unwittingly masking perceptions of cruelty to animals. In a literal rather than in a metaphorical sense, no shepherd is so good as to spend his life merely leading his flock safely to green pastures and sweet waters. The sheep are used: for food, for fleeces, and in biblical lands for milk. In the real world the shepherd protects his flock from other predators, so that he has no competition. The ultimate cruelty may be in the betrayal of the animal's trust. Thus the naive view of a moral debt to animals, associated in some cases with religious instruction of young children, may come sharply into conflict with reason as children mature, posing both educational and moral problems in the transition to a more generally rational stage of development.

There are debts to animals, it is said, which 'mankind can never repay'.[35] Is there anything to be rescued from the bland deceptions of the naive view? Is there a sense of moral debt which can give point to our attitudes to animals in a practical morality? In ordinary language 'debt' has various senses related to duty or obligation: it is these that provide the moral connection. When we are indebted to someone who has cared for a companion animal while we have been away from home, we feel under an obligation to repay him for his favour to us (not necessarily to the animal at all), perhaps to do the same for *him* in similar circumstances. If we are unable to return the favour, the sense of obligation to him may persist. In some cases it is not possible for the obligation to be reciprocated: we expect no repayment in giving help to an elderly parent. This is a more distinctly moral case than the first, which is rather a matter of convenience. In the sense that the moral duty is owed to the parent, it is itself a debt, a moral obligation. Like all moral obligations, it commands attention but is without the authority of legal obligations. In relevant circumstances the repayment of a moral debt depends on the moral character of the debtor, just as – in the language of gambling – repayment of a debt of honour is without legal enforceability and has to rely on the trustworthiness of the debtor. In a personal rather than a public morality we prescribe for ourselves our own moral obligations. We may act independently of social values, feeling a strong sense of obligatoriness with respect to animal suffering: a bounden duty, for instance, to oppose the indiscriminate slaughtering of pilot whales off the Faroe Islands. Thus, in the ordinary language of moral relations, 'debt', 'duty' and 'obligation' are related and frequently interchangeable. The moral debt is nothing other than moral duty or obligation towards a person (or sentient animal).

With respect to our relations with animals, the moral debt may be applied in several ways: first, and prior to a moral act, to a perception by us as moral agents of what we *owe* to animals; second, to what is perceived as owing to animals after human acts of cruelty have already been committed to them, and when the debt may in some circumstances be partly repaid with kindly acts, but in other circumstances may never be repaid; third, to what is perceived as owing to animals for services they have rendered to us – no more than appreciation of the extent to which they have helped us – without any intention of repaying them, and usually without any possibility of making fair compensation to them. The first sense is forward-looking; the second is backward-looking, and in some circumstances then forward-looking as well; the third is almost exclusively backward-looking and very rarely forward-looking.

To summarise the argument up to this point, several emphases may be made. First, repayment of a moral debt depends on the morality of the debtor – his moral principles, or his moral attitudes and values. Second, in practising a personal morality we may take the initiative in binding ourselves in an obligatory sense to objects calling for moral attention. We do not need a dependence on social values: we may give ourselves a *duty* to act in certain ways. Our morality is our own, of our own making. We may perceive moral debts to animals which others do not. Third, though debts imply some sort of debtor-creditor relation, or a doer of harm and a receiver of harm, moral debts are distinct from legal debts inasmuch as they are not always repaid or repayable. It is the character of moral acts that they be performed when the moral agent experiences a sense of *owing* something to another, a duty to act to serve another's interests in particular circumstances rather than pursuing his own. When we act in benevolence to prevent or alleviate the suffering of invalids or the suffering of animals, the sense of a debt is in *our* minds, not necessarily in the minds of the invalids and not in the consciousness of the animals. A moral debt does not therefore require awareness of the debt by the recipients of moral acts or favours, and in this sense we are justified in using the expression 'moral debt to animals': it conveys this very notion that it is not necessary for a duty or obligation to be *repayable* to qualify as a moral debt. Indeed, in a practical morality one acts in accordance with what one feels is *owing* by one as a moral agent. It would contradict the very notion of a practical morality if every such act were to be performed in expectation of reward or any form of repayment. Moral debts are not to be confused with non-moral debts, which may be monetary, or favours on a contractual or quid pro quo basis, and where some expectation of fair repayment is understood by each party. A moral debt is a one-way process: the transaction is completed when one has discharged the debt through an appropriate moral act.

On the other hand, when we *fail* to act morally in situations when we ought, such as by indifference or neglect, we may incur a continuing moral debt. With respect to animals there is no redress; the moral offence is compounded against ourselves. In the case of other persons there may well be an awareness of the moral debt accumulating in their favour – political prisoners, for instance, minorities, abused wives or children, slaves, nationals humiliated by colonial powers. In such situations the sense of legal debt, of possible restitution for wrong committed, merges with the sense of moral debt. That does not change the condition of the moral debt as a one-way process: it is simply that with some persons and in some situations there is a perception of what a moral agent owes to them. Some have attempted to strengthen the case for a moral debt to animals by ascribing rights to them. Do they require moral rights before we can give them status as moral objects?

Animal rights

When we refer to a failure to respect animals, the moral focus is on interests founded on their respective natures, not on their rights, which are no more than artificial ascriptions to animals, adding nothing to our understanding of the moral situation involving them. The advantages of using the language of rights are political, not moral or rational. The ascription of rights and the use of rights slogans have become useful means to an end, both educational and legislative. Their justification is pragmatic, measurable in terms of success in decreasing the maltreatment of animals and in promoting their wellbeing. To that extent the end may be said to justify the means.

The means are false *in principle*. If the pressure groups employing the weapon of animal rights use it with the understanding that it is an 'as though' approach that they are adopting, their strategy is defensible pragmatically, since history shows how difficult it is for a few to influence the many in improving the wellbeing of animals. If they believe that animals *have* rights, their position is not so clearly defensible. For the rights they are claimed to have are simply attached to them by us, without throwing any further light on their interests and what we owe to them in considering these interests. The propaganda value of rights is strong in a rights-conscious world, where political activism is sometimes more successful in bringing about change than quiet reasoning. It is strong because it borrows an aura of authority from the law; it is weak because moral rights are not analogous to legal rights, which have the support of prohibitions and sanctions. Even with moral rights there is an individual understanding, in a community of persons sharing the rights, of what the rights are, of what one can assert or stand up for, expect or claim from another. Such an understanding animals do not have. The moral position of ourselves in relation to animals is entirely one of respecting animals for the interests they have and considering these interests instead of concentrating exclusively on our own. The moral position is no more, in other words, than an appreciation of our *moral debt* to animals, of what we owe them, or of our obligations to them. It would be absurd to argue that before we can appreciate this moral debt we have to ascribe *rights* to animals. Rational thinkers need no political means to a moral end. To be clear and unambiguous in our moral discussions involving animals it is preferable to avoid the use of 'animal rights' altogether, for to deny that animals have rights is often to provoke further confusion.[36]

One of the humanitarian leaders at the turn of this century,

Henry Salt, was very conscious of the propaganda value of the word 'rights', whether applied to humans or to animals, for the New Charter of the Humanitarian League was directed towards the alleviation of suffering whenever 'the weak are oppressed by the strong'; it was in that context that rights language was employed, although one or two members deprecated the use of 'rights', preferring to speak of 'duties'. Salt commented that 'the man who knows best how to assert what is due to himself will also know best how to respect what is due to others', explaining that if the correlative term 'duties' be preferred, the same conclusion will be reached in a different way.[37] But in the apparent disagreement on the use of rights or duties applied to animals, Salt failed to explain that animals are unable themselves to assert what is due to them; or in other words to *have* rights with understanding, or an expectation of what is due to them from another. By contrast, the idealist philosopher Bradley insisted about the same time that neither rights nor duties exist outside the moral world, which requires mind as an 'inner morality'. An animal is merely 'the object of duties, not the subject of rights'.[38] Salt's purpose was not merely to explain, but also to influence others, to arouse sympathies. Bradley's purpose was no more than to clarify, to increase understanding by explanation.

IMPARTIALITY: IDEAL AND PRACTICAL

While attention to preventable animal suffering will undoubtedly remain our greater moral concern, we may wonder how far it is possible for us to proceed by taking steps to promote general animal wellbeing beyond the point of preventable suffering. Ought we to protect domestic animals from attack by predators – foxes, dingoes, coyotes and so forth? Ought we to allow domestic animals to return to the wild if they so prefer, at least giving them a chance to enjoy some liberty in their lives? And to invoke still further practical difficulties, with respect to wild animals (those not held captive or domesticated by us) ought we to attempt to provide veterinary care when needed, to move some to new areas when food resources are near exhaustion, to protect them from bushfires and drought, to restore natural habitats by returning to forestland some of the earth that has been used by us for agriculture, to give special protection to endangered species, to develop more extensive wildernesses so that more species can live out their lives under conditions natural to them?

The two main problems in attempting to answer questions of this kind are: first, the limited human capacity for impartiality; and second, purely practical difficulties of organisation, manpower, expense and so forth. To appreciate the first of these in particular, we shall contrast ideal moral theory with a practical morality which takes into account what is achievable. We shall attempt to adopt Mill's benevolent and impartial spectator stance as rigorously as we can, with a general understanding of those interests which make for *human* wellbeing when satisfied, and those which make for *animal* wellbeing: armed with relevant knowledge, that is, of human nature and of animal nature. We shall need a constructive imagination to get outside our humanness in order to attain the utmost in detachment, imagining an ideal spectator, a being of perfect intelligence or rationality, benevolence and knowledge, and so with powers of observation exceeding the human; one, further, who is completely uncommitted in any human affairs, living somewhere externally.

From this imaginary perspective we shall consider first a positive morality of promoting or improving human and animal wellbeing where there is little or no apparent suffering; and second a morality which concentrates on freedom from suffering, or suffering avoidance, as a common animal and human interest. It is important to note that Mill's benevolent and detached spectator was very much an individual of *this* world. The ideal spectator has a perfect detachment which is more meaningful when we imagine him standing outside this world. He serves as a model to remind us of the gap between ideal detachment and the utmost detachment of which we are capable in practice.

Promotion of wellbeing

With his command of relevant knowledge, including knowledge of the evolution of human and other forms of life and of human nature and animal nature, the completely uninvolved external spectator sees life forms as a unity. He understands the interests of the species, the struggle for survival, the advantages of the strong over the weak. He recognises that humans alone, of all

living things on earth, have sufficient intelligence and knowledge to promote both their own wellbeing and that of other
animals, but that – rather than sharing resources in fairness to all
– they have lived competitively with other animals. He has no
doubt that humans and animals are deserving of equal respect
according to their respective human and animal natures,
understanding that *homo sapiens* has simply been fortunate in the
relatively recent development of the human brain; and that
there ought to be an equality of consideration of interests,
regardless of whether they are human or animal interests. From
his ideal external stance humans and animals are seen as much
closer than they are in human perceptions.[39] This impels him to
the view that there ought to be a regulation of life on earth so
that the interests of the weak are not overridden by those of the
strong. He sees humans as far exceeding their moral claims in
their destruction of animal habitats to make room for the
expansion of other humans, for this does not give to animals and
humans any equal consideration of interests. He appreciates
that any regulation of life on earth by humans continues more
than ever to be in humans' favour, but sees no moral justification
in those life forms, blessed with superior intelligence and
creativity, using others to increase their control over the earth
and its resources. How can it be said that moral worth is to be
measured in terms of evolutionary success?

With the ideal detachment of a non-human and a non-animal,
the external spectator now asks: How can the wellbeing of
animals be promoted, recognising that interests are simply
different, according to natures, but deserving of equal weight?
He directs his attention to two things: first, human practices;
second, an ideal situation in which humans regulate their affairs
with an equal consideration of the interests of animals along with
their own.

First, he perceives that animals do not need to be killed by
humans at all, except in situations of self-defence. He acknow-
ledges that animal killing will go on, for some animals are
carnivores. But he understands that in the contemporary
human situation of science and technology humans are no
longer dependent on animal flesh for good health and vigour,
and that an animal with life satisfactions before it from the
fulfilment of its interests is never better off by being killed. He
notes with understanding of human limitations the recurring

rationalisations of involved humans: the irony of Fowler's claim that morality was 'progressive' by the end of the last century, while still contending of animals that 'man has a right, within certain limits, to use them, and even to kill them, for his own advantage';[40] Paley's acknowledgement of 'a right to the flesh of animals' as one of the general rights of mankind, finding excuses for 'the pain and loss which we occasion to brutes' from the belief that we are 'intended to feed upon them' as they were 'created to prey upon one another', that they would overrun the earth if let alone, and that we repay them for what they suffer by our 'care and protection';[41] Bentham's admission that if we could dispense with the infliction of suffering, 'there is very good reason why we should be suffered to eat such of them as we like to eat', for, as he went on, 'we are the better for it, and they are never the worse'.[42]

The uninvolved, ideal spectator rebukes humans both for killing animals in sport, and for their management plans to make the killing more plentiful: the habitat manipulation which creates extensive clearings for the hunting of deer, ignoring the interests of other animals not wanted for sport; the flooding of land to transform it into a duck-breeding area, ignoring the drowning of many mammals in the process; the poisoning of egg-eating racoons before placing wild turkey eggs in hunting zones, not for conservation of bird species but for the sport of shooting at the turkeys when they mature.[43]

As for captive animals, in the best of circumstances the ideal spectator sees that the balance of interest satisfaction weighs heavily in favour of humans; that the animals themselves in the most 'open' of zoos would find greater satisfaction at liberty in their natural habitats, foraging for their own food, free to exercise according to their natures. (He may have reservations about some of the smaller and more defenceless animals, subject to predation by larger animals, but he understands that all surviving species have been adaptive in nature despite their losses, and does not overlook the needs of carnivores themselves.) As a general principle liberty is seen as promoting animal wellbeing, though once domesticated and 'bonded' to humans he recognises that it is sometimes not in the animals' interests to be set free. Again he penetrates the human rationalisation that because animals in zoos have regular meals, veterinary care and security, their wellbeing is promoted better by man than by nature.

The ideal spectator perceives that animal experimentation is not justified when it is used to promote human wellbeing alone, on obvious grounds of an inequality in the consideration of interests of humans and animals. When it benefits humans and animals alike, and in cases where human subjects are available as well as animal subjects, the ideal spectator is fair-minded between and among species, as we shall find in Chapter 4. From his standpoint also, genetic manipulation of animals is an unwarranted presumption, since surviving species have established their own adaptability. He finds no justification for animal scientists' attempts to increase the weight of pigs or cattle for economic reasons: since it is one-sided human benefit that is being promoted, such designs are to him merely exploitative.

Let us now quickly change the perspective from the ideal to the practical. This will be the stance in practical morality of a person who strives to achieve moral relations with animals, but inevitably lapses from impartiality because of his humanness: he cannot completely cast off his human biases, for he sees the world through human eyes; he has some limitations in his knowledge of both humanity and animals, though he has the capacity to explore and to expand his knowledge; he is strongly self-interested, though as a moral agent he tries to consider the interests of animals as much as possible; he has moral values, though he cannot always act in accordance with them because of conflicts of values.

Practical morality falls short of ideal theory, with its perfect combination of benevolence and impartiality, to the extent that practical morality refers to the morality that is humanly *practicable*. How does this affect the *moral debt* to animals? Does it restrict what we owe morally to animals, bringing the debt into a realistic correspondence with what we are capable of giving to animals or capable of fulfilling in moral obligations to them? The answer is plain: the moral debt remains unchanged. It is simply perceived clearly by the being of perfect benevolent detachment, and less clearly by humans who are limited in both benevolence and impartiality. As Hume observed, the struggle for limited resources[44] is another factor reducing man's capacity to live a perfect practical morality by forcing him to pay urgent attention to self-interest for the security of himself and his family. The way morality is perceived – perfectly or imperfectly, with unlimited impartiality and benevolence, or with limits to each – is distinct from any human capacity to put it into practice. While it is appropriate to consider the goals of a practical morality as practicable, in the sense that any expectation of *perfectly* fulfilling our moral debt to animals, for instance, is readily frustrated by conflicts with our own interests, it is also appropriate to keep the model of perfection in mind. Since the bounds of human impartiality can always be improved, the effort to reach upward towards the ideal is worth sustaining, even though no one can prick through the world of imperfection, in the Platonic sense, to glimpse the Form of the good as he understood it.[45]

How may we promote animal wellbeing within the imperfections of a practical morality? Why should we try, when we are incapable of the perfect detachment or disinterestedness of the ideal spectator? To answer the second question first, the positive moral debt to promote animal wellbeing is one we owe because we alone, as the ideal spectator perceived, have both the knowledge and the capacity to do this, even if we do it imperfectly. If we believed in increasing *human* wellbeing, distributing opportunities for further satisfactions as widely as possible, that alone would be a merely selective benevolence, as it would also be if we restricted our benevolence to relieving the suffering of animals without extending it, where relevant, to the promotion of their wellbeing as well. To act on a consistent principle is to give equal consideration to the interests of both humans and animals. In answer to the first question, then, we strive for as much impartiality as we can whenever there are conflicts between humans and animals, guided by the principle of an equality of consideration of interests.

Let us consider briefly some of the difficulties of practical morality in attempts to promote animal wellbeing. In the present international situation we have to admit that we have had very limited success in promoting *human* wellbeing. Basically we remain competitive, nationalistic or territorial, suspicious of others, nervous and defensive. We have improved in recent years in aid to starving millions in Africa and in international disaster relief, but we are a long way from promoting the wellbeing of humans *generally*. Because of our insecurity and other aspects of our natures, self-interest is dominant. Can we reasonably expect more in attempts to promote animal wellbeing *in general*? Suppose, for instance, we considered it a moral debt to animals to restore some of the vast territories we have taken from them for exclusive human use (or for selected animal use where the animals themselves are used by us), or attempted to acknowledge a moral debt by reafforestation schemes so that animal habitats are restored, or sacrificed extensive agricultural land for animal wilderness areas, without any hunting or mining rights claimed by us. Sharp conflicts of animal interests with our own become obvious. We claim special duties with respect to our kin, so that if by such actions intended to promote the interests of animals we found that we were sacrificing our family's health and the future livelihood of our children, we would fall back on the human interest and the animal interest would lapse. This situation is not merely a limited human generosity and benevolence; it is also, and just as fundamentally, a lack of human impartiality or capacity for a totally detached fair-mindedness.

Suppose our disinterested and benevolent spectator also had executive powers to regulate all human and animal life on earth. Totally impartial himself, being neither human nor animal, his attention would certainly be drawn to the size of the human population, the great increase in population in the last few decades and the great decline in animal population. An equal consideration of interests would not lead him to favour human life despite our greatly superior intellectual capacities. Would he not see that such capacities ought to be turned rather to promoting both human and animal wellbeing? A check on human population growth would seem an early imperative. Similarly our observer would take notice of the wellbeing of some *wild* animals: the lives of wild horses, for example, their health and vigour and vitality in environments such as the Camargue of France, Central Australia, the Mongolian plains, the Nevada desert of the United States; and the contrast between the lives of wild camels and donkeys and their lives in captivity in the service of man. Would our executive spectator not favour a freeing of as many animals as possible from man's control?

The difficulty is obvious. Man has not this degree of impartiality. He is not capable of promoting the wellbeing of animals whole-heartedly when his own vital interests are threatened. Man is impelled, but not irresistibly, to regulate animal life in his favour. In more specific management policies man has not the resources to proceed very far. Some species would benefit from greater security, for instance. Should man allocate species to particular areas, fencing some off from predators? Should he follow up all animals in the wild, and in times of drought and scarcity of food supply these according to need? Both schemes are clearly impracticable. Even the reallocation of land so that animals are given a more generous share than they have at present is a luxury few countries could afford without severely impairing self-interest, and in impoverished countries where both humans and animals strive to survive together, the proposition is, as seen by the inhabitants themselves, even insulting. Practical morality demands only that what can be done *ought* to be done, that some of the moral debt be discharged to animals, even when some sacrifice by humans is necessary, a sacrifice which can be borne by benevolent people without inducing intolerable suffering. But decisions on these matters can be taken by few people only, even decisions that will lack perfect impartiality: these are not politicians, but the morally and intellectually best, who at present have no executive power.[46] Though taking account of public opinion, they would not allow their judgements to be impaired by powerful self-interest groups. Though still human, they would face the daunting task of deciding what is 'tolerable' in human sacrifice and what is not, remembering that in recent emergencies people have learned quickly to adapt to hardships that are equitably shared. The task of decision-making will be considered further in the final chapter.

Prevention of suffering

The ideal external spectator with the powers we have assigned him judges moral situations on principles which he applies with equal favour to humans and to animals. To him pain is pain, suffering is suffering, and the moral debt to prevent suffering among humans is no greater than the moral debt to prevent suffering among animals. Questions of how much total suffering is felt, and whether there is 'like' suffering among animals and humans, he regards as irrelevant to the application of the principle of equal consideration of the interests of each.[47] To strengthen the perspective of perfect impartiality and to contrast it with imperfect human impartiality, let us glance at some of our human practices from his detached perspective, returning to our previous attention to eating habits, hunting, amusements and so forth.

First, from the standpoint of animal suffering he judges against killing animals for food, quite apart from its unnecessariness as noted earlier. Temporary exceptions only are people who still need to live on animals for daily sustenance: in those circumstances he considers that other humans on the planet ought to rescue them from their predicament, so that the moral debt to this minority of humans, once paid, relieves the moral debt to animals. He observes the dependence of the Lapp people on reindeer and of the Masai in Africa on their cattle, but is aware also that a similar dependence on animals among the Ewenki people in China has recently been broken with external aid.[48] He does not accept that the suffering of animals in slaughter, and prior to slaughter, is justified, noting that some improvements in techniques have not completely removed the suffering.[49] He is aware of the threat to animals from the contemporary human craving for variety in foods, with its implications for a widening of animal species to be killed.[50] As he focuses on animal suffering, the comprehensive assessment from his totally disinterested stance is not that suffering ought to be diminished, but that since animal slaughter is unnecessary the suffering from that source should end.

Similarly the suffering of animals in the hunt, both from distress and from the killing, earns summary condemnation, as does cruelty in trapping practices. From his perspective, killing for sport or for vanity is equally senseless, as unnecessary as killing for food.[51] High on the list of amusements condemned from the ideal spectator's stance are the rodeo, described in Chapter 1, and the bullfight. Even in its milder forms the bullfight is seen to cause unnecessary suffering. If there is to be amusement between humans and animals, he judges, there are opportunities for shared play with companion animals, for then there may be an equal consideration of the interests of both humans and animals.[52] The one-sided pleasure of human amusements involving animals is what impresses him also in zoos, with extensive animal suffering persisting, especially in private zoos and menageries;[53] as well as in many separate activities when animals are hunted to exhaustion from powered vehicles: coyotes over snow, wild camels over sand dunes, buffaloes or wild horses across plains.

Let us now turn to the standpoint of *practical* morality, and to the actual world in which humans alone are moral agents, owing moral debts to sentient animals as creatures with interests they are sometimes incapable of fulfilling entirely from their own resources, dependent to some extent on man's benevolence, his knowledge of their natures and their needs, and his own limited capacity for taking even Mill's disinterested spectator stance, much less that of the ideal spectator with his total impartiality. The intention now is not to provide instances of our 'limited generosity', in Hume's language, but to suggest what we *ought* to do, as humans, to prevent animal suffering. Though the normative stance we take is human, we shall assume that as moral agents our task is to extend both our benevolence and our capacity for impartiality ever closer to the ideal in an effort to prevent animal suffering. Sooner or later we realise that in relieving or preventing animal suffering we are causing some loss of our self-interest, and in this way some suffering to ourselves. At this point we have to ask whether it is morally appropriate for the sacrifice of interest to be made by ourselves or by animals. Let us see how this applies to the areas we have considered – killing animals for food or trapping them for furs, hunting them for recreation, using them for our own amusement or abusing companion animals – and then extending these to intensive farming, transport of animals and other commercial activities such as fishing.

Both as rational beings and as moral agents we take stock of relevant facts: first, that on scientific evidence humans can be healthy and vigorous on a vegetarian diet, but that some would find it – especially during a period of adjustment – less palatable; second, that generally speaking animals killed for food suffer at some point in the process – in distress if not always physically. But for the sake of the argument we shall consider the situation as we find it. Which presents the stronger *moral* solution: complete removal of the probability of animal suffering by abandoning the practice of killing them for food; or retaining the general meat-eating preference while refining slaughtering techniques still further towards an increasing reduction of stress and pain? In the second alternative there is a concession to human self-indulgence which, on present trends, might lead to an extension of animal suffering in attempts to satisfy a craving for novelty in foods. In the first, some humans may suffer mentally from frustration and may suffer temporarily from loss of appetite. Some others may be deprived trivially of the enjoyment of restaurant eating, and some engaged in the meat industry, as well as some restaurateurs and their chefs, may suffer from loss of employment or from the need for temporary retraining. Indeed, the complete change from meat-eating to vegetarianism would produce far-reaching social and economic changes, requiring careful planning to prevent sharp dislocations of habitual cultural practices which would inevitably lead to some human suffering. Unlike the situation of the benevolent and impartial external spectator, now we are left with a *human* judgement. Must we resolve the conflict in our favour?

An understandable response in this dilemma is that a practical morality cannot realistically demand the impossible. But detailed practicalities do not need to be weighed. All we need to show is that *in principle* vegetarianism is practicable for all mankind. The moral solution must also be rational in the sense that it considers the relevant facts and is as impartial as is humanly possible. If meat-eating continues, it seems that two wrongs are committed to animals: first, they continue to suffer; second, they are denied the satisfaction of some of their interests according to their natures. The first is the more serious consideration; the second is merely a potential loss, one they can never be aware of, and so one that does not constitute a form of suffering. If a vegetarian diet is introduced gradually for mankind, the human suffering involved may, on the evidence of some who have undergone the experience, gradually diminish and disappear. If the evidence is proved unreliable, further research may be needed before deciding in what way, and how gradually, the change away from meat-eating is to be introduced. But in the last resort the solution from the standpoint of practical morality is to assert a preference for a temporary human sacrifice of pleasure over a continuing animal suffering. This conclusion conveys the moral debt to animals in killing them for food. It is the debt of civilised man everywhere on the planet.[54]

From a similar rational and moral stance, practical morality quickly leads to a similar conclusion with respect to hunting, amusements and certain commercial practices. We have sufficient benevolence and impartiality, and sufficient knowledge of ourselves and of animals, to see that recreational shooting of

animals and trapping of animals for furs are both wrong, and
that our amusements at the expense of animal suffering are also
wrong. The reasoning is simple: in each case there is human
pleasure, but in each case there is animal suffering inflicted
unnecessarily. If there is satisfaction to some in testing their skills
in marksmanship, simulated targets may easily replace live ones,
as in the case of clay pigeons and moving images on rifle ranges.
If the substitutes do not provide the same degree of temptation
or zest, then the shooters expose either their inclination to
cruelty or their dullness of perception. Trapping animals for
furs is similarly unnecessary either to keep people warm or for
fashion. Those who persist in wearing the coats of mink, otter,
red fox, beaver, sable, seal, muskrat, coyote, lynx, opossum,
racoon, leopards or jaguars expose the quality of their sensibilities.

From the standpoint of practical morality, in brief, similar
conclusions are reached to those reached by the perfectly
impartial and benevolent spectator. Limited as we are, we have
sufficient reason, impartiality and knowledge to distance
ourselves from cruel practices and to take a moral stand on
them. The same applies to perceptions of animal suffering in
factory farms and in commercial fishing.[55]

Most humans are still unready for this standpoint of practical
morality. To them any suggestion that animals' interests are
worthy of equal consideration with humans' is a contradiction,
for animals are clearly below us. This is the partiality and the
presumption observed by Montaigne. It is a reflection of our
lofty preoccupation with self-interest. Practical morality requires
that we *act* on our moral principles, moral understandings or
perceptions. It is in respect of an incapacity for moral acts in
relations with animals that many humans, though compassionate in human relations, live a morality that fails to stand up to the
crucial test of a serious conflict of interests. To these it is only in
principle that the interests of humans and of animals call for
equal consideration; in practice animals' interests receive secondary consideration.

A practical morality often requires extraordinary effort to
concede to other *humans*' interests. The task of conceding to
animals' interests, whenever our moral convictions indicate that
we ought, is even harder. This is because of, first, the anthropo-
centricity which expresses habitual human partiality rather than

detachment and fair-mindedness; and second, human ignorance of animal natures, which is taken up in the following chapter.

SUMMARY

The nature of morality has been considered from three different stances: Mill's disinterested and benevolent spectator stance; Kant's imperatives of duty based on a rational will; and Bentham's classical form of utilitarianism with the modified form of the Preference Utilitarians. A practical morality may combine two or more of these approaches, with benefit to a perception of moral relations with animals. Mill's stance helps to remove some of our human presumption; Kant's to appreciate our intuitive moral duty not to be cruel to animals; the utilitarian to an understanding of the importance of satisfaction of *interests* – both human and animal.

Attention to the capacity of sentient animals to experience pain owes much to Humphry Primatt and soon after to Jeremy Bentham, but these evoked a response, it seems, especially in the *already* compassionate. Observation is sufficient to infer the experience of suffering in vertebrate animals, without insisting on the impossible by actually witnessing the register of sensation in the brain as it is transmitted by the nervous system. Pain or suffering is evil inasmuch as it inhibits or prevents the fulfilment of interests according to human or animal natures; pain avoidance is itself an interest. The conscious infliction of unnecessary suffering is *cruelty*, its severest forms *torture*, though the distinction between the two is arbitrary.

Human interests and animal interests have a common element in 'wellbeing' and share general interests such as health and security. Social animals such as mammals and certain birds share with humans an interest in social relationships, including rearing and protection of the young. But each of the general interests takes on a specific meaning according to human and animal natures, with their markedly different *needs*. Avoidance of suffering as a common interest does not imply that there is *identical* suffering in each case – something which cannot be claimed even with respect to different humans. Prevention of unnecessary suffering is the moral consideration. The utilitarian calculation of intensity of duration of pain, or even a general impression of its impact on all concerned, is not necessary to conclude that the suffering is wrong. Any malicious violation of another's interests is wrong, and leads to suffering.

As a moral standpoint, respect for persons is based on a measure of benevolence and impartiality, and on some knowledge of human nature. Respect for animals is also a moral standpoint, based similarly on a variable benevolence and impartiality, and also on a relevant knowledge of animal nature, especially its distinctiveness – according to species – from human nature. Practical morality is a consideration of others' interests – practical inasmuch as it goes beyond a theoretical understanding of what these interests are, to acts aimed at helping others to satisfy *their* interests, while recognising that as moral agents we have interests too which are not to be ignored. Moral conflicts between duties are common, and their rational resolution requires that Kant's dogma of perfect or unconditional duties be relaxed as the interests of those concerned are considered. But the resolution of moral dilemmas or problems is never achieved by reason alone. As humans we reach moral decisions, conclusions or judgements as our complex dispositions interact with reason.

The moral debt to animals is a duty, or obligation, to them: something we owe to them by way of giving a fair or benevolent consideration of their interests. It is a *human* awareness. The moral debt by its nature does not require reciprocal acts by animals. Since animals are not moral agents, the moral debt is discharged by an appropriate human act. The strongest application of 'moral debt' is in a forward-looking sense. It is usually too late, and therefore meaningless, to speak of discharging a moral debt in a backward-looking sense for cruelty committed to animals in the past, for no amount of benevolence to present animals will discharge a moral debt to former victims of our cruelty, now dead. But in some cases our moral reflections may lead us to reconsider our attitudes and to adopt a forward-looking moral stance with respect to animals that have survived our cruelty, treating them subsequently with a supposedly compensatory benevolence. Moral debts must not be confused with legal debts even in such acts of remorse: obligation in the former does not entail compensation; a moral slate of cruelty is not wiped clean by subsequent moral action which is no more than appropriate for the current situation.

There is no increase in our appreciation of the moral debt to animals by ascribing rights to them. The gain is political: rights language has strong emotional appeal through association with the authority of legal rights; animal rights have become a propaganda weapon of (perhaps well-intentioned) pressure groups. From a rational standpoint 'animal rights' is a confusion. From a pragmatic standpoint alone, on a principle of the means justifying the end, the language of rights serves a purpose in attempting to win a struggle against strong opposition, such as in attempting to achieve legislation against the steel-jaw trap or the fur trade. But in the logic of a moral relation between humans and animals the ascription of rights to animals is either pretentious or confused.

Impartiality in our moral approach to animals may be considered from both *ideal* and *practical* perspectives. For explanatory purposes, and to give emphasis to the supreme importance of impartiality, Mill's disinterested, benevolent spectator has been elevated to an ideal, made both non-human and non-animal, and given a perspective even external to the earth. It is more readily understandable that such a being can achieve a perfectly unbiased perspective on all forms of life and thereby can give equal consideration to the interests of humans and animals according to their respective natures. It is not presumptuous to claim the power to *imagine* such an external being with perfect impartiality. The difficulty is not one of imagination: it is one of a shift of stance as soon as we assume an involved position when confronted with animal interests in an actual situation. It is then that the moral compass needle swings sharply back to the human zone.

The moral bearing that is so difficult to sustain for most people is towards an equal consideration of interests. This does not imply that humans and animals are *equal*: indeed, the very question of equality is meaningless unless we make comparisons according to specific criteria. The criterion of moral respect as we apply it to humans is not helpful, because human and animal natures are different: moral respect is related to the natures of the particular objects of our respect. So, to the question, Are humans deserving of more moral respect than animals? the answer given from a human standpoint is often Yes, because humans alone are capable of acting as moral agents. But from the ideal standpoint of a perfectly impartial being, the answer is No, because humans and animals are different in natures, each deserving of equal respect for the interests they happen to have. The wider non-moral question, Are humans worthier than animals in the scheme of life on earth? is unanswerable, unless criteria for non-moral 'worthiness' are specified. Animals are not on an evolutionary ladder which will take them to man's eventual state of intelligence: they are simply different from humans, and will never become human, or have human powers of moral agency.

The interests of animals may be considered in two contrasting ways, so that the ideal and the practical perspectives are each subdivided into positive and negative aspects: the first refers to *promoting* the satisfaction of animal interests; the second to preventing loss of such satisfaction by reducing or eliminating animal suffering as far as possible, and by refraining from acts of cruelty to them. Illustrations of such suffering are to be found in the human demand for animal meat, recreational hunting, various amusements, animal experimentation, commercial enterprises such as trapping for furs and the indiscriminate netting of fish, genetic manipulation by animal scientists, transporting animals to market, and above all, in our times, in the intensive methods of factory farming. In practice it is much more difficult to promote animal wellbeing generally than it is to attend to unnecessary animal suffering. Though we are imperfect moral agents, unable to match the perfection in benevolence and impartiality of the ideal external spectator, we are sufficiently rational and benevolent to perceive that we are *not* giving an equal consideration to the interests of animals if we kill them unnecessarily for food, cause suffering through recreational hunting and various amusements such as the rodeo, or use them with indifference to suffering in the experimental laboratory, in intensive farming and in certain other commercial activities such as fishing.

Practical morality is changing. The moral convictions which, along with reason, give us bearings in practical judgements on what we ought to do are individually held, learned by us in various ways, sometimes in childhood. There is evidence of much compassion towards animals, but also of a need for much clearer understanding of practical morality, including the need for the utmost impartiality in considering animal interests against the pressures of commercialism. An understanding of the meaning of equality in the consideration of animals' interests along with our own, according to their respective natures, demands that we understand what animal natures are. A rudimentary understanding is that animals are not merely things for human use. As Bentham understood, all animals 'stand degraded' when their interests are neglected.[56] A second rudimentary understanding is that they are not inferior because their natures are different from ours. If they are to be compared with humans they are inferior only in specific respects, notably in intellectual powers, but the moral debt to animals cannot be adequately discharged by us until we take better advantage of our intellectual powers than we have in the past.

Two centuries ago Holbach urged that morality is to be understood only by following nature, not the supernatural. Not that nature itself makes man 'either good or wicked': man's moral dispositions have to be cultivated, but the important thing is to study the nature of man.[57] In his time sentient animals were excluded from the sphere of practical morality, now they are included. So Holbach saw only half the truth; the other half is the need for a practical morality to be based on the nature of animals as well. It is to this subject that we turn in the following chapter.

3 Morality and the Nature of Animals

In rejecting the 'state of nature' as a 'mere fiction', an invention similar to that of the golden age of the poets when there was no war, no violence and injustice, no avarice, ambition, cruelty or selfishness, Hume proposed as certain that in the actual world justice derives from the concurrence of man's 'selfishness and limited generosity' with an external situation of 'the scanty provision nature has made for his wants'.[1] His limited generosity notwithstanding, man was also a creature of *sympathy*, Hume observed. The objects of our sympathy are other human beings, for we sympathise with those who resemble us; indeed, 'the minds of men are mirrors to one another' (book 2, part 2, section 5, p. 365). Yet from a broad perspective of all life on earth – 'a general survey of the universe' – Hume also noted 'the force of sympathy thro' the whole animal creation, and the easy communication of sentiments from one thinking being to another' (p. 363).

Hume was saying little of the natures of animals but their natural tendency to seek association with other animals (except, as he qualified, for those that prey upon others). He did not urge man to extend his sympathy from other humans, perceived as mirror images of himself, to animals, which could not be so mirrored. As for *benevolence*, he believed this to be of two kinds: either 'implanted in our natures', like 'the love of life and kindness to children', or 'the general appetite to good, and aversion to evil' (section 3, p. 417), considered rather in the abstract. He went on to explain that benevolence (like other passions supposedly natural to mankind) is contagious, passing 'with the greatest facility from one person to another'. Benevolence has many different forms, all excited by sympathy (or love) as in the case of friendship, and because of this common element of sympathy it is easy for us to change from one object to another (book 3, part 3, section 3, p. 605).

Hume's thoughts on sympathy and benevolence raise a fundamental question in practical morality. Why do we not

67

more generally change the object of each of these to an *animal*? By implication Hume believed the answer to lie in human nature. But his psychological account of the way things are, according to his observation, can easily be refuted in experience, as in many instances of reciprocated human affection for companion animals. By his account, if it were validated, the transition of human sympathy from one object to another – easy when the various objects are human – would be a contradiction of our natures if the object were animal rather than human. That would make impossible also a practical morality of considering the interests of animals, or any appreciation of a moral debt to them.

Here Hume was in error in his observations; and the moral question of whether we *ought* to extend our sympathy and benevolence to animals, enlarging the moral sphere beyond humanity, has been answered in the previous chapter in the discussion of interests, as well as in the emphasis on understanding the distinctiveness of animal natures in giving them our moral respect. Sentience implies that animals have awareness – at least a minimum of awareness of suffering. (Some, such as mammals, have much greater awareness, as we shall enlarge on shortly.) This minimum awareness is the criterion for excluding trees and other plant life from the moral sphere, though they undoubtedly have a place in other, non-moral areas of our thinking, such as the scientific, the economic and the aesthetic.

Hume's thoughts on sympathy and benevolence have a characteristically human ring. It was not merely that he was limited by the influence of eighteenth-century thought, or by any personal stinting of the limited generosity he attributed to everyone. (On the contrary, Hume appears to have been a more than usually generous man.) What is humanly characteristic in Hume's moral thought is the strong human inclination to confine practical morality to our own kind – a tendency that is understandable up to a point inasmuch as it restricts practical morality to those who alone are capable of acting as moral agents. Illustrating this tendency, towards the end of the last century one moral philosopher explained that 'the law of Benevolence, or brotherly love, is universal, and knows no limits but those of the race for whose benefit it was established'.[2] He too could see no object of benevolence other than another human.

MORAL JUDGEMENTS

Regardless of the object, practical morality requires an under-standing not only of the nature of morality, or of what it is that we do when we act morally, but also of ourselves as moral agents. Hume has drawn attention to our human imperfections, which may act as serious impediments to moral conduct in the *actual* world of avarice, ambition, cruelty, selfishness. What is it that leads a grazier in Australia to declare kangaroos to be vermin, needing to be exterminated for our own good; or a rancher in the USA to declare unqualified war on all coyotes as trash? What makes a representative of the fur industry say that animals caught in steel-jaw traps cannot be said to feel any pain; or a representative of trappers assert that those who are agitating to end the use of steel-jaw traps belong to 'animal worship cults' and that countries already banning their use 'are still in the dark ages'?[3] In some instances such as these it appears that reason itself is being challenged, or at least that there are other powerful components of our moral thinking as we make our practical judgements. What are they?

Any account of the psychological elements of our moral thinking is in itself no more than descriptive: it does not, in itself, indicate what we ought to do. Its value is in enlarging self-understanding in such a way as to increase the *probability* of some persons acting with greater moral sensitivity in relations both with other persons and with animals. First, it is apparent that in moral thinking one of the elements invariably present is reason, however rudimentary it may be. Further, at least some of our intuitions are rational to a degree, though we express them spontaneously, such as that cruelty is wrong or telling lies is wrong. As we saw in the previous chapter, when we speak in their language, asserting an already-formed moral conviction, we are sometimes said to be speaking categorically by respond-ing to the call of duty. In the background, nonetheless, reason has been an active formative agent. If cruelty is intuitively wrong, preceding the conviction is the reason that it causes suffering; if suffering is intuitively wrong, embedded in the conviction is that it is contradictory to cause suffering to others when one wishes to avoid it oneself; if telling lies is intuitively wrong, it is breaking one of the rules that make human communication practicable. There is justification therefore in referring to these as instances of 'rational intuitions'. In terms of Kant's moral imperatives 'reason determines the will to action': moral duty commands us to obey a law which all *rational* beings will respect since it applies equally to each of them.[4] Behind duty is a will 'which of itself conforms to reason'.[5] While it was important to acknowledge the place of reason in moral judgements, though, Kant exceeded this recognition by giving it an overriding, transcendental place in his account of the way all rational beings conduct their moral lives, taking reason outside ordinary experience. The strength of reason in moral deliberations on what one ought to do – as in the making of moral judgements of a more direct nature based on already-formed convictions – is clearly variable, not uniform, among rational persons.

What are the other elements in the mental complex prior to reaching moral judgements, decisions or conclusions? Let us consider some of the wide range of perceptions people may have of animals, and what factors seem to influence those perceptions. Graziers and ranchers who perceive some animals as merely destructive and worthless are influenced by their emotions and the motives of profit which have generated them. Sometimes it may be a matter of economic survival and protection of a precarious livelihood. Experience of losses or diminished profits may have been repeated sufficiently for stubbornly defensive prejudices to have developed against animals competing unwittingly with their sheep and cattle for pastures. Knowledge of predators' interests is almost extinguished by personal self-interest. The emotional and sometimes irrational defence of the trapping of furred animals with steel-jaw traps is also related to a threatened livelihood. Visitors to zoos express a variety of attitudes to animals, related to their personal experiences, degree of curiosity and knowledge of animal natures. A lion in a pit may be seen as an object of derision, reduced by the superior force of human skill and ingenuity to impotence and harmlessness, despite its physical strength. A powerful gorilla sitting disconsolate in a corner of a barred cage, without the company of others of its kind, may be seen as a dull and torpid bulk.

The way we perceive animals is a complex of our attitudes to them – including our ideas, our knowledge, our interests – as well as of motives and emotions. Those attitudes may be moral:

then we are aware of animal interests to be considered by us. They may be immoral: then there is a denial of animal interests, as in the abandonment of companion animals. They may be amoral: then we are unaware of animal interests and indifferent to them through ignorance. In other words, before we make judgements concerning animals, we are already *predisposed* towards a response of a certain kind by a complex of attitudes, motives and emotions, associated with information or misinformation about them, relevant knowledge of their natures, or almost total ignorance. In these predispositions the place of attitudes and values is central.

Attitudes and values

If the moral debt to animals is left undischarged by us because of certain predisposing tendencies, we need to become clearer about what these tendencies are as a means to more sensitive self-understanding. When we value an animal (or animals generally) we have a distinctly favourable attitude towards the object. When we place no value whatever on an animal (or on animals generally) we have a distinctly unfavourable attitude to the object; that is, we have developed a prejudice against it. In either case we are predisposed to act in a way appropriate to the attitude: to give an animal attention or affection, for instance, or to hurt it, abuse it or even destroy it. Emotion is part of the predispositional complex, helping to give it the cohesiveness and stubbornness characteristic of attitudes, especially when the orientation towards the object is strong and there is a degree of personal involvement. When attitudes and values form a powerful composite force they incline us towards defensiveness, even at times in contra-rational directions.

The factory farmer's attitude towards veal calves (in their worst conditions) or pigs or battery hens may lead to rationalisations, as he proclaims that they are in better health than they would be in the wild; or, like all animals, need no more than food and rest; or, being 'only animals', never realise what is happening to them. Whatever the attitude is towards an object, its various components – ideas, impressions, opinions, preconceptions, familiarity or unfamiliarity with relevant facts – become a binding, habitual influence which may lead to a hasty judgement or decision unless checked by reason. And further, from the standpoint of an animal's wellbeing, an unfavourable attitude may lead to a harmful act, to severe and sometimes protracted misery. Self-understanding is therefore crucial to moral relations with animals: an understanding of our motives, the frequent dominance of self-interest in our goals, the cruelty that may be inflicted on animals for no better reason than that we do not understand the nature of our moral thinking. It is common observation that many humans are merely *potential* moral agents, responding to objects or situations according to habitual attitudes that remain inadequately informed, without an appropriate capacity for self-criticism.

Our moral thinking is in fact both rational and dispositional, the dispositional component referring to all components of a mental configuration which inclines us towards a decision, judgement or act of a certain kind.[6] While Jews and Moslems believe in ritual slaughtering, with an animal bleeding to death from a cut throat, others believe that stunning should precede slaughter, for the reason that it prevents as much unnecessary suffering as possible. From the standpoint of devoted Jews and Moslems there is no better reason for ritual slaughtering than that it is decreed by tradition and holy doctrine. In each case attitudes and values, comprising powerful moral convictions, lead to spontaneous judgements. Indeed it is exceptional to deliberate with reasons for and against before reaching a moral conclusion whenever we are personally involved in situations. Slower deliberations of this kind are reserved for situations when we are not personally involved, so that we are better able to stand off and to attempt as much impartiality as we can; or when it is necessary, as in a quasi-legal situation, to mount arguments against those of an adversary.

Individual judgements are made, in most instances, in response to attitudes and values already predisposing one in a preferred direction.[7] Those attitudes and values are sometimes formed with reasons, especially those strongly favourable to an object, for then it is usually necessary to have some reasons in the course of preferring one thing to another. In other cases attitudes (without values) are formed as almost blind habits, especially those strongly unfavourable to objects such as reptiles or rats, when emotions rather than reasons are apparent. There are occasions when careful deliberation and the marshalling of arguments conceal well-entrenched attitudes, so that conclusions do not follow from the reasons given, but instead substantially reiterate preconceived positions. It is in such situations that rationalisations occur, as in the *Report of the Committee on Cruelty to Wild Animals* in 1951, discussed in the first chapter. It is recalled that the conclusion reached by the committee was that hunting 'should not be interfered with except for some very good reason',[8] partly because it provided recreation for people. A defensive self-interest, a long-standing cultural attitude, had made it very difficult to bring about change, no matter how good the reason. The moral reason was evident only to those with appropriate values: namely, that the hunting of foxes, rabbits, hares, deer, otter, badgers and other creatures inflicted unnecessary suffering on them; but for a significant proportion of the population the reason was over-powered by a traditional preference for 'field sports'. Demonstration of the force of attitudes in our moral thinking gives further weight to the need for a disciplined effort to improve in *impartiality*, as well as benevolence, returning to a major emphasis of the preceding chapter.

In the interaction between reason and the complex of dispositions which include attitudes and values at their core, reason is not always dominant even among ordinarily rational persons. Moral sensitivity is kept alive by a continual awareness of our imperfection in this respect and by a resolve to allow reason a proper place in moral judgements whenever there is a danger that it will succumb to habitual attitudinal pressures. Moral judgements of other persons require us to assume Mill's disinterested and benevolent spectator stance as far as possible, so that we are better able to see the world from the standpoint of those other persons, to perceive *their* interests and needs. This is central to respecting persons. In a similar way it is central to a moral respect for animals, as explained in the previous chapter, seeing the world as far as we are able from *their* standpoints, appreciating that they have their pattern of interests and needs, including health and security and, for some, social relationships with their kind.

No commercial photographer for a popular magazine could have a moral respect for a hunted stag swimming desperately across water with a pack of hounds almost upon it, eyes bulging with terror, his personal thoughts being no higher than his reputation and profitable return. No exporter of sheep from

Australia to the Middle East could possibly have a thought for the interests of the animals or look at the world from their standpoint, knowing that several weeks of travel at sea in crowded pens will itself lead to suffering and the death of many, quite apart from the primitive slaughter of the survivors at the end of the voyage. The trappers of jungle animals for zoos and the agents who engage them and profit from their success, often transporting them carelessly to their destinations in colder climates, see the world from their own commercial standpoints. They are dealing in *things*, commodities for trade, and things have no standpoint of their own worthy of consideration. When there is no moral respect for animals as such, there can be no moral decisions or judgements made with respect to them.

In the making of moral judgements, or the reaching of moral decisions or conclusions leading to moral acts, there is no critical faculty which regularly intervenes from a higher level to keep our wayward or disorderly dispositions, at a lower level, in moral shape. Though it may help at times to reflect on the need for a kind of rational vigilance, we are more usually swayed by habitual attitudes and values, at least in the initial stages of the interaction with reason.[9] Sometimes there is a marginal success to the dispositions, sometimes to reason; but tragically, in some cases, for the human or animal objects of our moral judgements, dispositions towards cruelty sometimes overpower reason, leading to suffering in the acts that follow. Our moral judgements are made at one level only, and reason belongs to that one level. It has no transcendental power to eclipse the dispositions entirely.

It cannot be over-emphasised that the moral point of view on animals is dependent not only on impartiality and benevolence, but also on appropriate *knowledge*, both of animal natures and of human nature. Regardless of how much we consider ourselves superior to animals in the types of awareness of which we are capable, there are times when we are singularly unaware, with reason and understanding almost subdued by an habitual cluster of emotionally reinforced false ideas or beliefs. When Livingstone, the missionary, wrote of blacks in Africa as 'degraded', to be uplifted only by Christianity and commerce, he set them apart as inferior beings despite his benevolence. Similarly animals may be walled off as inferior in many human perceptions. The abuse sometimes shouted at a murderer or a rapist when he is making his first court appearance after the offence is frequently the word 'animal'. That is the ultimate derogation. Miserable, neglectful treatment may pass for a dog, since it is only an animal, but a 'dog's life' is inhumane when it is a human who suffers.

Animals are the reference for debasement: it is always human status that suffers in the metaphors, not animal status. The view that animals belong to one world, humans to another, is pre-scientific, characteristic of the centuries-old Christian doctrine which sought to set human life, with the gift of reason, sharply against animal life, devoid of reason and governed only by desire and instinct. Yet some peoples, considered sometimes as primitive, have brought animals into their one-world perception of living things, as the Australian aborigines still do. Thus human attitudes towards animals have been formed with a variety of ideas and beliefs, some based on assumptions of supremacy over animals, others on assumptions of kinship with them. Darwin introduced a scientific perspective which changed the way many looked on animals, demonstrating that animals are indeed one with us, sharing with us an ageless process of evolution. 'After Darwin', it has been said, 'man could no longer avoid considering himself as an animal.'[10] But the scientific view of animals has tended to be élitist rather than popular, though strengthened by increasing evidence in its favour from palaeontology. By and large the popular perceptions of animals continue, based on inadequately informed traditional attitudes of degradation.

The effect of ignorance in the formation of prejudices against animals, and the destructive effects of this on moral conduct, are reflected in the view that those in man's service need to be 'punished' as a way of indicating what is expected of them. In countries where horses are still used as draught animals they continue to be whipped and beaten, and the language used is reminiscent of some recorded in the UK in the last century: 'I'll teach you a lesson!'; 'Now you'll learn what your business is!' It is assumed that continual punishment is needed because a horse is incapable of learning in any other way. The arrogant and autocratic notion that punishment is to teach someone obedience to the punisher assumes that the punisher's standpoint is just or fair. While the principle is sometimes supported in the case of legal punishment, where the institution of the law with enforceability may be seen as a social instrument to make men 'better disposed to obedience' (in Hobbes' words[11]) whenever they have offended against the rule of law as promulgated for society, it is clearly a denial of justice to punish a person or an animal for an offence which he has not committed. Since the animal has not offended, the question of desert, or *how much* it deserves to be punished, does not arise. Reformism is also irrelevant, for in this instance, without a lapse of some kind, there is nothing to be reformed. The driver's arbitrary infliction of suffering in the name of 'punishment' is a form of rationalisation to suit his own purposes, not a supportable case falling under conditions of punishment, such as those formulated by Hobbes. The fundamental source of such an amoral position is ignorance of the animal's nature, combined with moral insensibility.

The presumption of a total separateness of the animal world from the human is also based on inadequate knowledge, though exceptionally perceptive persons such as Montaigne needed no acquaintance with palaeontology to correct the presumption. That we too are animals is something now that 'no informed person can doubt any more'.[12] It is this informed humility, based on an understanding of ourselves as animals (without denigrating our intelligence and creativity) which may be turned to moral advantage. Even man's uniqueness is no longer as conspicuous or as many-sided as it was once thought to be, especially since detailed observation has begun to replace conjecture. Ability to make inferences, to use tools and to communicate in sounds, for instance, are not peculiar to man, though the extent of our reach in each respect far exceeds the capacities of animals. Since the powers conferred by the complexity of the human brain are realised differentially by us, it is appropriate to reflect on the distribution among us of lives characterised by almost total slavishness to habit, with very little intellectual effort or skill; and of other lives dominated by passion, bent on destruction, violence and needless killing, or relishing aggression, hurting others, valuing physical strength and cunning above critical capacity, moral or aesthetic sensitiveness, or inventiveness. In brief, to become more effective moral agents we need to understand both animals and ourselves better. It is to relevant aspects of animal natures that we now turn.

ANIMAL NATURES: GENERAL OBSERVATIONS

A knowledge of animals' natures, including their interests, is in itself morally inert: a description of the way living things are in nature does not establish any 'oughts'. Knowledge of animals is made morally active as it is brought into conjunction with our moral convictions, or our attitudes and values, as well as with self-understanding and understanding of the nature of morality. To illustrate, we shall consider first knowledge obtained from general observation of companion animals, domestic or farm animals, captive animals (especially in zoos) and wild animals. Then we shall turn briefly to ethology, or the science of animal behaviour; to sociobiology, which attempts to use biology to explain social behaviour; and briefly to animal behaviourism. In this way the progression will be from broad but confirmable general observations to an expectedly more rigorous scientific observation, with the prospect in principle that the second will enlarge and perhaps even rectify some aspects of the first.

Companion animals

It is common for those with companion animals to anthropomorphise, perceiving them as human too, with almost human powers in intelligence, memory, communication and so forth. The careful general observation we have in mind excludes such distorted perceptions, but in making this general observation, and in setting it against scientific observation, the danger of leaping to conclusions, of attributing qualities or achievements to animals which are in excess of their natural propensities, remains. One of the biasing factors may be the motives and values of the perceiver; another may be simply devotion to one's own animal; another careless observation; and in some situations these factors may combine.[13]

Like ourselves, dogs and cats have fundamental interests of health, security and social relationships. From a moral standpoint companionship is a two-way process, not a one-way view of an animal merely serving as a companion to a lonely or handicapped person. The moral threat to our responsibility in taking an animal into our care is that we may owe it much more in health and reassurance than we may be prepared to give it. On the other hand the moral debt cannot be total in its consideration of an animal's interests: in most circumstances our obligations need to be limited to some extent by our own interests. When both parents work and children spend the day at school, all may return home with energies spent. In such circumstances, and as work pressures mount, a companion animal may become more and more taken for granted, its needs neglected progressively until its interests are scarcely considered at all.

It is for that reason that the initial moral debt to companion animals, before we take them into the home, is knowledgeable planning and preparation to ensure that throughout their lives, and not merely when they are young and often most appealing, we shall be in a position to consider their interests fairly as well as our own. The moral debt is itself lifelong, a continuing appreciation of *their* needs so as to prevent unnecessary suffering and to promote, as well as we can, their life satisfactions according to their natures. That first commitment includes some very elementary knowledge, such as that dogs and cats with long coats need to be combed frequently to prevent skin disorders and the harbouring of parasitic insects; that they need vaccinations and boosters each year; that dogs require regular daily exercise; that both dogs and cats require nutritious food and clean water for good health; that over-eating leads to obesity; that training of dogs can control the excessively exuberant behaviour that sometimes leads to rejection and neglect; that desexing or neutering dogs and cats does not itself lead to obesity or reduce playfulness or affection for humans; that both dogs and cats suffer emotionally if neglected and not given regular assurance by human contact; that cats may suffer continuing distress when their claws are cut (to prevent them from scratching furniture or carpets).

The moral debt to dogs may be aggravated by failure to understand what is sometimes described as 'pack psychology'. Perhaps (though inconclusively) descended from wolves, the present breeds of dog are sometimes observed as thinking of an adult human as a leader of the pack, the biggest and strongest of the children then fitting into a hierarchy according to size and strength. During rough play with children the dog may attempt to locate itself within the hierarchy, perhaps trying to assert itself over the smallest. In such circumstances it may be misunderstood as aggressive, and in the worst situations given a reputation for bad temper and unreliability as grounds for abandoning or destroying it. Such treatment is a form of cruelty through ignorance or indifference: every owner has a responsibility to seek veterinary advice when uncertain, and summary rejection may be no more than a rationalisation when an animal is no longer wanted. Moral relations with animals depend partly on a knowledge and understanding of their distinctive natures; projection into them of human weaknesses is as damaging as falsely attributing human strengths to them. There may also be a failure to appreciate differences of temperament between breeds as well as within breeds; to understand, for example, that dogs from the one litter may show marked differences in temperament. If an owner finds that his dog is mischievous and difficult to train when he would have preferred a docile animal, there would be no more moral justification for abandoning or neglecting the dog through disappointment than there would be with a child in similar circumstances.

At the level of general observation the more solitary and independent nature of cats may also be misunderstood, as well as the considerable differences between and within breeds and within individual litters. The moral debt to them is fundamentally to avoid cruelty through ignorance of facts such as these: because of the strength of the sexual drive in male cats, they are often restless, unsatisfied, prowling and fighting at night; neutering the male cat makes it more contented. Female cats are restless when on heat and if allowed outside the house may wander far from home, calling for a mate, and attracting public attention as nuisances; the neutering of male and female cats – far from being immoral as an intervention in nature – therefore prevents the suffering of millions of unwanted animals which would otherwise be born to abandonment, starvation or destruction.[14]

General observation was sufficient to lead Hume to the conclusion that animals (like ourselves) learn many things from experience and, although incapable of reasoning, do make simple inferences that 'the same events will always follow from the same causes'. Even in responding to its name a dog 'infers some fact beyond what immediately strikes his senses'.[15] Dogs and cats store in their memories many such learnings from experience, both pleasurable and unpleasurable: a ball is a time for play, a key for going out in the car, a particular knock on the door a time to greet a family member; but also, regrettably, a stick is a signal for punishment, a chain a signal for day-long restraint. While their perceptions are animal and not human perceptions, the scope of their understanding merits recognition as part of their distinctive natures, to be appreciated by us as we give an appropriate moral consideration to their interests.

General observation is sufficient to realise that many animals are territorial. When a dog barks in answer to a neighbour's dog it is ignorance of its nature to punish it as though it had committed an offence; more usually the 'punishment' may be an act of human irritability or a refusal to accept personal responsibility for inadequate training. From general observation too dogs and cats are understood to enjoy play, providing an outlet for energy as well and an opportunity for a dog, in particular, to have necessary exercise. (Whether play fulfils a further natural need, especially among the young, is a matter for further scientific study.) Opportunity for dogs and cats to play is a moral debt to them, based on their natures, as it is also to children. The responsibility in caring for companion animals includes affording them, as far as possible, life satisfactions according to their natures, even if we have to make some small sacrifice in time and effort ourselves. The companion relationship is not a moral one if it is entirely one-sided.

Domestic or farm animals

The factory farmer's success depends largely on satisfying his own interests and ignoring the interests of animals. Mechanisation has relieved him of all but occasional visits to the factory: he can enjoy the sunshine or open air, exercise according to his needs and eat according to his liking, but his confined and overcrowded animals are denied natural exercise, opportunities to groom themselves, to breathe fresh air, to benefit from sunlight, to forage for food. The vitamins obtained from sun or grass are not available, though some deficiencies are made up with artificial substitutes. To view restless hens in battery cages, crowded with several others so that they are unable even to stretch their wings (the wing span of one hen usually exceeds the width of the cage), and then to consider that when one laying cycle is completed they may be forced to undertake another after moulting is induced by starvation and thirst for up to ten days, is to be left with repugnance for the factory farmer's unrepayable moral debt. Another distasteful moral debt is evident in the sight of veal calves, as described in the first chapter, confined for life in stalls barely wide enough for them to lie down, never able to touch the earth but standing or lying on slatted floors, never seeing the sun or grass, fed only on a milk diet, taken from their mothers long before the natural mothering period is over. How could man, with all his pride in his unique intelligence and with his capacity for moral agency, consider his own interests and needs according to his nature and almost completely fail to consider the interests of other living things that depend, as he does, on sunshine and fresh air, at least some freedom of movement, and food and exercise according to their natures?

General observation suggests that the moral debt to animals on the traditional farm is significantly less. There horses, cattle and pigs are usually in a better position to adjust to their environment, but ignorance of their natures may still lead to unnecessary suffering. Horses are exploratory by nature, especially when young, so to keep them in close confinement is to act contrary to their natures. Horses too are social animals, preferring the company of their own kind. They frequently groom each other, pairing for age and size. They have a social hierarchy, the larger and older animals establishing a dominance over others. Mares and foals derive satisfaction from their association. That the moral debt to domestic or farm animals depends partly on understanding their natures is evident too when there is a failure to appreciate the horse's sensory peculiarities: that its vision is limited by 'blind spots', but that its hearing and tactile senses are both acute. Cruelty to a horse is often preventable by appreciating its nervous and highly-strung nature, and by simple knowledge of its physiology.[16] Responsibility for the care of domestic or farm animals implies that ignorance of general matters such as these is not a moral excuse for any failure to consider their interests. The onus is on the farmer to make himself adequately informed.

Both foals and calves are playful (calves especially) and even if theories of play (such as that play is a means of acquiring adult behaviour) prove inaccurate, the obvious enjoyment of a calf as it kicks out its legs, shakes its head and snorts, chases others about and improvises its prancing, means simply that a denial of opportunity to play by unnatural confinement is a failure to promote the interest of social relationships for those animals capable of enjoying them. General observation shows that it is natural also for calves to explore; that like adult cattle they are social animals and at times groom one another; that cattle establish a social hierarchy, as horses do, related again to size and age; that fighting may occur in the process of establishing dominant positions in the herd; that intensive farming causes stress in dairy cows when the number of cows is increased in a restricted space for part of the year, due to difficulty in adjusting to competitive feeding situations. Appropriate knowledge of the nature of cows shows that the wellbeing of all animals in the group is safeguarded by a careful consideration of stock density in relation to stress.[17] We owe to cattle, as to all farm animals, a respect for their interests founded on this kind of general knowledge and understanding of their natures, thereby preventing unnecessary suffering, as far as possible allowing them to live out their lives with the satisfactions natural to them, and even promoting the interests of health and social relationships by any means at our disposal.

Similarly, necessary general knowledge and understanding of the nature of pigs includes the fact that they are exploratory, especially at night when they are active. General observation shows that they rest in huddled groups for long periods in daylight hours, and that their exploratory drive finds expression in rooting into the earth, following scents in the search for food, nibbling leaves, roots and fungi. Their natures too are ignored in the factory farm, where they stand or lie on wooden or metal slats, well fed but unhealthy, obese and unexercised. For their responsible care by farmers it is significant that they have poor skin insulation; that the separation of piglets is therefore detrimental to their health since their huddling is necessary to retain sufficient body heat for survival; that pigs need wetting of the body surface to avoid heat stress. (Covering of the skin with mud is common among feral pigs, as has been noted, but mud wallows are not always available on farms.) From general observations there are facts on the nature of sheep too to be understood by those taking responsible care of them: that the frisking of playful lambs is characteristic, as is their attachment to their mothers; that the maternal drive of ewes is so strong that they accept, with rare exceptions, only their own young, staunchly rejecting attempts of others' lambs to feed from them.

To summarise, a moral consideration of the interests of farm or domestic animals, especially those of health and social relationships, places certain demands on the farmer to provide suitable conditions or facilities: opportunities for the young especially to play, and for all to explore whenever appropriate to their kind; sufficient freedom and space to exercise and to perform natural functions; opportunities to associate with other animals of their kind; facilities for rest, sleep and grooming according to their kind; nutritious food and clean water. An overlapping demand is for 'satisfaction of minimal spatial and territorial requirements'.[18] It is because the factory farm disregards some of the natural needs of animals and the fundamental interests of health and social relationships according to their species that it functions single-mindedly to promote economic goals only, and not moral goals.

The use of 'natural' in reference to the interests, needs or functions of animals is not to be construed as an indication that what is 'natural' among companion or farm animals is necessarily good. What is natural for humans, such as obeying certain impulses or inclinations, is not good either. If left entirely to nature, some companion or farm animals would die of disease, or overproduce their kind, or engage in harmful agonising behaviour. The main moral offence is so to deny them the fulfilment of their interests in health, security and social relationships as to lead them to distress of some kind, so that avoidance of their suffering remains the chief animal interest to be considered by us. But we have gone further than that, as explained in the previous chapter, by arguing that it is also a moral offence to deny them opportunities for satisfaction in interest fulfilment which exceeds the suffering barrier, or any mere equilibrium reached between suffering and enjoyment, when such satisfactions can fairly be accommodated to the pattern of our own interests. Neither humans nor animals can expect to have their interests satisfied perfectly: there are social constraints on all of us, for instance, so that we sometimes acknowledge that common social interests deserve priority over certain individual interests. The rule of practical morality is to consider the interests of others (including the mammals we are now focusing on) as well as our own, in a fair appraisal of the needs of each, applying as well as we can (but necessarily imperfectly) the impartiality of a benevolent spectator.

Captive animals in zoos

How does a knowledge of the natures of formerly wild animals, now held captive in zoos of various kinds or bred in them, promote a consideration of their interests, or conversely deny or neglect their interests? The zoos of the world differ so much in their capacity to satisfy the animals' interests, based especially on their needs for health and social relationships, that generalisations are apt to be unjust to a few and to be excessively generous to the many. None satisfy *all* the demands, as set out in the previous section, for all kinds of animals, though at their best they may satisfy some of the demands for some kinds of animals. A knowledge of the social interests of some animals may lead to provisions for some to associate with their kind. Sometimes there may be sufficient space for certain kinds of animals to exercise and to perform natural functions, and for their young to play according to their natures. But some animals, especially larger ones such as giraffes and elephants, have very restricted opportunities to satisfy their interests, though we have sufficient knowledge from observations in the wild to know what their interests are. For instance, there is inadequate space for their foraging, even in the best of circumstances. Animals with drives to establish territorial claims are similarly circumscribed by economic requirements. Comprehensive zoos catering for a wide range of animals cannot exist without a substantial moral debt, and generally we enter into arrangements for their confinement with a knowledge of what the debt will be and the extent to which, in the forward-looking sense, it will be impossible to discharge it. We appreciate, that is, that animals in zoos live artificially in poor simulations of nature, sometimes deprived of free association with others of their kind, continually stared at and unable to escape, with little zest for play or interest in procreation, and their environment so stale and narrow in its bounds as to leave nothing in it to be explored.

Improvement in zoo conditions likely to affect animals' wellbeing has been slow. A little over a century ago the monkey house at London's Regent's Park Zoo was described as 'a wonderful improvement on the old building, where ventilation was the last thing thought of, and the atmosphere was raised by artificial heat sometimes to 150 degrees'. Little wonder that the monkeys 'were found half-baked and several of them dead by such mismanagement'.[19] Yet the 'old building' would have done credit to some of the small menageries or roadside zoos to be found today, where even lions, chimpanzees and bears are kept in small, often dilapidated cages, without room to exercise, without bedding and often without shelter from extremes of weather. Knowledge of animals as they are in the wild, gained by general observation, is not used to promote the wellbeing of captive animals in such places, except in the superficial sense of providing the bare essentials for survival. Animals may be confined, like factory-farmed animals, in broad-gauge wire mesh cages, including floors of the same material to facilitate cleaning, faeces dropping through the mesh. Privately owned and often designed to attract tourists to such places as gift shops or motels, these zoos cannot afford to engage expert keepers. They are a sideline, no more than a business lure. In one instance in a roadside zoo a chimpanzee, naturally a social animal, was left in solitary confinement for life in a concrete cell measuring ten feet by six feet; in another instance a bobcat, which in the wild covers about five miles a day in its wanderings, was found confined in a cage about six feet by four feet.[20]

The moral debt to captive animals is eased but not entirely removed by the attempts in open zoos or safari parks to allow them as much extended space as economic and other constraints permit. There may be grazing areas for American buffalo or for zebras, for instance, several acres in size; there may be a small pine forest for timber wolves, or a more open area for the Cape hunting dogs or the Australian dingoes. These are better than mere mockeries of natural conditions and do attempt to follow general observations of the animals in the wild. But the animals' interests are only partly considered: they are still not free to explore and to forage for food according to their natures; the environment is circumscribed and over-familiar. In privately-owned safari parks animals are found to benefit, or to suffer, according to the profitability of the enterprise. One investigation in the UK found more than half to be substandard.[21] Lions were still caged in some instances and the grass in one deer field had been eaten out. When animals in safari parks suffer in proportion to the adequacy of the owner's resources, attempts to serve their interests from a knowledge of their natures is of secondary importance. Only a few species of water birds may be fairly described as living in natural conditions. To have a hippopotamus pool which freezes over, or giraffes dying of cold in a European winter and those surviving feeding off the ground rather than from trees, or elephants in bare enclosures and necessarily hand-fed: all of these serve as indicators of undischarged moral debts through inadequate attention to the needs and interests of the animals as they are found to be in the wild.

The behaviour stereotypes of animals in confinement in zoos are reactions to impoverished environments, without the exploratory opportunities and the variability and stimulation of changing visual perceptions, as well as perceptions of sounds and scents which arouse curiosity or lead to a range of food satisfactions. When the conditions are confined and unvaried, animals are worn down psychologically and succumb to stress. Lions, tigers and panthers may be seen performing repetitive, compulsive movements, pacing from one side of an enclosure to another, circling, performing figures of eight or weaving. Wild dogs and other carnivores exhibit similar restlessness. Primates suffer stress that may lead to vomiting. Chimpanzees may push pieces of straw into their ears, elephants may nod their heads incessantly; other animals may pull out their hair, bite or even mutilate themselves.[22] Among some animals under the environmental stress of confinement, depression becomes deep-seated and lasting, affecting the immune system and leading to disease. Others may simply give up, lying on the floor of their cages if closely confined, fundamentally uninterested in the life forced on them, merely existing in a state of 'learned helplessness'.[23] The name conveys only a remote sense of the psychological experiences of confined animals which slump into chronic depressive states. So widespread is depression in general circumstances that many animals do not breed or care for their young. When there is no means of communication between captor and captive, or when communication is discouraged, the hopelessness has no opportunity for relief.[24]

The travelling circus is in part a mobile zoo, with animals such as tigers and bears confined in small cages. Elephants, horses, dogs, monkeys and so forth go through their conditioned routines in return for food and, when not performing, are tethered or confined in cages. The moral debt needs no elaboration.

Wild animals

The capture of wild animals for zoos has a long record of cruelty, based on ignorance of their natures and on motives amounting to moral indifference. In most instances little is known of the circumstances of their capture, since it is usually performed by unskilled villagers or farmers used to hunting and killing animals for food and without sufficient understanding of the animals' natures to handle them with care so as to avoid injury and minimise stress. Many animals trapped or snared by improvised methods are known to die in the process; others die soon after as they succumb to shock and stress when transferred to cramped containers. Stress continues among survivors as they are passed from one middleman to another; it may be two or three days before they reach the exporter, himself often without a knowledge of the animals' natures sufficient to consider their fundamental interests in both physical and mental health. Shipping by air or sea leads to high mortality: sometimes the animals are diseased or too immature to be exported, and have not been checked for good health by a veterinary officer; sometimes their crates are inadequate, being too small or otherwise inappropriate for the species; sometimes there are injuries from overcrowding, long delays in transit, unsuitable stowage on aircraft; and sometimes the obvious requirements of food and water, of adequate ventilation to prevent suffocation or of the means to cope with temperature extremes are not met.[25] In these circumstances the moral debt to animals is compounded by human indifference to suffering, as responsibilities are delegated to those who cannot bear them because of ignorance of animals' interests and of what the moral debt in the forward-looking sense entails.

In general wild animals are used for business or for pleasure: for animal traders they have commercial value; for recreational hunters they provide 'sport'. In each case they are objects of moral indifference. Insensitivity to suffering is duller still in those gamblers who find amusement in live coursing with wild animals. In the training of greyhounds for coursing, rabbits, jack rabbits (hares), possums, poultry or even piglets may be tied to a mechanical arm; they are knowingly subjected to distress, responding with squealing or screeching as they are dangled only feet from the pursuing dogs. Near the end of the course the operator slows down the lure sufficiently for the dogs to seize their reward.[26] (Another method is to release a live rabbit or hare within a fenced area, to be pursued by several greyhounds competing for the prize as a training exercise.) In both forward- and backward-looking senses, the moral debt to animals in these circumstances is self-evident.

Hunting wild animals for sport is at the very low end of a scale of human sensibilities. The human participants would appear totally insensible but for the contradictory fact that some do show a consideration for the interests of other *humans*. The hunter has no respect for animals as such and on other grounds is not a moral person: indifferent to animal suffering; careless of the interests of animals in social relationships when he takes a prominent stag as a trophy, disrupting the social structure of the survivors and leaving a legacy of distress in the herd; proud of his display of 'kills' in home or hunting lodge. The hunter *as* hunter focuses exclusively on self-interest.

To summarise, from general observations the natures of companion animals, farm or domestic animals, captive animals and wild animals are all sufficiently known to form the basis of a practical morality based on a fair consideration of their interests in the context of our own. Those interests are apt to be heavily biased against animals with respect to their suffering at our hands and with respect to promotion of health and social relationships. (In these considerations the focus has been narrowed from the class of vertebrate animals to a sub-class of mammals without implying that fish and reptiles are not also capable of suffering from conditions imposed on them in artificial situations.) We now ask if scientific studies can enlarge our knowledge of animal natures from general observations and point more clearly to animal interests which have tended to be misunderstood or ignored by us.

SCIENTIFIC STUDIES OF ANIMAL NATURES

From the time when the first steps in scientific thinking were taken by the Greeks to displace some of the religious and mythological beliefs concerning animals, there have been some who have been so attracted to particular similarities between animals and humans as to perceive a continuity from one to the other, especially to see in some animals rudimentary forms of behaviour which are more highly developed in man. Aristotle was one of these, yet his own observations were sometimes little better than hunches or general impressions. His outstanding merit against the background of his times was to focus on the natural world. He observed in 'the great majority of animals' what he called 'traces of psychical qualities or attitudes' which in humans were 'more markedly differentiated'.[27] In a number of animals there are qualities similar to human qualities, he explained, such as 'gentleness or fierceness, mildness or cross temper, courage or timidity, fear or confidence, high spirit or low cunning, and, with regard to intelligence, something equivalent to sagacity'. It is simply that man has more or less of the qualities than animals, but they do not differ *qualitatively* in animals and people. Other psychical qualities in man and animals are not identical, but rather similar or analogous (588[b]).

Ethology

Much of contemporary ethology is founded on a similar conviction, enlightened with knowledge of genetic inheritance and of evolution, that among humans and animals there are identical qualities which have a genetic basis associated with our evolutionary origins. What moral import would there be in such a discovery? We shall return to the question when the trends of ethological research have been more clearly drawn. Following a delineation of these trends in their broad interpretative aspects, we shall then look at specific aspects of animal behaviour as studied by ethologists: intelligence and instincts, the question of animal awareness and emotions, communication and play. Of these specific aspects we shall ask too if the knowledge they adduce has moral import inasmuch as it enables us to perceive the animals as *they* are, not as inferior creatures overshadowed by man, but as beings with interests which invoke a moral debt unless we consider those interests as impartially and as benevolently as we can, in much the same way as our practical morality insists that we consider the interests of other human beings.

Konrad Lorenz has been regarded by some as 'the father of modern ethology',[28] though as one of his former associates, Niko

Tinbergen, has conceded, there is much that is clearly ethological in Darwin's work.[29] Lorenz interpreted ethology as 'the *comparative* study of behaviour', explaining that its method of comparison is to investigate similarities and dissimilarities of related species, thereby attempting 'to elucidate the evolutionary process by which living creatures and all their characters came to be as they are'. Only an expert, someone 'thoroughly familiar with a group of related species', could have achieved this, he claimed.[30] His observations of birds were close and detailed, with the focus on specific units of behaviour. But his studies were impelled by a powerful presupposition that the behaviour of all vertebrate animals was caused by *instinct*, with a necessary *genetic* basis. Certain ritualised or formal patterns of behaviour were seen to develop during evolution. Even human behaviour, he believed, obeys laws of natural causation (*On Aggression*, p. 190). Though he recognised the place of reason in human behaviour, he emphasised the place of 'natural inclination' in conflict with it. Never, he believed, would pure reason alone lead to a moral imperative. There is always 'some emotional, in other words, instinctive, source of energy supplying motivation' (pp. 212–13) – a view in conflict with the explanation in the previous chapter that the influence in interaction with reason is not instinctive but rather *learned* attitudes and values.

Though Lorenz contributed significantly to our knowledge of animal (specifically bird) behaviour in particularised patterns, his conclusions were so much the products of preconceptions about genetically based instincts that at times he became incautiously speculative. He ended his work *On Aggression* with a utopian belief that 'reason can and will exert a selective pressure in the right direction', until 'in the not too distant future' our descendants will be endowed with a faculty enabling them to love one another (p. 258). If this unguarded guess were ever to become true, it would make morality merely a matter of living out our genes; or, more strictly, it would remove the need for the moral effort that accounts for all practical morality – the impartiality, the benevolence, the determination to consider others' interests and not only our own. Further, if all 'natural inclinations' opposing a moral judgement, decision or conclusion could ever be shown to be genetically based, and not learned dispositions, what would that signify morally if reason and dispositions remained to contend with such inclinations? Whatever the source of these inclinations (instinct, learned dispositions or a combination of the two), the nature of practical morality remains unchanged unless the inclinations are given such force as to overpower reason and any dispositional component there may be. That would make us moral automata, rendering futile any attempts to consider others' interests.

Had Lorenz restricted his work to 'the application of ortho-dox biological methods to the problems of behaviour', his own definition of ethology (*Studies in Animal and Human Behaviour*, volume 2, p. 280), some of his more speculative conclusions would almost certainly have been avoided. The course of ethology has been outlined briefly by Tinbergen, who saw Lorenz, in stressing the function of the central nervous system, as elaborating a modern version of Darwin's treatment of animal behaviour patterns as constituting equipment for survival (*The Animal and its World*, volume 2, pp. 132–44). The search for 'internal behaviour-specific determinants' has led to explora-tions described as half way between ethology and neurophysiol-ogy (p. 144). Some have observed a 'pre-set expectancy' in animals, making them, at particular stages of development, especially responsive to certain stimuli. Tinbergen himself leaves no room to doubt the evidence of evolution and of man's animal heritage 'which must be there because we have de-scended from animals' (p. 174), and returns to Lorenz's em-phasis on the need for a biological study of human behaviour as a means of better understanding irrational tendencies such as aggression. It is when people give way to passions and act 'against better judgement' that 'our animal roots can perhaps be seen best' (p. 171). He too cannot resist extrapolating from detailed studies of animal behaviour to the possibilities in man, though recognising that human ethology is very different because we are so different even from our closest relatives (p. 163). From the moral standpoint the very description of acting against better judgement implies that the capacity for better judgement is already there, that even if there are hidden mechanisms which incline some to passionate outbursts, or to dominant assertions of self-interest against others' obvious interests, such inclinations can be opposed by reason and our dispositions (especially attitudes and values). In other words, to this extent at least ethology is irrelevant to practical morality, because the grounds of innate tendencies – whatever they are – are irrelevant to it. Tinbergen admits that whether or not human aggressiveness has an innate basis is not known (p. 158). Practical morality expects some resistance, some effort by the moral agent. All animal to human hypotheses detract from our central concern with *animal natures* as such.

Others in the Lorenz tradition, such as Eibl-Eibesfeldt, have persisted with his belief that the most important task of ethology is to contribute, through knowledge of animals, to a better understanding of human behaviour.[31] No one has yet justified this claim in a way which throws light on moral conduct. The notion of an 'innate releasing mechanism' has some application to animal behaviour: the ability embedded in the animal's evolutionary history (phylogenetically acquired) 'to react to stimulation with specific actions that are appropriate and of advantage to the species' (p. 431). For instance, two hundred young turtles which hatch by the seashore, the eggs previously covered over by the female turtle which then deserts them and makes her own way back to the sea, behave as though they know exactly what to do to further their own best chances of survival (low in any case because of predators): they scurry for the water's edge and the protection of rocks or seaweed. Some unknown innate mechanism appears to function when each infant turtle makes its way to the surface of the sand, never failing to go in the appropriate direction. No 'time-consuming, risky learning experiences' are needed. Indeed to experiment by trying out various avenues of escape from predators overhead would quickly prove fatal (p. 217).[32]

Ethologists who attempt to apply discoveries in animal behaviour to humans have had very limited success, but among some the Aristotelian hunch persists of identical qualities sufficient to confirm a conviction of the continuity of animal and human life, and in particular, following Darwin, of an evolutionary inheritance in man from other animals. There is no convincing evidence of innate releasing mechanisms which lead to either moral or immoral conduct, such as violent aggression towards others causing suffering or inhibiting others' life chances. Here the vagueness of the language matches the uncertainty of some ethologists' convictions – the use of expressions such as 'seems to be', 'could be', 'might be', 'perhaps' and so forth. A thesis is proposed, for instance, 'that both aggressive and altruistic behaviour are pre-programmed by phylogenetic adaptations and that there are therefore preordained norms for our ethical behaviour'. Preceding this is the admission that the inheritance of any behaviour pattern or disposition 'by no means implies that it is not amenable to conditioning'.[33] So in the end any 'preordained norms' for ethical behaviour can be no more than tendencies or inclinations, and a practical morality remains free to oppose them by the force of their interaction with reason and with whatever attitudes and values may be learned.

The source of human aggression has been widely debated among ethologists, with various analogies observed between animal and human behaviour: from the 'pre-programming' of animals to respond with aggressive reactions when territories are threatened, to man's own 'fencing off' of groups and the formation of social hierarchies; from chickens fighting to establish a ranking order, to similar tendencies among humans. But when generalisations are made such as that 'many features of human territorial behaviour point to our ancient primate heritage' there is insufficient evidence for the inference; and more importantly, even if the ethologist believes that the source of aggression in man and animals is phylogenetic or within an evolutionary background, nothing follows for practical morality. To repeat, regardless of how powerful the natural inclination may be, those with appropriate moral sensibilities and capacities can oppose it. In these preoccupations the ethologists again take us away from our primary interest in *animal* natures.

Some of the ethologists' strongest, and in many respects most cogent, criticisms have been of experimental psychologists who have sought to demonstrate that behaviour is learned, not innate. If the origin of aggression and of altruism and other morally-related behaviour is not phylogenetic and innate, is it possible that it is totally learned within the culture; that is, of environmental origin? If this could be shown to be true, there would be clear implications for practical morality, for then there would be a chance of achieving a moral standpoint on animals, and avoiding the moral debt, by a suitable programme of education. Lorenz stated his firm opposition to the behaviourists, and other ethologists in his tradition have repeated that opposition. From their standpoint human behaviour is not explainable universally as 'a bundle of learned responses' (*Studies in Animal and Human Behaviour*, vol. 1, p. xx). Claims for heredity had to be asserted against the behaviourists' claims for the environment, for in the search for general laws of learning to apply to people, based on experiments with animals such as rats, mice and pigeons, behaviourists themselves claimed to be scientific.

Like the early ethologists in particular, behaviourists attempted *total* explanations from the insufficient evidence before them: each made discoveries about animals and went on to extend some of them universally to embrace humans as well. Several illustrations will explain their general position in this regard. Much of the impetus for research on animals in experimental psychology came from Pavlov's discovery of the conditioned reflex in dogs.[34] In experimental psychology Thorndike found that very hungry animals such as cats could learn how to escape from puzzle boxes by trial and error, so that food *reinforced* or rewarded their efforts. He too leapt to a universal explanation, a law of general nature applying to all animals.[35] This demeaning view of the animal mind was surpassed by J. B. Watson, whose experiments with rats in mazes led him to the view that animals were no more than manipulable 'stimulus-response machines'. His total explanation was that all behaviour is the result of conditioning, human behaviour included, and that behaviourism could discover general laws of learning. Skinner required his pigeons or rats, imprisoned in the 'Skinner box', to press a lever to be rewarded with a pellet of food. He became convinced that the *environment* shaped all behaviour through its provision of rewards and punishments.[36]

In their preoccupation with discovering laws of learning of universal application, and the reduction of animals to stimulus-response automata, behaviourists gave animals little chance to show more than one part of their natures. It was the behaviourist who made them mindless. Have animals intelligence of a kind, or are they creatures of instinct only, or of genetic pre-programming or inner-releasing mechanisms or pre-set expectancies? We shall now ask if ethologists can depart from genetic preconceptions on both heredity and morality and lead to more open enquiries on animal natures.

Intelligence and instinct

From their own biological standpoint ethologists had a right to be contemptuous of any behaviourist who could bypass direct observation and depend on a device to record data.[37] The experimental conditions imposed by the behaviourists were very different from the animal subjects' natural conditions. Experimenters saw animals as very limited because they were not allowed to be anything else. Further, the experimenters' inferences from some species to all species were often unwarranted, as were inferences from animals to humans.[38]

To categorise animals as creatures of instinct only has a significant bearing on our attitudes to them. Indoctrinated with this dogma, we are not likely to be disposed towards extending our understanding of their interests and needs, especially when the view is held to be scientific. We can be caring in our attitudes to plant life, treating diseases, promoting growth with nutrients and so forth, and similarly caring for animals if we believe them to be no more than mechanical expressions of instinct. But we would be unlikely to have moral attitudes of *benevolence* towards them, for there is little point in wishing an animal well which is no more than an automaton. And there would be little point in being *impartial* towards an animal if it does not have interests in competition with our own interests. We do not normally speak of being impartial to plant life.

It is uncommon now for ethologists to give animals the bad name given them by behaviourists, but some are still sufficiently tradition-bound to focus almost exclusively on instinct. Within recent years one of these has defined ethology as the study of instinct, so that animal behaviour is largely a matter of responding to genetically-based releasers which it is the primary object of ethologists to discover. Further, the familiar inferences from animal to human are continued, with an exhortation to study *human* behaviour in a similar way: 'looking hard for putative releasers, critical periods, drives, cases of imprinting, motor programming, and so on'.[39] Despite such traditional standpoints, and with acknowledgement of the central place heredity and instinctive responses to sign stimuli or releasers have had in ethology, there have been sharp reactions from other ethologists to any assumptions that the behaviour of animals and humans is dictated either by instinct or by reason: humans too have instincts, and suggestions have been made that animals have the rudiments of reason in their ability to make simple inferences.

The lumping of animals and humans into sharply divided groups, the one instinctual and the other rational, has been supported in some Christian theology and by certain historical philosophers who were influenced by it, such as Descartes,[40] with a reluctance to grant anything like mind to animals, including consciousness and even desires and intentions and the capacity to make inferences. From the moral standpoint of respecting animals' natures for what they are found to be and considering their interests accordingly, such rigid preconceptions have been a comforting excuse to those who want to use animals merely as a resource. The simple inferences made by dogs as they learn from experience were noted, as we have seen, by Hume.[41] Others have been as impressed as he with the great variability in human intellectual capacities, so that as one observer commented in the early part of the last century, there is as near an affinity between the lowest human intellects and that of the 'most sagacious brute', as there is between the lowest and the highest of human intellects.[42]

Indicating the extent to which attitudes towards animals are apt to be influenced by the preconceptions and prejudices of one's age, the same writer denied reason or intellect to animals, while acknowledging the confusion in his time, even among 'the learned', on the reason-instinct question: some gave reason exclusively to humans and instinct exclusively to animals, but others 'of no mean authority' saw no sharp division between them (p. 7). His own account of the supposed distinction between reason and instinct is worth noting for the questions it raises concerning animals' minds: 'while Reason acts with intelligence and design, (variably indeed and inconstantly,) profiting by experience, comparing motives, balancing probabilities, looking forward to the future and adapting itself to every change of circumstance; Instinct operates with uniformity in all individuals of the same species, and performs its office with unerring certainty, prior to all experience' (p. 15). But some animals clearly do profit from experience. A hunted fox quickly considers probabilities in the avenues of escape open to it. Some animals clearly also prepare for the future, as they carefully select secure shelters. Some adapt to changes of circumstance as they respond to ravages of fire or storm. What are the signs in these conditions which merely set off supposedly genetically-acquired releasing mechanisms?

By the end of the last century, partly under the influence of Darwin, there were increasing doubts that animals are merely instinctive in their behaviour. Questions were raised about gulls and crows, for instance, which carried shellfish high in the air, then dropped them on stones to break their shells. Darwin himself reported the instance of a caged bear which deliberately drew to it a piece of bread floating outside the cage by making a current with its paw.[43] In the early years of this century there seemed little reason to doubt animal 'intelligence' of a kind, not only from instances of problem-solving, but also from dogs' 'conscious intelligence' in acting for 'the protection, relief, or satisfaction of those for whom they feel affection'.[44] Now we have become more aware than ever of the problem-solving ability of some animals and of their use of simple tools. Chimpanzees from Tanzania use twigs which they push into termite holes, and on withdrawing them eat the termites that cling to them; other chimpanzees have been observed to make ladders by piling boxes on top of each other to reach high objects.

There are many further questions to be asked about both intelligence and instinct. Each is apt to be defined from within a particular conceptual framework. Lorenz accepted the definition of Ziegler to explain the difference between instinctive and intelligent activities: 'the former are based upon *inherited pathways* and the latter on *individually-acquired* pathways'. It is significant that Ziegler added, to Lorenz's satisfaction, that 'the psychological definition is thus replaced by a *histological* definition', thereby making it clear that somehow animal behaviour is physiologically-based, in the nervous systems of vertebrates – not only that which is inherited and therefore genetic, but also behaviour that is acquired by individuals and repeated. Despite this inbuilt rigidity of animal behaviour, Lorenz stressed his conviction that 'conscious insight is the definitive feature of intelligent behaviour' (*Studies in Animal and Human Behaviour*, pp. 57–8). To some degree that was an easing of the ethologist's association of animals with instinct only, calling to mind Julian Huxley's explanation of man's uniqueness as lying partly in his capacity for abstract and general thought, when he contrasted the 'relative unification of man's mental processes' with the 'much more rigid unification of animal mind and behaviour'.[45] Now at least there was a concession to animal *mind*, and Huxley's attempt to clarify the very wide and substantial differences between animal mind and human mind was in no way in contempt of animals.

By contrast with ethologists in the Lorenz tradition, psychologists have found the greatest difficulty in defining 'intelligence': some refer to the ability to understand abstract relationships, some to quickness in reasoning or in other intellectual functions such as learning; though few nowadays accept the operational definition of intellectual achievement as measured by IQ tests. All such approaches are conspicuously human-centred and make no reference to what might be called 'animal intelligence'. Indeed whether human intelligence is a unitary or a general ability or made up of a number of different abilities is irrelevant to animal behaviour, but it does draw attention to the many varied abilities within the animal world, abilities in communication, navigation, adaptability, problem-solving and so forth which are characteristically *animal* abilities, not human abilities, despite the similarities between the human and animal mind (of primates in particular) which have led some to the conclusion that the differences are of degree, not of kind.[46] Between psychologists and ethologists there is little to dispute concerning instinct: both agree on it as innate and as fulfilling biological functions, though some ethologists attempt to locate it in the nervous system. Like intellectual abilities, instincts vary in strength and influence over animal behaviour: if they induce merely a *tendency* to behave in a certain way they do not, as in the song of the chaffinch, preclude learning by imitation of adults.[47]

It is not surprising that experimental psychologists and ethologists find it impossible to agree on what animal intelligence is, for there is no clear agreement on what constitutes *human* intelligence. What we are left with is an understanding that animals do have mind (we have limited our enquiry to mammals in this respect) in the sense of a variety of mental qualities and functions relating particularly to their adaptations for survival. To understand the reach of their mental abilities is to appreciate something of the animal's nature from a *moral* standpoint, for then we are better able to see the animals as they are in their own world, not as poor copies of ourselves. In his own world, for instance (that is, in the wild), the chimpanzee is in some respects close to primitive man: he lives in a social group, caring for young and for elders; he hunts for food, makes tools and demonstrates his experience of emotions such as anger and fear. He is biochemically closest of all animals to man.[48] But it is *not* his similarity to man that makes him worthy of our moral attention. By preserving his habitat in the wild we can serve his interests (security, health, social relationships); by destroying it we can destroy the fabric of his social life. By isolating him in captivity we can cause further distress. The moral debt is what we owe to him because of what his nature happens to be. If 'intelligence' is an unsuitable word to apply to him (confusing also to humans) at least we can say that he has awareness of the world around him, can experience emotions, can use tools and solve simple problems. He has interests of health, security and social relationships, like all mammals, as well as awareness and abilities which justify a moral respect for him for the kind of animal he is.

Awareness and emotions

What exactly is the awareness of an animal? How do we know that it is as it is? Up to now the science of animal behaviour has helped little with such questions, but at least it has dispensed once and for all with the prejudiced notion obtaining for centuries that animals are merely mechanisms of instinct. To Descartes we have consciousness for as long as we are experiencing; when we cease experiencing we necessarily cease to be. Only humans have souls, and consciousness, with the intellect and the will, belongs to beings with souls.[49] To him not even the chimpanzee in a family group would have been seen as conscious or experiencing.

It has been considered by some ethologists to be equally a dogma to assert that animals *do* have consciousness, *are* aware and have emotions. How can anyone possibly know what such subjective experiences are like, if indeed they exist? Tinbergen's reply was that the biologist has no means of knowing, and for that reason 'is not entitled to say anything on the subject'.[50] Tinbergen asks of the animal, 'does it feel anything akin to what we feel when we are, say, angry or sad or amused?' But the question is not whether we can know *precisely* the state of mind or awareness of an animal when it is angry or sad, for instance; but rather whether we can ever know *that* it is ever angry or sad, or has sufficient awareness of a situation in which it finds itself to experience such emotions. We infer that a person or a dog is angry without knowing the exact shade of intensity of anger it is experiencing. There are different means of expressing anger: a dog may bark fiercely, bare its teeth, assume aggressive postures; a human may breathe heavily, become flushed in the face, change the tone or speed of his speech and utter words with hostile connotations. In each case it is simply a matter of reading the signs, *different* signs, the signs characteristic of either an animal or a human. The conclusion *that* either the dog or the human is angry is part of our normal perceptual processes. It is a way of knowing by experience, a way of inferring from observed behaviour, just as it is (again without the possibility of direct observation) when we learn that someone has a toothache or a cramp in the leg or an itchy back.

Though Lorenz could claim Darwin as the patron saint of ethology, Darwin himself was more clearly aware of a continuity of emotions from animals to man; Lorenz, Tinbergen and others were concerned rather with directly observable behaviour patterns which could be shown to have 'an evolution exactly like that of organs . . . the same sort of heredity'.[51] Darwin compared expressions of hatred and anger in animals with similar expressions in various human races. Among mankind, in sneering and defiance, the uncovering of the canine tooth on one side of the face, and whether it was a playful sneer or a ferocious snarl, he observed that each 'reveals his animal descent'. In comparing the mental powers of man and animals in *The Descent of Man*, Darwin concluded that 'most of the more complex emotions are common to the higher animals and ourselves': a dog becomes jealous of his master's affection if he lavishes it on another creature; it shows pride in carrying out a duty for its master; it experiences shame, and at times even a sense of humour in enjoying a practical joke, as when it waits until its master arrives before racing off with a stick it had previously retrieved.[52] What reason have we to doubt that such emotions reflect a situational awareness, or that in the animal mind the awareness is *functional*, as Tolman described it, not merely unrelated 'raw feels', but rather throwing a spotlight on some area of an 'environmental field'.[53] The animal's total perceptual field may be very limited compared with that of humans in similar situations of jealousy, pride, hate or anger, but a rudimentary perception of a relation between dog and master in Darwin's example is a far more convincing explanation of its behaviour than one of blind emotions or 'raw feels'.

An animal that is whipped or beaten by a master does not

merely experience a sensation of pain: the situational awareness seems likely to include some recognition of a relation with the human. When repeated whippings lead to hostility and resentment the response seems to be anything but that of a mindless automaton. Yet that was as Descartes saw it, even though he understood at least the elements of the brain and nervous system of vertebrate animals. Such animals had been dissected (alive) for centuries. In his time Descartes was able to refer with confidence to the sensation of pain in his foot as 'brought about by means of nerves scattered throughout the foot; these are stretched like cords from there to the brain . . .' (*Philosophical Writings*, p. 122, 'Sixth Meditation: Existence of Material Things'). Proof that animals are totally lacking in understanding or reason is that they cannot talk, he argued, something even lunatics can do. They are likened to a clock 'composed merely of wheels and springs': 'it is nature that acts in them according to the arrangements of their organs' (ibid., pp. 42–3, 'Discourse on the Method of Rightly Directing One's Reason . . .'). In a memorable passage in his *Philosophical Dictionary* Voltaire seized on the contradiction between Descartes' avowal of physiology and his rejection of mind in animals. Dissection of a dog shows that it has the same organs of feeling as in man, he explained: 'Answer me, machinist, has nature arranged all the means of feeling in this animal, so that it may not feel? Has it nerves in order to be impassible? Do not suppose this impertinent contradiction in nature.'[54]

It is sufficient for present purposes to note the universal aptness of Voltaire's rebuke of Descartes, for it has relevance to all who persist with the denial of animal awareness and emotions in the face of the physiological evidence. Darwin confessed to difficulty 'about the proper application of the terms, will, consciousness and intention'.[55] Consciousness implies some mental registering of environmental elements which are significant to an animal in a particular situation. At least an animal's consciousness must be 'responsive to adverse circumstances' or it would not have survived in evolution.[56] The consciousness of the wide range of individual animals probably varies vastly, from the lowest which is still an expression of the animal interacting in some way with its environment, according to signals warning it of bodily danger, to the highest in man with his creative imagination and powers of abstract thought. There is an obvious

gap between being aware of physical danger in primitive
survival responses, and being aware in a flash of the solution to a
complex mathematical problem. But *different* consciousness
does not imply *no* consciousness; the highest forms of consciousness do not extinguish the lower. Any emotion implies an
awareness. No animal is angry over nothing, any more than a
human is.

Acknowledgement of awareness or consciousness in animals
is an important first step in establishing moral relations with
them. Any moral debt is aggravated by a denial of their mental
experiences or of any purpose in their activities. It would be
arbitrary to deny them intentions[57] on the grounds that we
expect that they have nothing like human capacities to plan
ahead. In the awareness of the monkey which breaks shellfish
with stones, or of the lioness preparing to hunt and kill in order
to feed her cubs and the rest of the pride, there is an
unmistakable sense of purpose and expectation. The differences between man and some of the higher apes in their
emotions may be of degree, intensity and duration rather than
of kind: perhaps this is one respect in which the psychical
qualities or attitudes noted by Aristotle have a continuity from
animals to man.[58]

Communication and play

Animal awareness, with purpose, is indicated partly by their
communication. If language is taken as requiring a working
knowledge of syntax and rules and grammar, they do not have
it. But Descartes' inference that because they cannot talk they
have no understanding is unwarranted: that they would talk if
they had understanding or reason, because 'many of their
organs are analogous to ours' (*Philosophical Writings*, p. 43).
Animals communicate in *their* way. Vervet monkeys can discri-
minate between a wide variety of sounds[59] which some of their
own kind make: some are alarm signals to warn others of
approaching predators, and the predators may be differentiated
by particular sounds for each. In the expression of emotions
some animals intentionally display anger or hostility, as in
Darwin's example of the baring of the teeth; others intentionally
make overtures to convey appeasement, as do fighting wolves

from the same pack. Communication is itself a demonstration of awareness.

Animal communication is still the object of much speculation, and there may be far more to be learned about it by a close and direct observation of animals rather than by some ethological diversions which seek to locate the hereditary basis of all language in the communication of the higher apes.[60] Comparisons with human communication have led to some false perceptions of animal communication. From the discovery that cetaceans (whales and dolphins) communicate in high-pitched squeaks with one another some have inferred that they are more 'intelligent', or have greater mental powers, than some other mammals; there is no scientific evidence for this.[61] The threat to a moral standpoint on animals in conveying groundless enthusiasms is as great as it is in degrading them with inadequate evidence. The learning of Ameslan (American Sign Language, hand signs used by the deaf) by chimpanzees and gorillas has enabled them to communicate a few thoughts or feelings, such as 'time to eat', but the range of learning is limited and there is no scientific evidence that the animals have sufficient flexibility of mind to do more than produce a few of the same repetitive movements.[62] For present purposes in practical morality it is sufficient to note that, within the limits of their capacities, some animals do communicate with others of their kind in an aware and purposeful way, and that this elevates them above the demeaning notion of mindless creatures of instinct.

Animal play also seems to refute any assumption that it is no more than a response to genetic impulses. It is never so rigid or stereotyped as to be expressed in species-specific patterns: gyrating in circles, for instance, or leaping in the air in regular fixed-action movements. At least some animals improvise, taking advantage of the environment and what they find in it. Some believe that by ascertaining the *purpose* of play we may become better informed on ways of fulfilling animal interests. One view is that play has immediate costs but delayed benefits in the development of adult behaviour. (It is costly inasmuch as the animal may expend a great deal of time and energy in it and there is always risk of injury.) Some social animals do not play, but for those that do it is assumed by some to be beneficial by providing the exercise needed for survival fitness, including the development of specific skills. Recent studies provide strong support for a relationship between early social play and later behaviour. Certain social animals raised in isolation and so deprived of play opportunities have been found to be slower in some of their activities than others of their kind raised normally.[63] Both scarcity of food and overcrowding have been found to lead to a significant reduction in play. While it is not *necessary* for animal survival, there are some grounds for believing that for those species engaging normally in it there are benefits in behavioural development. It has been observed that the biting of young kittens in play and their pawing movements against each other lead to predatory activities as they advance in maturity, whereas the arching of the back and chasing are related rather to subsequent aggressive acts within the species.

But if the biological function of play remains an enigma, if those animals that do play can do without it, there remains the possibility that the benefits are largely immediate in the enjoyment or satisfaction which the young in particular find in it. Whether it is social play in which conspecifics engage, play directed at sticks or other inanimate objects, spontaneous activity of a locomotor kind within the animal's environment or predatory play with prey such as insects, the young show both awareness and emotion as they engage in it. In the case of companion animals, domestic animals and animals in captivity, one way of assuming moral relations with them – especially the young – is to facilitate rather than take away their opportunities for play, since this is to acknowledge part of their natures even when the behavioural explanations remain uncertain. The science of animal behaviour, or ethology in its more open definition, is helpful in this respect, even when the gains in knowledge seem small.[64] Since it is we who are the moral agents, not the animals themselves, our practical morality relating to them needs *knowledge* to supplement the benevolence and impartiality of our moral approach. Before we condemn them as unintelligent, unaware, unable to talk, emotionless, instinct-impelled automata, we need to know much more about them than we do, but also to take account of what *is* known. It is unlikely that any ethological discoveries will be totally valueless in understanding the moral debt to animals. Samuel Johnson's view, that for all we know animals' faculties may produce no more than 'motionless indifference' and human beings provide 'sufficient matter for curiosity' without any 'superfluous in-quiries' into animals' powers, is both unscientific and potentially harmful to an understanding of their natures as a basis for a moral consideration of their interests.[65]

Sociobiology

When sociobiology is defined by E. O. Wilson as 'the systematic study of the biological basis of all social behaviour',[66] it is clear that we have already crossed into its territory. Ethology is narrowed to social behaviour, again from a biological stand-point, but the 'new synthesis' which sociobiology was claimed to be a decade or so ago had pretensions to constituting a new science. It is not distinct from ethology in its fundamental attempt to find a biological origin for all social behaviour and in its backward-looking approach to the genetic basis of heredity accounting for social behaviour in animals as well as in early man (and indeed in 'the more primitive contemporary human societies'). But it is sharply set off from *sociology*, whose approach is non-genetic. The appearance of disciplinary presumption is relevant to our study only because of the claim by the same author that even ethics should be 'removed temporarily from the hands of the philosophers and biologicized' (p. 562). Like sociology, ethics awaits a full explanation of the human brain and its nerve cells: 'Only when the machinery can be torn down on paper at the level of the cell and put together again will the properties of emotion and ethical judgement come clear . . . A genetically accurate and hence completely fair code of ethics must also wait' (p. 575). Such claims have little rational appeal from the standpoint of practical morality because they fall into a familiar 'is–ought' fallacy. If a total genetic basis for all moral judgements were ever discovered, that in itself would not indicate what one ought to do. It would effectively eliminate any need for an 'ought', for again we would be genetically determi-ned, mechanistically responding to our genes. Then we would be left simply with the 'is', the facts about ourselves as we happen to be.

Similarly, to discover the hereditary basis of animal behaviour with respect to such expressions as aggression leaves the 'is' in a quite distinct field from the 'ought', whether the ought is directed towards animals themselves or towards other humans.

If we have innate aggressive tendencies explainable by inherited genes, that is to say no more than that as moral agents we may need a stronger effort to oppose such natural inclinations. Whatever they are, and however powerful they may be, they do not *make* a person totally disregard the interests of another when moral principles indicate clearly that he ought not; and with respect to our relations with animals, however aggressive some may be by nature, the only moral relevance is that such a knowledge of their innate aggressive tendencies may help us to make allowances for them, realising that they do not have the understanding and self-mastery to be otherwise.

As with ethologists, so now with sociobiologists, the language of uncertainty eventually prevails: 'might well be', 'could be', 'perhaps is'. Against the flamboyant claims for the ultimate discoveries to be made by the 'new science' there are now tentative concessions, acknowledgements that the behaviour of animals and humans is influenced not only by genes but also by the environment. By separating young rhesus monkeys from their mothers soon after birth, for instance, researchers have demonstrated that their behaviour in adulthood is distinctly abnormal.[67]

To this point sociobiology appears to have little to add to our knowledge of animal nature in a way that would enhance our moral relations with animals. Some see a special moral relevance in animals' *altruistic* behaviour, behaviour literally 'for others' rather than for the individual alone, usually at some risk or loss to the individual. In all human societies, it is claimed, the underlying altruism which helps to give them cohesion is genetically endowed. Similarly among animals there is said to be an inherited impulse to help others, sometimes to escape from predators with apparent unconcern for the escaper's own safety, but successfully drawing predators away from others who may be threatened; sometimes to share with others a newly-discovered food supply. Elephants go to the aid of injured group members. Whales go to the help of others in difficulty. How is it that in 'kin altruism' we help those of our own family first? Is there a biological basis for this behaviour, as in animal behaviour? How is it that we seem to be strongly motivated towards helping those who help us, rather than helping those who do not? Has 'reciprocal altruism' also a genetic basis, with animals in groups helping others (as in grooming) because it is the natural but unthinking thing for them to do? Is our own behaviour in 'group altruism' (as in helping victims of earthquakes or cyclones) a response to a genetic impulse? To the extent that it is, it too is a blind allegiance, not a moral one, for the moral impulse is always a conscious effort to consider others' interests. If – as some sociobiologists are now saying – there is *both* a genetic impulse and a moral impulse, the two in sympathy, it is no credit to the moral impulse to claim that it is supported by the former. Whether the genetic force is supportive of a moral act or opposed to it is likely to make a difference only to the morally weak and indecisive. It is the nature of moral conduct that it does not follow merely the easy way ahead: indeed it is frequently most conspicuous when it is otherwise.

Those who seek to 'biologise' ethics are confused on the nature of morality,[68] assuming that the discovery of natural tendencies will explain what practical morality is. No person can be accounted *good* because he has a particular evolutionary or genetic background. Whatever the influence of dispositions may be found to be, he is judged to be good by the way he acts, either contending with those dispositions or being morally supported by them.

Thus much of sociobiology, like much of ethology, focuses on humans rather than on the nature of animals. With its various moral presumptions and confusions, we must ask if it has any contribution to make to our understanding of the nature of animals and our moral consideration of their interests. By relying less on evolutionary and genetic speculation it may, like some ethology, extend our understanding of animals in morally relevant ways. But sociobiologists who concern themselves with aggression and altruism, and focus on speculative interpretations from inadequate evidence, demonstrate how little their so-called scientific approach has added to a knowledge of animal natures which we have gained from general observation. Their enthusiasm has caught up others outside their ranks for the mere *possibilities* that lie within their field of interest.[69] Yet, excesses aside, it would be foolish to block off any avenues to knowledge of animal natures because of the misdirections of the past. Sociobiology may yet have something relevant to impart on both animal and human natures; and moral relationships with animals require, as we have noted, a knowledge which includes an understanding of human nature as well as of animal nature.

Its signal failure in the context of the present enquiry is to add significantly to our knowledge of *animal* nature.

Animal behaviourism

The third of the scientifically-inclined approaches to animal behaviour stems from the behaviourism of Watson, Skinner and others which, as we have noted, earned the reprobation of early ethologists who were emphasising genetic influences on behaviour. In the end the doctrinal environmentalism of the behaviourists proved as unreliable as the dogmas of some ethologists and of sociobiologists on genetic influences. Behaviourism as it was founded by Watson was a branch of experimental psychology which aimed to make the study of behaviour (both animal and human) as exact as the physical sciences. To achieve this supposed goal of scientific objectivity Watson saw that it was necessary to concentrate on the careful measurement of animal responses, so both he and other behaviourists turned animals into stimulus-response machines. Their enthusiasm led to excesses in claiming laws of learning of universal relevance to both animals and humans, and in the process they degraded the natures of each.

Animal behaviourists adopt a similar attitude to the careful measurement of animal responses. Many clinical studies of animals are now being undertaken which are fragmented to such an extent that separately they contribute very little to the knowledge of animal natures. They pursue limited objectives, each stated precisely as though it were an end in itself. Just as the behaviourists leapt to the conclusion that they had accounted for all animal behaviour from the results of their stimulus-response experiments in learning, reducing animals to mindlessness and leaving out much of the whole animal (such as social relationships in play, communication, emotions and so forth), so the animal behaviourists now, in their accent on precise measurement of animal responses, neglect the synthesising of their findings and the perception of the animal as a whole to which its *nature* refers. Nonetheless, like sociobiology or genetically-oriented studies in ethology, animal behaviourism may yet have a contribution to make to an understanding of animal natures, as fragments of knowledge from a wide variety of sources are eventually pieced together. There are many other studies of animal behaviour which are not behaviourist,[70] and the most useful to an understanding of the nature of animals depart from measurement-oriented studies of specifics.

SUMMARY

A practical morality based on an understanding of animals' natures is founded on appreciating the sentience of vertebrate animals and their capacity for suffering. With respect to mammals in particular, and to some social birds, it is based also on *promoting* their wellbeing according to a knowledge of interests other than avoidance of suffering: interests of health and security, for instance, and social relationships. Moral judgements concerning animals depend also on understanding *ourselves* and the nature of our moral thinking, especially the interaction of reason with the predisposing tendencies of attitudes and values. As we may have a moral respect for persons (understanding their aspirations, struggles and conflicts in pursuing their goals) so too we may have a moral respect for animals as such, acknowledging that they too – according to their kind – have interests and needs which if unfulfilled may lead to suffering, if fulfilled to satisfaction. Prejudices against animals, unwillingness to consider them appropriate objects of moral attention or to recognise any moral debt to them, have their sources largely in ignorance, tradition and dominant human self-interest. Some believe animals to be mere things, without mind; others believe in the Cartesian supposition of humans elevated above animals, so failing to acknowledge our own evolution from animals and perpetuating the presumption of animal inferiority.

Although there is still much to be learned about animal natures from observations of their behaviour, we already have sufficient knowledge of the interests and needs of companion animals, domestic or farm animals, captive animals (as in zoos, menageries and travelling circuses) and wild animals to clarify much of the forward-looking moral debt to them, especially when we combine this knowledge with self-knowledge.

Much knowledge from general observation might be expected to be strengthened by scientific studies of behaviour. Yet the moral perspective on animals has not been significantly sharpened with knowledge from genetically-based ethology, with its emphasis on evolution and heredity. This has taken the emphasis away from a consideration of animals' interests to a preoccupation with the *causes* of their behaviour – fixed action tendencies, innate releasing mechanisms, and so forth – which collectively have left an impression of animals as little better than automata, going about their lives as though programmed by evolution. Experimental psychologists in the past have aggravated this tendency to view animals as driven by innate forces, exceeding the ethologists in their mechanistic characterisation of selected laboratory animals.

In one specific respect the ethologists' emphasis on inheritance has relevance to the nature of the predisposing influences which exist prior to making moral judgements. While some ethologists have argued that the predisposing influences are genetic, we cannot replace their dogma with another by contending that the only such influences are motives, attitudes and values. We *do* know that attitudes and values may be learned in various ways, so there is no justification for yielding entirely to the ethologist's assumptions. The sources of the predisposing influences may well be a combination of heredity and learning. On the assumption that we remain free to oppose whatever predisposing influences there may be, the *sources* of our inclinations are not of critical moral import as we make practical judgements.

Studies of animal intelligence are far from conclusive: indeed 'intelligence' is not appropriately attributable to them, but at least some of the higher mammals are capable of problem-solving and the use of tools in ways that suggest mental powers beyond mere responsiveness to instinct. Awareness and emotion can be inferred from behaviour: the attitude of solipsism is discredited by empirical knowledge of both animals and humans. The inability to know *precisely* what an animal's state of mind is, to engage in a perfect empathy, is no different in principle from the inability to know precisely what another *person*'s state of mind is at a particular time, and is distinct from knowing *that* the animal has awareness of its environment.

Some animals are shown to have purpose, to be forward-looking in their activities. Although there may be much to be learned about animal communication, some of the higher animals communicate in purposeful ways, and with a range of sounds, which are best understood as *their* ways, not inferior attempts to talk in the human sense. In animal play, especially in the young, both awareness and emotions are evident. From the moral standpoint, to learn of play as a source of satisfaction to some animals, or of its denial as a subsequent loss to the animal in its adult behaviour, are further indications of the significance of our learning as much about their distinctive natures as possible, without forced comparisons with humans.

Sociobiology has become confused whenever an attempt is made to explain morality in biological terms, failing to distinguish between possible influences on behaviour and the freedom to oppose those influences in a practical consideration of others' interests. The third scientific approach, that of animal behaviourists, has contributed little at present to our knowledge of animal natures in ways that make them integrated beings, with their own patterns of needs and interests. The scientific approaches generally have been marred by speculations on relationships between animal and human natures. The exceptions are those ethological studies which depart from rigid adherence to genetic presuppositions and are more open in their controlled observations of animals in their natural habitats. Studies of cetaceans and some of the higher primates, for instance, have been conspicuously successful, especially in relation to social behaviour. It is these studies too which have added to our understanding of animal awareness and emotions, of animal mind in play, communication and use of tools, giving us a firmer basis for a moral respect for the distinctiveness of their natures.

Yet those ethologists who are still bent on discovering inherited traits, as well as sociobiologists concentrating on the biological bases of social patterns and animal behaviourists whose main concern is with accurate piecemeal measurements, may all be found to have something to contribute as the total configuration of animal natures emerges.

4 Experiments on Animals

INTRODUCTORY

First let us review the moral argument up to this point. Chapter 2 discussed the principle of an equal consideration of the interests of animals and of humans, according to their respective natures. Chapter 3 has now thrown further light on this principle in demonstrating the importance of a moral standpoint on animals being armed not only with benevolence and impartiality, but also with relevant knowledge of their natures. Moral debt was explained in the earlier chapter as denoting no more than what is owing to an object (animal or human) with possible application in several ways: first, in a way that is forward-looking, as when our moral principles indicate what we owe to an animal prior to the performance of a moral act relating to it; second, in a way that is backward-looking, and then occasionally forward-looking, as when we refer to human acts leading to animal harm or suffering, leaving us with a debt that only in some circumstances may be repaid; third, in a way that is backward-looking in appreciation of an animal's past services to us, and still more seldom forward-looking, since we normally have no intention of attempting any kind of compensatory benevolence. The third, as we have seen, is often naive in the sense that the animal has no choice but to do as we train it or compel it to do. In this chapter moral debt will be applied in the first two ways, especially in the backward-looking sense with reference to suffering inflicted on animals as we use them in experiments, and then in the forward-looking sense as we make moral judgements on these past performances and take a moral stance on what we consider we ought to do in the future.

From the principle of an equal consideration of the interests of humans and animals, according to their respective natures, there arise a number of questions which foreshadow some of the morally sensitive aspects of animal experimentation. The most general and far-reaching of these is whether human interests ought to override animal interests in any circumstances: that is, whether exceptions ought to be made, with respect to some animal experiments at least, to the principle of an equal

112

consideration of interests. Backward-looking applications of the moral debt raise questions such as these. Can unavoidable infliction of suffering on animals be justified in experiments designed to benefit solely human wellbeing? Is the justification easier if the expected beneficiaries are both humans and animals? Can unavoidable infliction of suffering on animals be justified if the primary object of the experiment is animal health? A number of pseudo-questions may be framed to supplement these sensitive aspects of animal experiments, but the answers to these are self-evident. Can animal experiments be justified to satisfy vested interests, such as to attract financial support for a university research department, or as a means of postgraduate students qualifying for higher degrees? Can the commercial trading in animals for research be justified?

Forward-looking applications of the moral debt often depend on a prior backward-looking appreciation of a moral debt in past experience, raising sensitive aspects of animal experiments which again may be expressed as pseudo-questions. Is there a moral debt to animals to use alternatives to animal experiments whenever possible? If alternatives are not always available, do we owe it to animals to radically reduce their numbers in experimentation? Ought there to be strict controls at national and international levels to prevent unnecessary repetitions of the same experiments? Are we morally obliged to prevent animals being used in experiments by schoolchildren (including adolescents) and for purposes of training junior staff in research techniques or to develop research skills? Is there a moral debt to animals, whenever their use in experiments is considered absolutely necessary, to accommodate them in optimum conditions for health, for exercise natural to their species and for enjoyment of social relationships with others of their kind?

Since moral judgements or conclusions cannot be reached without reference to relevant facts, the approach to the moral appraisal of the use of animals in experimental research will be as follows. First, we shall develop or revive awareness by presenting selected evidence of animal suffering in experiments. Second, we shall consider various viewpoints on whether or not there is a moral problem, or on whether there is a problem at all. Third, we shall bring the first and second approaches together from an ideal spectator standpoint, with special reference to the principle of an equality of consideration of interests. The moral perspective will then change to a more practical one: the standpoint of practical morality, which considers not only aspects of animal experimentation as it is in fact practised, but also practical morality itself within the context of human imperfections. This will raise questions of motives as well as of attitudes, with application to vested interests, abuses in the planning and conduct of experiments, the law in practice and the availability and pursuit of alternatives.

Is there animal suffering?

A hundred years ago there was an outcry at the practice of 'dissecting alive, cutting to pieces, baking, injecting with poisons, torturing in a thousand different ways, living horses, cats, rabbits, pigeons and dogs'. The operating table followed a model that was likened by one critic to a rack: an animal was firmly tied to a table by legs and nose, and immobilised in this way, the animal's suffering was secondary to instruction in the anatomical system.[1] About the same time a prominent scientist operated on dogs after paralysing them with curare, which still left them with the sensation of pain, each experiment lasting most of the day.[2] Evidence of prolonged pain was reported to the Royal Commission which led to the UK *Cruelty to Animals Act 1876*. In one experiment nearly two hundred rabbits and dogs were given various injections which led to 'severe spasms coming on with great suddenness, accompanied by bending backwards of the spine and pawing movements of the fore limbs. The spasms continued for nearly thirty minutes.'[3]

Chapter 1 suggested that our humanity to animals has not increased in a century. More than matching the earlier account, animals have recently been subjected to amputations and other mutilations, electric shocks, crushing, poisoning, freezing, burning, dissection, deprivation for long periods of food and water, irritation to the eyes, broken bones and gunshot wounds, and isolation in 'depression pits'. Rats have been submerged in freezing water, put on hot plates to measure how long it takes them to jump, plunged in scalding water, asphyxiated with fumes from burning plastic or furniture.[4] Monkeys have been used by car companies in crash tests of their products. Cats and rats have been deprived of sleep for weeks to study physiological effects and to ascertain how much they can tolerate before they die.[5] Rats have had the spinal cord severed to demonstrate that under such irreversible conditions their sexual reflexes actually increase. Animals have been subjected to electric shock for a variety of purposes, sometimes to study responses when they have no means of escape, eventually succumbing to 'learned helplessness'. More specifically, in one of many different experiments on head injuries, a monkey has been immobilised in a tank of water by means of a yoke around its neck, and with a breathing tube inserted down its throat to prevent drowning. Then the tank has been rocked by means of a vibration table until brain damage has ensued.[6] Another contrivance has been invented to ascertain what happens to an animal thrown about inside a revolving drum with internal projections. Drawn up the side of the drum during a revolution, the animal is then dropped onto another projection and the procedure continued at the experimenter's discretion. Injuries from the battering have been broken bones and teeth, ruptured internal organs and tissue destruction.[7]

In order to determine if irregularities in teeth can be corrected by applying force to the jaw, normally active monkeys have been deprived of movement for three months (some for almost seven months), fitted with a headgear appliance and fixed in restraining chairs so that the appliances are not damaged.[8] Primate infants have been separated from their mothers and others have been forced into states of depression through isolation. In the case of separation, the experimenters have been fully aware of the 'extremely stressful event for both mother and infant', have observed the ferocity of the mother towards attendants as she attempts to protect the infant, and with the infant eventually taken from her by the superior force of two or three men, have noted the manner of her pacing about the cage and her attempts to escape, as well as the shrill screams of the infant almost continuously during the separation period. The separation may last for several weeks.[9]

Another experimenter has invented a vertical chamber with sides of stainless steel sloping inwards towards the base so that an isolated monkey cannot climb the sides to reach the wire mesh roof. There is nothing for it to cling to. After several days of futile activity the confined monkey has been found huddled on the floor, and after four to six weeks has developed serious depression.[10] The effectiveness of the 'depression pit' has led to its repeated use by other researchers. Rabbits are used in the Draize test to ascertain if particular substances – including cosmetics and household products – are likely to be harmful to human eyes. The suspected irritants are dropped into one eye of the rabbit, an animal selected as suitable for the test because its eyes do not produce sufficient 'watering' to dilute the irritant. Sometimes eyes are burned and animals are blinded or left with severe inflammation or sores.

Experiments in electric shock avoidance and 'punishment' have shown how animals suffer not only from the pain, but also from the distress caused by constant fear of the shocks, and by conflict when escape is seen to be impossible.[11] Indeed some experimenters attempt to measure the fear: in one experiment rhesus monkeys have been given 'five seconds of inescapable electric shocks every thirty seconds for twenty-five minutes through the floor of an electrified box to measure the effect of previous punishment (electric shock) upon how fearful the animals become of this pain'. In another experiment three squirrel monkeys have been given electric shocks every twenty seconds 'until they learned to press a lever which would prevent the shocks'. But when they had learned this, the lever itself was wired so that it too would deliver shocks.[12] There have been burn experiments in which unanaesthetised baboons have been burned over fifty per cent of the body by immersion in scalding water, then observed for eighteen hours for liver damage; guinea pigs have been anaesthetised and burned over twenty per cent of their bodies by immersion in boiling water for twenty seconds, then injected with bacteria and observed until death several days later. In an acceleration experiment unanaesthetised pigs have been immobilised and spun in centrifuges at speeds nine times the force of gravity for one hundred seconds, five times a day, three times a week, for up to six months, to simulate aerial combat manoeuvres and the effects of physiological stress. Heart damage was discovered.[13] Dramatic examples are not uncommon, though these are among the worst and some of them have been replaced recently with alternatives. But the total scale of animal suffering from the millions of experiments conducted each year throughout the world is incalculable, and unnecessary suffering, on any humane criteria, is unquestionable.

Use of animals: is there a problem?

Broadly, and to some extent superficially, those who see no problem in the use of animals in research are often researchers themselves. The perceptions of some are masked by career ambitions, the desire for personal reputation and reward, or by obsessive preoccupation with scientific curiosity of a kind which tends to extinguish humanity. Those who do see a problem usually have more influential humane attitudes and values in their attempts at least to reduce the suffering. But in the first category there are some who do have compassion for suffering animals, though believing that some sacrifice of their wellbeing is justified for the sake of greater *human* wellbeing; and in the second category there are a few who oppose the use of animals in research on scientific as well as on moral grounds.

The purpose of this section is therefore to approach the central question of a moral justification of animal experiments by bringing to the surface some of the various viewpoints taken by relatively well-informed individuals. Some of these viewpoints parallel those of more than a century ago, when the issue was even then contentious: first, as it was said then, there are those who object to the destruction of any animals unless in self-defence; second, those who object to experiments on living creatures even if the pain could be established as minimal; third, those who support animal experiments which are claimed by physiologists to be necessary, when there is no pain involved at all; fourth, those who believe the interests of human beings may demand the *occasional* infliction of suffering on animals; fifth, those who are prepared to leave the nature and number of experiments to the discretion of physiologists, while still objecting to 'wanton and reckless suffering'; and sixth, those who are prepared to allow any amount of pain 'in the interests of general humanity'.[14]

In brief, some object to the infliction of any suffering, presumably on the grounds that infliction of unnecessary pain (or distress) is evil; others are divided on the criterion of whether human interests transcend animal interests, though except in the last group of all individuals express various degrees of uncertainty as they see the need for restricting the permissible pain. From the moral standpoint shall we say that pain is pain, regardless of intensity or duration, and therefore never to be inflicted on animals; or shall we say that it is proper to use animals in the service of humans, as long as the suffering is not excessive, 'wanton and reckless'? These are the beginnings of the moral probes into animal experimentation. One of the fundamental questions to be asked is, How *impartial* can we be? Even Bentham, for all his humanity, could see no objection to 'the putting of dogs and other inferior animals to pain, in the way of medical experiment, when that experiment has a determinate object, beneficial to mankind, accompanied with a fair prospect of the accomplishment of it'.[15] The difficulty unforeseen by Bentham is the frequent indeterminacy of the benefits to mankind, but that is overshadowed by the larger question already intimated of whether animals, because they are animals and not humans, should be regarded as merely instrumental to the wellbeing of mankind. A further moral question arising is whether experimenters are to be trusted to give the utmost humane consideration to animals, for there is evidence to the contrary. Indeed some experimenters have seen the pain of an animal as of much less moral significance than human pain, even rationalising to the extent of arguing that 'a little pain' endured by animals will 'prevent human pain much more severe and lasting'.[16]

It is probable that some researchers still view animals as usable commodities for the sake of human ends, partly because they cannot talk. Immobilised in restraining harness, when they do feel pain they are unable to speak in protest, and when it becomes acute they cannot press a button for relief or ask for an analgesic. That they cannot talk is of crucial significance to a moral understanding of their position, for it permits the easy rationalisation, the indifference to their pain which presents no obstruction to the researcher's single-minded plan of action. In a prize-winning essay written in the USA in 1908 entitled 'Our Dumb Animals', it was claimed that 'the borders of medicine are enlarging and animals will be called upon in increasing numbers to serve humanity'. The writer recalled the part played by animal experiments in the discovery of the secrets of malaria, yellow fever, typhoid and other diseases. But another who argued from a moral standpoint rather than a scientific one asserted a preference to die from these and other diseases, rather than be responsible for the offences against animals committed in the experiments that led to the discoveries.[17]

It is a moral question whether human interests ought to override animal interests completely, and if not, whether there are particular conditions under which animal interests ought to give way to human interests. What are the implications for equality in the consideration of interests? In the experiments considered in the preceding section, it would be unthinkable to use human subjects, even with their consent: these are things that are simply not done to humans – even to pathological killers or to the terminally ill. So we *do* see animals differently, and as inferiors. Is that a moral standpoint?

One of the arguments sometimes advanced – at least with a moral face – is that a number of animal experiments are unjustified because the benefits to humans are small, or even negligible, in proportion to the costs in animal suffering. That itself is a presumption of human superiority – of a distinctly unequal consideration of interests. Few would seriously think of *human* pain as a cost for the sake of animal wellbeing (though minimal temporary suffering through denial of some satisfactions – as in accepting a lower standard of living in order to preserve animal habitats – may be considered by some as morally justifiable). In the case of animal experimentation the analogy with economic cost-benefit analysis is misleading: the scales to weigh animal suffering on the one side, and on the other side human benefit, are false because totally unpractical. The quantification of units of suffering is no more achievable than the quantification of units of human benefit. It is Classical Utilitarians who believe that such arithmetic is practicable: Preference Utilitarians acknowledge the difficulty and fall back on general impressions. It is the general impression that we are left with too; but the practical judgement made is dependent on an individual's capacity to view the situation with impartiality and benevolence. If the judgement is made by the experimenters themselves it is likely to be influenced by research objectives and by personal goals of various kinds.

The cost-benefit notion has application particularly to *extreme* cases – to those where even some experimenters realise that they are exceeding all bounds of moral decency in causing animals to suffer when no one is likely to benefit except the researchers themselves. In the Royal Commission on Vivisection in the last century some witnesses expressed their concerns in cost-benefit terms, as in the use of animals to verify previous findings. Then it was said by one witness, 'the question comes to be whether the advantages of the practical verification of fully described phenomena which involve pain are counterbalanced by the injustice done in the production of pain itself'.[18] Today certain well-qualified researchers who have developed a moral sensitivity towards some of the gross excesses of recent times, especially (but not only) in experimental psychology, have defended cost-benefit analysis 'as an appropriate way to determine the ethical justification of a study involving animals', though acknowledging that there are some procedures such as prolonged maternal and environmental deprivation in infant primates which are 'inherently objectionable independent of such an analysis'.[19] At least some advance is made by these researchers in insisting that research planning should include a thorough analysis of *specific* benefits rather than the supposed benefits couched in generalities such as the increase of knowledge. But even then it is possible for 'highly aversive or injurious' research, involving considerable animal suffering, to be justified by setting it against 'equally strong' claims for human benefit.

The appearance of an equation is illusory. How can human benefit be as great as, or equal to, animal suffering? Comparison of opposites – a large quantity of pain with a large quantity of pleasure – may lead to various conclusions because of its inherent imprecision: there may be a lot of X and a lot of Y, with quantity the only thing they have in common. A lot of elephants may be compared with a lot of mice, or, with similar purposelessness, a lot of whales with a lot of minnows, a lot of anxiety with a lot of peace of mind. But what follows? By what criteria are we able to judge when a certain amount of animal suffering is enough to justify the human benefits? Or in cases where humans endure physical hardship to rescue starving animals, when is human suffering enough to justify the animal benefits? In either case the judgements are apt to be made in our favour, on a concealed assumption that human and animal interests are not to be considered equally.

Instead of weighing disparates, for which there are no logical scales available, is it more appropriate morally to weigh the benefits in human terms with the benefits in animal terms, or human suffering with animal suffering? Though more meaningful comparisons may be made with common elements on the two sides of the balance, when put to the test suffering usually weighs far more heavily on the animal side than on the human side; and on the human side, benefits usually weigh much more heavily than on the animal side. As a means to more precise quantification, these judgements may be made by sampling a wide range of experiments in which animals are used and making a separate judgement for each experiment, leading to a kind of algebraic sum of the various judgements. Considering benefits first, on the human side they are undeniably strong. There are a number of useful drugs, for instance, used in the successful treatment of disease and certain surgical procedures, such as the first kidney transplant, both developed from animal experiments. In defence of animal experiments it has been pointed out that had such experiments been stopped in 1950 there would have been no polio vaccine; in 1935 no knowledge of *safe* antibiotics; in 1910 no understanding of vitamins in nutrition. When diphtheria immunisation of schoolchildren began in the UK in the early 1940s a sharp decline in the notification of the disease occurred, until by the early 1950s there were no cases notified.[20] Similarly when immunisation of schoolchildren began against acute paralytic poliomyelitis in 1958 the number of notifications dropped sharply until by the mid-1960s there were none.

In animal experiments a wide range of vaccines have been successfully tested which have defended the health of millions of people throughout the world. (There are about seven hundred million people in third world countries suffering from parasitic diseases for which vaccines have not yet been developed. If animal experiments were to cease, these and many millions more would suffer indefinitely from them.) Humans have not been the only beneficiaries of animal experiments. Millions of animals too have been saved by veterinary treatment of such diseases as distemper in dogs, cattle plague (rinderpest) and pleuropneumonia, anthrax in cattle and sheep, and swine fever. Vaccines have been developed to protect cattle, sheep, dogs, horses, pigs and poultry from a variety of diseases. As in the case of human diseases, new viruses appear from time to time, requiring the discovery of vaccines and their testing before use. Understandably the funding of research projects has favoured those aimed at improving *human* health over those directed towards *animal* health, even with respect to farm animals, so the preponderance of animal experiments has been for human benefit rather than for animal benefit.

By widening the scope of experimentation from animal subjects to human subjects, the weight of evidence for animal suffering is seen to be overwhelmingly superior to that for human suffering. In one case individuals allowed themselves to be bitten by a tiger mosquito, which is responsible for transmitting yellow fever. They contracted the disease and recovered; then it was found that the one onset of the disease gave them immunity to it in the future. In World War II Japanese conquests in the Pacific almost eliminated available sources of quinine necessary for the treatment of malaria. Other substances were developed and tested on *human* subjects for effectiveness and toxicity, and suitable replacements for quinine in the treatment of malaria patients were discovered. One physiologist, aided by artificial respiration, allowed himself to be paralysed with curare to ascertain if this drug affected consciousness.[21] More recently human volunteers have been engaged for testing a variety of cosmetics, though never where the risks of permanent injury or of death are high.

Why is it relatively rare for human subjects to be used, except in times of national emergency? Why do we use animals for testing drugs and vaccines that might prove to be seriously toxic or to have serious side-effects? Clearly an animal life is valued more cheaply than a human life. The primary object of animal experiments in biomedical research is to sustain or improve *human* health (disregarding extraneous motives of a personal nature). Animals are our front line in the battle against disease, providing a protective shield for us in a similar way to the use of dogs as mine detectors during war. But since it is humans only who have the intelligence and skill to discover ways of treating and preventing diseases, thereby reducing vastly the total human (as well as animal) suffering in the world, would it be appropriate for humans to be used more extensively as voluntary research subjects? If so, which ones? Should experimenters use themselves? One who had tried prussic acid on himself was found dead in his laboratory. Soon afterwards another scientist tested the drug cocaine first on animals and then on humans, and this was described at the time as a wise precaution.[22]

It is a matter of prudence, not necessarily of morality, to preserve the lives of those scientists who are likely to benefit others, but there are many others – a large majority – of humans who do not have this capacity. Is it therefore a *moral* question as to whether volunteer humans should be used as experimental subjects as well as animals? These moral probes may appear more pertinent with respect to some particular research. Why are animals used in studies of the harmful effects of tobacco smoking, when thousands of human subjects are available to be studied, some at present in apparent good health, others who have already succumbed to diseases such as lung or throat cancer, heart disease or emphysema? Why should animals be forced to ingest alcohol, when there are similarly ample human subjects available, some at present without diagnosed diseases, others with diseases of the liver and other organs?[23]

It is claimed that there is no alternative to using animals in some particular circumstances, notably in testing new drugs and vaccines for toxicity and side-effects, or in developing techniques for organ transplants. Let us *assume* that it is proper to risk serious injury or death to animals in such testing, but improper to risk serious injury or death to humans in the same circumstances. When serious injury or death is highly improbable in human subjects, ought they to replace animals when they are the likely beneficiaries and when there are no alternatives available to using either animal or human subjects? Is it prudence or morality that inclines us to answer that human life and wellbeing ought to be protected at all costs, because only humans can undertake beneficial research or in other ways ameliorate the condition of human and animal life alike? These are questions which test the human capacity for impartiality, as well as the human perception of presumption.

On the use of animals as models (that is, on the assumption that what is found to be the case in animals will also be the case in humans) there are both moral and scientific difficulties. To the extent that some inferences from animal to man are false, much animal suffering is unnecessary and should have been avoided. Testing of a drug in animals does not always guarantee its safety in humans. One of the most conspicuous examples is thalidomide, which appeared safe from animal tests but caused both human and animal birth deformities. Penicillin has proved invaluable in the treatment of diseases, but it was not developed in animal experiments. (The impetus to its discovery was the chance event of penicillin spores reaching Fleming's culture

plates through his open laboratory window.) Had it been tested
on guinea pigs, to which it is toxic, it is possible that it would have
been viewed, for a time at least, as suspect for human use.
Similarly aspirin is selectively toxic in animals, being toxic to cats,
but that was discovered after it was found to be safe in other
animals and in humans. As for thalidomide, it has been claimed
that had it been tested by one of the alternatives to animal
experiment (namely tissue culture) the product might never
have been developed commercially, and great human and
animal suffering would have been avoided.[24]

Animals as models in human research thus raise practical and
moral problems. When the animal model is used with supposed
psychological or psychiatric relevance to humans, as in the use of
infant primates in separation and maternal deprivation studies,
a contradictory moral position is reached. For on the one hand
the animal is seen as inferior, without the gift of human mind;
but on the other hand inferences of supposed relevance to the
human mind can be made only on the assumption of some
degree of mental affinity between animals and humans. That
very assumption raises moral questions about using animals at
all.[25] In biomedical research there are moral questions too in the
use of animal models, particularly with respect to the risks
involved in animal to man inferences. One of the most sensitive
areas is the effect of new drugs on pregnant women or women
of childbearing age, for this, it is held, 'cannot be reliably
predicted from the animal studies'.[26] If it is true, as has been
asserted, that there are no adequate methods of testing new
drugs for the capacity to produce birth deformities, the moral
questions refer, first, to the possibility of subjecting unborn
children to a lifetime of handicap; and second, to the continued
use of animal models in testing when in the case of teratogens
(deformity-producing agents) such tests may be largely a waste
of time.[27]

It is wastefulness that is the more serious moral question with
respect to animals, for it is they who may be subjected to much
unnecessary suffering. Animal models for research into human
cancer and human heart disease are sometimes suspect on the
grounds of unwarranted animal to man inferences. Cancers are
artificially induced in animals, leading to prolonged suffering,
but claims for any significant advance in the treatment or

prevention of human cancer have been strongly disputed by some.[28] Similarly it has been claimed that 'animal models of cardiovascular disease are only vaguely similar to the human diseases and have failed to make a significant advance against congenital heart defects, hypertension, stroke and coronary artery disease'.[29] The experiments continue at the cost of animal suffering. To the extent that this research area is contentious, with some physiologists supporting animal models, it is sufficient to observe the probability that some at least of the research is wasteful. (From the researchers' standpoint it has to be acknowledged that whether research is going to be fruitful or otherwise is not known at its beginning.) If the futility of some research is strongly indicated, the continued use of animals in that area constitutes both a moral and a social problem. It is a moral problem from the social standpoint, inasmuch as society's resources used to fund futile research would be better used to relieve suffering in other areas.

In summary, the recurring moral questions are: first and fundamentally, whether human interests ought to override animal interests; second, whether any humans can make this crucial moral judgement with sufficient impartiality and benevolence; third, whether the justification of animal experimentation rests on the consequentialist argument that it benefits both humans and animals; fourth, whether the end of human and animal wellbeing in the future justifies the means, *any* means, devised by researchers using animal models, regardless of animal suffering; fifth, whether there are adequate regulatory controls at present, imposed either internally by researchers or externally by legislators, to put an end to *unnecessary* animal suffering in research that is recognised as futile or redundant.

The central moral theme of this book relates to the second question: namely, to the human capacity for *sufficient impartiality* (with benevolence) to make moral judgements on the way we use animals, whether in research or in other ways. That is why we now return to the imaginative standpoint of the ideal spectator, as in Chapter 2, and then contrast it with the standpoint of practical morality to demonstrate both the limits of human moral practice and the far-reaching improvement of which humans are capable, given greater knowledge and understanding, and modified moral attitudes and values.

IDEAL SPECTATOR STANDPOINT

The ideal spectator has an umpire role. But to equip him for that role he has to be more than ideally rational, with a perfect command of all relevant knowledge. He needs also to be perfectly impartial and benevolent, and we shall return therefore to the notion of the non-human and non-animal being with the perfect powers we have already attributed to him. As an umpire, and along with his other attributes of impartiality and benevolence, the ideal spectator is fundamentally *rational*. He is not given to ad hoc judgements. Though with his ideal powers we might expect him to make infallible intuitive judgements, he has reasons to support them. His approach will then rule out summary pronouncements of Kantian imperatives of duty. His qualities give him the power to respect humans for what they are, and without bias to respect animals for what *they* are too. What is so difficult for most humans to achieve is easy for the ideal spectator: to see the world from the animal's standpoint, with a perception of the animal's awareness, its emotions, the things that give it satisfaction and the things that cause it suffering, according to species differences. But above all else he has what humans generally do not have: the capacity and the readiness to perceive humans and animals in the one animal kingdom, and to give to all, regardless of species, equality in the consideration of their interests.

Equality of consideration of interests

From his uncommitted standpoint, to the ideal spectator it makes no moral difference whether the animal is human or non-human; two-legged or four-legged; a running or hopping or flying animal; living in houses, nests or burrows, in rock shelters or perching in trees; hairless or covered with a protective coat; a primate, a rodent or a cetacean; omnivorous, carnivorous or herbivorous. All are seen to have their own separate interests, none taking moral precedence over others on irrelevant criteria of intelligence, cunning, craftsmanship, sociability, learning ability, manipulative skill, powers of mimicry or any other. None are placed on an inferior–superior scale, for no such scale is contemplated. None are placed on an undeserving– deserving scale, for again there is no such moral scale. With his knowledge of human nature and of animal natures, supported by a knowledge of the place of each in the evolutionary struggle, the ideal spectator takes each animal (human or non-human) as it is, perceiving some as more fortunate than others in the development of the brain and the nervous system, with the mental powers associated with that development. To him good fortune in natural endowment justifies no preferential consideration: equality of consideration of interests is simply an equal consideration of the interests of each as they happen to be in nature, without favour or prejudice.

How does the ideal spectator approach the questions posed at the end of the previous section? To the question, Ought human interests to override animal interests? the answer is obviously No, since it is a contradiction of the principle of equal consideration of interests. The second question, on who is to make this judgement, will be considered in the following section on practical morality. To the third question, on the validity of a consequentialist approach which weighs benefits both to humanity and to animals, the ideal spectator does not give an unqualified answer. He sees a justification if the beneficiaries are both animal and human (as with testing of vaccines for diseases common to both) only on condition that among the experimental subjects are human volunteers who carry the burden of risk and suffering roughly in proportion to the advantages likely to accrue to humans compared with those likely to accrue to animals. (On the use of animals in experiments when they are to be the only beneficiaries, as in the treatment of uniquely animal diseases, the ideal spectator has no doubts since he understands the benefits, even though the animals do not volunteer as subjects and have no capacity for weighing the risks and the suffering involved.) He does not see all experiments planned or executed by humans to be justified: this is another consideration to be weighed in the next section on practical morality. Similarly, on the fourth question, it is clear to him that the end does not justify the means in animal experiments: he sees at once that the interests of humans and the interests of animals are most ill-balanced when acute and prolonged animal suffering is involved. The last question is a contradiction to him: since he understands that some experiments are futile or redundant, it is self-evident that they should cease. Again there are practical implications to be deferred for the time being.

How does the ideal spectator approach a further question: are animal experiments justified when *humans* are the sole beneficiaries? Just as there are diseases unique to animals, so too there are diseases unique to humans. The foremost contemporary example is AIDS. Chimpanzees have already been infected with the virus in an attempt to find a successful treatment for the disease in humans. As with humans (assuming that the virus 'takes' or grows in the animals) if they do contract the disease and are not merely carriers, this will sharply reduce their lifespan and will also lead to suffering as they fall victim to other diseases which they are unable to combat for immunological reasons. From the standpoint of an equality of the consideration of interests the ideal spectator insists that the problem is a human one and not an animal one, and that therefore the solution must be found by means other than animal experimentation. (Alternative experimental techniques will be considered shortly.) From his standpoint of perfect detachment and disinterestedness, all animal life – human and non-human – is of equal worth; he is aware too of human powers for not only contributing to the wellbeing of all animal life, but also destroying or harming all animal life – indeed, for destroying most of the habitable earth.

It is to the practical world of conflict and imperfection that we now turn, and to the question of the moral justification of animal experimentation in human rather than ideal perceptions.

PRACTICAL MORALITY: MOTIVES AND ATTITUDES

In Chapter 2 'practical morality' was used in two senses: first to refer to its moral principles and its goals; second to what is humanly achievable. In the first respect it does not differ from the moral standpoint of the ideal spectator, except that the perception of its moral goals is limited by human imperfections in rationality, benevolence and knowledge. The ideal spectator has not been given any executive function, except for one particular purpose in Chapter 2, so a comparison of moral achievability is not now being considered. In practical morality, which is the morality of human beings in principle and in practice, it is not only our intellectual or rational imperfections which are observable by contrast with the ideal, but just as importantly it is our dispositions, those complex cognitive and emotional tendencies which together predispose us towards action of a particular kind, interacting with reason as judgements, decisions or conclusions are reached on what we ought to do in moral situations. The ideal spectator's world is not one of motives and attitudes: these belong rather to the more interesting world of practical morality – made interesting for the very reason of human imperfections and the moral complexities to which they give rise.

Animal experimentation is part of that world of imperfection. It is a world of dominant self-interests, of competitive goals, of ambition and envy. In animal experimentation, to live up to the principles of practical morality as effectively as possible, it is therefore not only necessary, as the two preceding chapters have explained, to understand animal natures; it is also necessary to understand *human* nature. The limitations of reason are perhaps more readily appreciated than our dispositional limitations, especially in terms of motives and attitudes (and possibly genetic influences as well), because these are sometimes concealed to observers and occasionally even to ourselves. Chapter 2 has also made it clear that equality of consideration of interests of humans and animals in practical morality is dependent partly on an understanding of the nature of moral thinking.

Motives are not simple mental states, but already have a complexity of desire and emotion from which they spring. If we want something, such as a reputation from research activities, we want it with some emotion, and we want it in a way that is directional towards the end in view. Even without the additional force of attitudes, motives themselves may overpower reason as they interact with it in our moral thinking. Then we may be led to moral rationalisations, sometimes only half aware of the strength of the motives that impel us into transparent excuses for acting or failing to act in particular situations. We may be clear in our motives, even arrogant and cynical as we ruthlessly pursue our ends in disregard of others' interests; or we may be unclear, confused, emotional, not fully understanding ourselves even if we believe we understand others. When we formulate intentions or purposes which have an orientation towards future action and goals, they too are motives.

It is sometimes said that people hide their true motives as a means of more readily achieving their ends. While this is true in some instances, it is equally true that there is often no attempt at concealment. But if they are not always hidden, motives are often mixed. The search for a single motive, even in animal experimentation, may be misconceived. Further, motives are much more than emotion and a vague desire: they relate to perceiving something, to an end; to having ideas or understanding of a situation. The cognitive content is variable, but when it is clear it gives the motive an additional force in the predisposing complex which interacts with reason. That complex includes attitudes and values, and when these and motives are in sympathy, as when a motive for gain from trading in animals for experimental laboratories reinforces an attitude of total indifference towards animals' suffering, then the combined dispositional inclination becomes a formidable force for reason to contend with.[30]

The awareness of the part of motives and attitudes in our moral thinking cannot but be helpful in penetrating any rationalisations about animal experiments. As foreshadowed earlier, we shall consider motives and attitudes as they are reflected, first, in vested interests; second, in various abuses of animals; third, in the extent to which alternatives are used to animals in research. Statutory provisions governing animal experimentation will be introduced briefly, leaving to the last chapter a consideration of possible motives and attitudes involved in *processes* of legislation.

Vested interests

Groups which have by now a long association with animal experimentation and seek personal gain from it are drug companies and some industrial chemists; university (and other) biomedical research departments; animal traders; experimental psychologists; and groups in agricultural and military research. Drug companies and relevant industrial chemists are organised by their executives for economic profit. Attitudes of executives towards animals are likely to be negative or indifferent, with animal suffering regarded as irrelevant to business performance. The motives of researchers in their animal laboratories may be mixed: like the executives they are paid to get results. Personal livelihood depends on the success of the marketed product, so animals again are a means to an end. Some researchers may have mixed motives and mixed emotions: some may have a degree of sympathy for the animals in their suffering, as well as a humanitarian motive in aiming to produce a substance that will relieve human suffering. (Some of the analgesics produced by drug companies *have* had widespread benefits, in some cases to animals themselves.)

Yet competition among companies has produced an abundance of drugs, many at best no better than others, some merely enlarging an oversupply already existing. Animals may suffer considerably in the process, for all new drugs have to be tested for toxicity. Further, the bulk of the products in some affluent countries are not drugs intended to relieve human suffering, but rather cosmetics, household and industrial preparations, each new one claiming to be better than its rivals, though for each there may be already an alternative on the market. Retailers and consumers are often confused, with no means of knowing which marketed product is better than another. Companies have their commercial travellers to take advantage of this client uncertainty. Even general medical practitioners are persuaded to try out new drugs claimed to be efficacious in the treatment of diseases, and unless they try them out on patients they have no means of knowing whether they are or not. (Some trials are justified because of individual patient reactions: drugs are not always equally suitable for all patients.) Temptations are put in the way of some hospitals by offering grants for research. Techniques for marketing drugs are as competitive, ingenious and ruthless as with any other commodity in large business organisations.

It is difficult enough to justify the end on moral grounds; it is more difficult still to justify the *means*, for these involve large-scale animal suffering. This is the case with both the LD 50 test and the Draize test – each long practised in the laboratories of drug companies and certain industrial chemists. The LD 50 is literally the 'lethal dose fifty per cent' test. It is intended to register the amount of a substance which will kill fifty per cent of a test group of animals within a specified time. Though originally used to test potent drugs (it was first used in 1927) in addition to testing medicines, it is now used in testing pesticides, cosmetics, new drugs, weedkillers and a variety of household and industrial products. Some of these are redundant; many others can readily be done without by consumers in the light of well-documented animal suffering.[31] While drug companies and industrial chemists are not themselves responsible for the introduction and continuation of the test (it is legally required in some countries) they *are* responsible for the introduction of an increasing number of unwanted products, with the consequent demand for an increasing number of animals as suffering subjects.

Similarly the Draize Eye Irritancy test has become, in some countries, largely a commercial instrument. Though used since 1944 the test is not regarded by scientists as reliable; from a moral standpoint, however, attitude to animal subjects may be quite indifferent. The test is applied to a range of products including pesticides, weedkillers, household detergents and shampoos. As indicated in Chapters 1 and 3, rabbits are used because they do not have tear ducts so cannot dilute the irritant when it is dropped into the eye. They are immobilised with their heads clamped in position. Metal clips or adhesive tape force the eyelids apart. When the substance is a severe irritant the rabbits struggle and sometimes scream. The test may continue for a week. The damage is observed and recorded, often in swelling, discharge from the eyes, blistering and destruction of the cornea. Subjective assessments on the severity of the irritation weigh heavily. While the test can usually distinguish irritants from non-irritants, it cannot reliably evaluate the extent of the irritation.[32] Some irritants which pass the test have harmful effects on particular humans.

Other commercial preparations are tested for *skin* irritation by the Draize Patch test. In this case the animals used are usually guinea pigs. The hair is shaved, then the skin scraped. A common technique is for adhesive tape to be pressed firmly down on the skin, then quickly lifted off. By repeating the painful process several layers of skin are removed. The exposed tissue is sensitive to the chemical irritants then applied, and eventually covered with a patch. The animal is immobilised for a day or two, unable to scratch or remove the irritant. If the preparation passes the test it will satisfy the consumer, should any questions be raised, that the marketed commodity – such as an astringent after-shave lotion – has been tested for safety. In neither the LD 50 nor the two Draize tests can the means be said to justify the end, particularly in circumstances when the short-term end is persuasion of consumers to accept an unneeded product and the ultimate end is commercial profit. When the product is of trivial relevance to any human benefit, as in the case of cosmetics, the motives and attitudes of drug companies and industrial chemists need to be seen in conjunction with the suffering of immobilised animals, unable to talk, to complain intelligibly, or to communicate their often desperate need for an alleviation of their suffering.

Equally pronounced, though not so powerful politically, are the vested interests of research departments, such as those in universities. One of the signs of firmly-held attitudes is a stubborn defensiveness against opposition and towards threatened change: a resistance by some to learning and applying alternative techniques, for instance. What may be hidden is the motive of ego-protection, upholding personal and professional standing in the community, expressed at times in a desire to conduct research in secret, away from the disturbing scrutiny of laymen who may be seen contemptuously by some as simply mischievous and uninformed. To some researchers only the research has value, and the possibility of publishable outcomes which will enhance the standing of both the researchers themselves and their institutions. There has long been a tendency for some in the medical profession (like any other profession in this respect) to close ranks against opposition. The Royal Commission which enquired into vivisection in England in the last century came to the conclusion that painful experiments are necessary for original research. While the RSPCA deplored such a stand, it had to admit that 'such opinion is predominant in the evidence' (mainly from medical witnesses).[33] In the USA a little later defensiveness among medical practitioners led to the rationalisation that 'vivisection is not necessarily cruel, or even painful', and the general attitude among them was reported as 'one that opposes concessions to a group of reformers whose ultimate aim is that of suppression'.[34] It is not unusual for some researchers to rally to the support of a beleaguered colleague, even when the evidence is strongly against him.[35] One of the most vigorous defences of researchers in universities has been that of academic freedom (though in some countries research proposals now need to be approved by ethics committees). When personal motives and attitudes are involved in using animals for research, no such freedom can be given a moral clearance without examination.

University research departments constitute vested interests to the extent that animals are used partly for personal and institutional gain. Some of the concealed motives may be administrative: to attract a sufficient number of higher degree students to strengthen a case for an increased staff establishment, or even for retention of an existing establishment. Other motives may be personal: to enhance reputations and career prospects; in the case of higher degree students, to earn a career qualification. Among the most conspicuous and competent researchers motives are mixed to the extent that there is also a genuine scientific curiosity directed towards an increase in human knowledge and human wellbeing. Animal suffering to gratify personal ambition, or to attract research grants, or to keep a flagging research department viable with demonstrable activity – these are the motives which can never be justified on moral grounds, for they call for much unnecessary animal suffering in experiments with factitious ends. When both ends and means are indefensible, the moral debt to animals is magnified proportionately.

These aspects of research merge into *abuses* in the use of animals, such as experimental repetition, futility and redundancy, which will be considered shortly. Others with a vested interest in animal experiments are animal traders, animal scientists and defence departments. Animal traders range from those who capture animals in the wild and the agents who sell them to laboratories, to large corporations which may make substantial profits from breeding rats and mice, hamsters, guinea pigs and monkeys for sale to drug companies.[36] Hundreds of dealers are licensed (in the USA by the US Department of Agriculture) to procure animals and to resell them to research institutions. Many of these animals are cats and dogs, once pets, which have been taken by control officers to municipal pounds, then usually put in the hands of dealers (though some pounds sell direct to laboratories). Humane societies have documented the prolonged suffering of the animals before they reach the laboratories; what happens in the laboratories compounds their suffering.[37]

The work of animal scientists has been noted: they represent the vested interests of livestock producers in factory farms especially. Their motive is fundamentally commercial. Nutrition research is not necessarily to promote animal health; it may be to increase the rate at which food is converted into meat. Physiological studies may be aimed at getting animals to reproduce at a higher and more consistent rate. Genetic research may be aimed at producing pigs whose feet and legs will withstand the stresses of standing on slatted floors in factory farms. Much of the research involves animal suffering; if successfully introduced into the factory farm the research does little later to reduce the prolonged suffering of animals living under artificial conditions.

Finally, defence (or military) departments constitute a vested interest in animals for research, with similar attitudes to animals as having no inherent value. Monkeys have been used to test nerve gas, cyanide poison, effects of radiation and effects of sustained acceleration on the cardiovascular system. In one research project the objective was 'to obtain accurate and reliable data reflecting the impact of nuclear radiation upon the performance capability of highly trained infrahuman primates'.[38] In the UK monkeys have been shot through the head with ball bearings to study the effects of high velocity missiles.[39]

Abuses in planning and conduct of experiments

Any unnecessary infliction of suffering on animals is cruelty, and all such acts in research count as abuses of animals. These include some of the experiments performed primarily to satisfy vested interests. With modern anaesthetics and analgesics it is possible to avoid pain in all, or almost all, cases; where it is not, there is a strong case for not proceeding with the experiment at all, but for using an alternative to animal experimentation should one be available. In the end, under present experimental conditions, judgements of what is necessary will be subjective, though reached in panel discussions with laymen. There is no guarantee that different panels will reach the same judgements of what is necessary and permissible, but decisions have to be made in some circumstances, and given human imperfections mistakes will at times be made. A practical morality allows for well-justified exceptions to the principle that infliction of suffering is an evil, such as veterinary attention to an injured animal which may have to be restrained for a lengthy period to facilitate healing, the pain relieved as much as possible with analgesics. Although *intentions* involve an awareness of means and ends, with a directional or forward-looking orientation,[40] they are not necessarily translated into actions with any consistent clarity or single-mindedness. In the previous chapter the question of animal awareness was considered. Now it might be wondered how aware *humans* are as they pursue their ends in animal experiments without proper attention to the means, or to the natures of the animal subjects.

The main category of abuses in animal experiments relates to futility and redundancy, including repetitions. In every such case there is animal suffering to little or no purpose, except to fulfil personal ambition. One of the most conspicuous illustrations is from maternal deprivation studies with infant primates. Since they began in the 1950s hundreds of similar experiments have been conducted in the USA alone.[41] Experimenters modify previous research with usually slight variations, such as into the timing and duration of the separation.[42] The repetitions have added nothing significant to the findings of the original research, which indeed was itself largely futile: first, because inferences from primate infants to human infants are in any case suspect; and second, because *human* studies of deprivation preceded the animal studies and therefore largely nullified their major findings. Sometimes researchers argue that research may produce surprising or altogether unexpected results; that it is therefore unreasonable for any individual, or for an ethics committee, to determine from the experimental proposal what experiments should proceed and what should not. If the experiments were on living tissues only, and not on whole organisms, alive and healthy, possible benefits from chance discoveries might justify some research. Certainly biomedical research has yielded important discoveries where the element of chance has been significant, as noted already in the case of Fleming's discovery of penicillin. But the additional factor in animal experiments is animal suffering: this cannot be justified by the mere possibility of making serendipitous discoveries.

The futility of animal experiments in maternal deprivation has been demonstrated on other grounds. Researchers continued to confirm findings of the harmful consequences of separation of infants from their mothers, but when a few departed from primate infants and used dogs, the problem of making inferences to humans was aggravated by the more obvious dissimilarity of the species. When there was a departure by a few researchers from rhesus monkeys to other monkey species, it was found that the species varied in their reactions to maternal deprivation. The relative unpredictability of the findings in the light of this variability might have dissuaded more discerning researchers from extending their deprivation studies. One analysis of experiments in this area undertaken to 1984 revealed that only one of one hundred and fifty experiments had significance for clinical practice.[43]

Repetition of experiments is sometimes defended by researchers on the grounds of the necessity to verify the results obtained. While it is true that in biomedical research verification is necessary, as in testing a new drug for toxicity, when animals are used in the testing the repetition should end when adequate confirmation has been established. In one study the effects of forced alcohol ingestion by animals were found to have been investigated in eight hundred and fifty experiments – even one of which would have been largely wasteful because of direct human studies already undertaken and the precedence these should have been given over animal studies.[44] Both nationally and internationally, computer banks readily indicate research already undertaken.

Duplication of experiments is not to be condoned on the grounds of the large number of research institutions in modern industrial societies and the difficulty of ascertaining exactly, at any one time, what has been done and is being done by researchers elsewhere. With many fewer research departments in the UK in the last century it was observed that 'the same experiment is repeated many times on different animals';[45] and in 1933 it was said that 'the same thing is tried over and over again, with the same results'.[46]

Researchers' persistence when the signs of futility and scientific invalidity are sufficiently plain reflects the dominance of self-interested motives. Their attention has been drawn, for instance, to species differences between and among animals in the speed and pattern of drug metabolism, and to the fact that even in monkeys (closest to humans in evolutionary history) drugs do not always behave in the same way. Animals continue to be fed with drugs over long periods, even when it is known that animals metabolise the drugs differently from humans. They continue to be used in cancer research when testing weak carcinogens, though animals are widely held to be unsuitable for this purpose.[47] Experimenters would be naive indeed if they could not foretell the effects of the suffering they inflict on animals in some of their experiments. In simulated car crash experiments, for instance, animals are sometimes strapped into sleds, then propelled at high speed into crash objects. It is a foregone conclusion that they will suffer severe injuries, as it is when heavy weights are dropped onto them as they are immobilised by restraining devices in one position. Time after time animals have been abused through the motives of the researchers; funding organisations are usually unaware themselves that the experiments may be merely repeating what has become a fashionable research activity, performed many times before. Thousands of *humans* are seriously injured each year in car accidents, and their injuries studied before treatment. Experimental animals are usually X-rayed, killed and their bodies further examined to study their injuries in further detail. If computer banks stored information gained throughout the world from *human* studies and made it readily available, animal suffering in this area of research might become unnecessary. Ironically again, the futility of the animal suffering is reflected in the admissions by many animal researchers that animal models are not particularly suitable in studying simulated crash injuries.

The futility has been noted of using animals in tobacco-smoking and alcohol-ingestion experiments. There are many other instances of animal abuse where the results of the experiments are foregone conclusions, or where trivialities are upheld as unusual or novel. Some of the experiments in sleep deprivation are in this category. What is the point of depriving animals of sleep until they die, or are so close to death that they have to be killed? Would not a normally perceptive human see that such experiments and suffering are unnecessary? What is the point of subjecting animals to the distress of addictive drugs to observe their response to food under these conditions, when there are many human subjects already studied in this and other respects? Is not sufficient known about human victims of house fires, bushfires, scalding accidents and chemical burns to make unnecessary the deliberate scalding and burning of animals, especially when it is acknowledged that animal to human inferences in these areas too are not reliable? Why subject animals to whiplash injuries (the animals accelerated in sleds, then abruptly decelerated, causing the head to be flung forward, then snapped back) when many humans have already been studied as victims of car accidents?[48]

When it is already known that primate infants are mothered, respond to fondling, are inseparable from their mothers when left undisturbed, and when it is already known that human infants too need mothering, what is the point of separating primate infants from their mothers to see what happens, or of isolating social animals from all association with their kind in contrivances from which they can see nothing of a social world outside and from which they soon learn there is no possibility of escape? The researcher who initiated deprivation studies with animals deliberately set about to contradict what was known in natural situations, setting in train as well many imitative studies which have not yet ended. It has been charged that he 'ironically reconfirmed the importance of love to personal health by utilizing gross abuse'.[49] His own attitude to animals is a matter of record, serving as a pertinent example of the influence of motive on attitudes towards animals.[50]

The abuse of animals in research has other foundations apart from the futility or redundancy of experiments, or false economic goals which are not related to human needs, as in the promotion of unwanted drugs[51] or the single-minded activities of vested interests. Other sources of abuse are experimental conditions; political rather than moral ends as in the case of military research; unjustifiable means such as the behaviourist psychologists' continued use of negative reinforcement. These will be considered briefly in turn. Laboratory conditions vary from sufficient space for free movement and exercise to very cramped conditions in cages. Active animals such as dogs and monkeys may be left caged for weeks or months. Not uncommonly cages have been found to be dirty, improperly and irregularly cleaned, without adequate food and water. There has been repeated concern at the inadequacy of external supervision of the facilities provided. After experiments some animals are returned to cages and continue to suffer as the effects of anaesthetics fade. The use of animals in military research is morally suspect on various grounds: subjection to radiation is not only wasteful, since much has been learned from human victims of Hiroshima and Nagasaki as well as from victims of peacetime nuclear disasters; it is also questionable for the ends that are contemplated, particularly involvement in a nuclear war that would probably destroy much of human and animal life. Their use in testing toxic liquids and gases directed towards possible use in biochemical warfare is also morally questionable in both means and ends. Finally, animals are abused when they are subjected by psychologists to negative reinforcement, inducing distress from anxiety or fear, or various forms of stress and pain such as from electric shock, in order to condition their behaviour.[52]

When so many questions are raised about the use of animals at all in research, and about the way they are used and the very large numbers used, why are they not dispensed with entirely in favour of alternative techniques and procedures?

Alternatives to animals in research

An answer to this question can be given only by referring to relevant facts, and in the last resort to the judgement of well-qualified experts, especially in the biomedical area, even though there is some danger of bias in the most well-informed of such judgements. First we must ask if true alternatives to animal experiments exist, and if they do, in what specific areas they are now available. Second we must ask, if researchers are not using alternatives open to them, what explanation can be given for inflicting suffering on animals. Third, if it is the most highly informed judgement that in some aspects of research animals cannot be dispensed with, we must enquire into the conditions under which such research is supportable morally or is least likely to be morally objectionable. We shall use a conventional interpretation of 'alternative' to apply to all procedures which can be used instead of animal experiments, either replacing animals completely or replacing them in part, without any necessary concern for animal suffering; or which in various ways do show a concern for animal suffering, either by reducing the number of animals needed or by paying greater attention to the humane aspects of the experiments. Some prefer to use what is a more logically consistent definition, by which alternatives are defined as the complete replacement of animals (sometimes called 'true alternatives'), other procedures being either complementary to them or able to provide some supplementary information helpful in using the true alternatives.[53]

Scientific opinion holds that replacement procedures for

animals do not at present exist for *all* research purposes, though they do for some. The strongest claims are made for in vitro techniques, referring to experiments conducted in test tubes. There are two types of tissue culture so used: cell cultures and organ cultures. In cell cultures a beginning is made with a single cell taken from human or animal tissue. This produces succeeding generations of identical cells and thus a standardised and reliable supply of test material. Organ cultures do not require the use of whole organs. A few different cells are used from the same organ, and because the different cells have a functional relationship, in a sense the structure of the organ is retained, and certain interactions can be ascertained without requiring that the whole organ be used.

Animals are first anaesthetised and suffer little discomfort from the removal of tissue; often the use of animals is unnecessary because of the availability of human tissue. Although tissue culture has now largely replaced animals for the production of viral vaccines, scientists claim that it is not useful generally when biomedical problems associated with the interaction between different tissues and organs are being investigated. For these whole organisms (animals or humans) are needed, and the choice of subject is traditionally *animal*. Tissue cultures are not able to replace animals entirely in toxicity testing, for once again interaction between tissues and organs needs to be tested with whole organisms, as in testing the possible side-effects of certain drugs. Tissue cultures have been useful in cancer research, though they have not yet been able to replace animals and are more strictly seen as complementary to their use rather than as replacements.[54] From the humane standpoint, though animal suffering has been reduced by limiting the number of animals used, there is reason to believe that numbers could be still further limited. One technique involves, for instance, using duck or chicken eggs with embryos. Even sea urchin eggs have been used to replace animals such as rats, hamsters and guinea pigs in toxicity tests in some circumstances. As replacements for tissues obtained from animals, cultured human cells are used for certain purposes.[55] Organ cultures may be grown from tumour tissue from lung or skin, for example.

In moral thinking generally, and in the making of moral judgements in particular, Chapter 3 has already demonstrated the importance of relevant *knowledge*, in addition to the need for the utmost effort in reaching for impartiality and benevolence. At this stage, therefore, a summary of factual information is unavoidable, without unnecessary technicalities, to enable us to answer the first question posed at the beginning of this section. Although in vitro techniques are the most widely used alternative to animals in biomedical research,[56] there are many others which collectively limit the numbers of animals needed. For example, single-celled organisms (without a nervous system and therefore unable to experience pain) are used for some purposes. Insights into genetics are still coming from a study of plants, and in genetic research they are widely used instead of animals. Computers are used instead of animals in some studies of heart attacks, of the functions of various organs and of entire anatomical systems. For teaching purposes computer models of the human circulatory and respiratory systems are sometimes used. Gas chromatography and the mass spectrometer together enable the detection of small traces of chemicals in the human body, such as harmful drugs, so that in drug research which at one time required animals the number of animals used has been restricted by this technology. Various imaging techniques and procedures save the use of many animals.[57]

Human volunteers are used at times to test new drugs, but only after the mandatory safety test has been applied to animals. Epidemiological studies provide evidence of the effects of diseases, and harmful agents such as tobacco smoke, by considering a whole population of humans within an environment.[58] Comparative epidemiological studies have indicated the risks of cancer in certain habitual practices such as tobacco smoking, or in fibre deficiencies in the diet, or in excesses in meat consumption.

There are many replacement alternatives to live animals for teaching purposes. Surgical procedures can be illustrated on videotape and by cinematography, often with a clarity individual students would be unable to perceive in an operation on a live animal (or on a living human). Dummies or mechanical models are now being used in some secondary school biology and in medical schools (as well as in car crash testing). The mechanical models or robots are made with increasing complexity for particular purposes: some with mechanical hearts which can simulate a variety of cardiac and other diseases; some simulating bleeding, breathing, coughing and vomiting. Car companies have sophisticated models to test car crashes at various speeds and to study neck injuries. The demonstration that simulators can be made with heart and circulatory system, lungs and a respiratory system, and with devices to test the effects of various drugs and the functioning of kidneys, indicates that animals can be replaced increasingly for some purposes.

We are now in a better position to answer the three questions posed initially on alternatives to animals in research. In answer to the first, replacements for animals are already available in a number of different research areas, but there are not alternative procedures to replace animals for all biomedical purposes, such as toxicity testing.[59] Though much has been learned of diseases from epidemiology, its findings do not generally reach to understanding relationships which lead to successful treatment of the diseases. The use of humans as research subjects has limits. Both the LD 50 and the Draize tests have been charged with inflicting unnecessary suffering on animals. There are alternatives which can achieve similar results,[60] though each with its own limitations. The reliability of the LD 50 test is seriously in question. Its continued widespread use is not justified except under very special circumstances, least of all with large animals such as dogs, monkeys and pigs.[61] In most cases carefully selected alternative procedures to the LD 50 test are capable of meeting experimental purposes.

Aversive procedures in experimental psychology, designed to extend knowledge of human behaviour, are of such a questionable nature from a moral standpoint that they call for the most rigorous examination by university or government commissions comprising all interested parties as well as selected laymen. That psychologists are being specifically trained in acts which amount to abuse of animals is morally repugnant. The most serious objection to any aversive procedure is on grounds of cruelty (with the supplementary consideration of the weakness of animal to man inferences). The record of achievement from aversive research needs careful examination, followed by a general cost-benefit judgement. On prima facie evidence aversive research cannot be morally justified. If the objective is to demonstrate classical conditioning with aversive stimuli, or learned helplessness, or the effects of drugs on behaviour, or the effects of surgical ablations or lesions, or the alteration of sensory capabilities, each can be taught to students by other means.[62]

We are now in a position to consider the second and third

questions together. When alternatives are open to researchers, why do some continue to use animals in their experiments? Two reasons have been a lack of training in alternatives and financial constraints within departments. Another has been a conservatism in adhering to known and trusted techniques and procedures, combined with motives of self-interest in preferring to achieve publishable results as quickly as possible, rather than take time to learn and master alternatives. Yet another reason is political, as noted, for largely to ease public fears it is mandatory in some countries to test new drugs for toxicity and teratogenicity even when the tests are held by scientists to have low predictability.

Under what conditions should animal experiments be permitted from a moral standpoint? These are now briefly summarised. First, all researchers should understand, and be prepared to consider, the *natures* of animals, and so an acquaintance with ethology (with special reference to the animals likely to be used experimentally) must be both a moral and a practical requirement. Included must be a knowledge of the physiology of animals in general and of the nervous mechanisms by which they experience pain. Included also must be a knowledge of emotional capacities connected with such things as social hierarchies, caring for the young, play and so forth. Researchers need a knowledge of anaesthetics and skill in using them, a knowledge of surgery and as much skill as would be required for human patients. They need a knowledge of principles of morality and an appreciation of humane values. Experiments with animals are not merely scientific activities: equally they are *moral* activities. Therefore all ethics committees need to include not only laymen, but also representatives of humane societies and moral philosophers with an interest in animal wellbeing and with both understanding and skill in presenting moral viewpoints.

Second, the massive duplication of experiments must be avoided by a required reference to data banks already existing or, in those countries without ready access to them, to all relevant journals, so that the scrutiny of ethics committees can justify them.[63] Third, the system of funding research needs amendment. Private sources such as drug companies are sometimes too readily persuaded that a research programme is promising when to them it promises no more than wide publicity or the chance of presenting yet another (often redundant) product to an already saturated market. There is an excessive number of researchers, particularly in psychology in some countries, all needing laboratories to work in and research that is likely to bring personal reward. Animal suffering must never be allowed to become an opportunity to solve a human vocational, social or economic problem.

Fourth, in reaching decisions on what experiments are to be permitted, the criteria need to be both scientific and moral, with availability of alternatives to animal experimentation a primary consideration and their use a requirement, regardless of time and regardless of expense, unless there is an emergency in human health which requires the urgent preparation and testing of vaccines in order to protect the population at large. It is the humane scientist only who is needed in animal experiments.[64]

Fifth, all prospective researchers need to be thoroughly trained in the use of alternatives, with an understanding of their many applications. They need to appreciate that animals are to be used *only* when necessity demands it, and as part of their professional training they need to be thoroughly exercised in presenting written and oral justifications for using animals on the grounds of *necessity* for human or animal health. Though familiar with anaesthetics and analgesics, they need to be exercised in the much more rigorous justification of inflicting any pain at all or any distress on animals. Sixth, and associated with the problem of animal distress, their training must include a planning of laboratories for animals, making use of their knowledge of ethology; and practical experience in animal care which takes account of the animals' natures according to their respective species.

Seventh, all economic incentives to trade in laboratory animals must be removed. Government-controlled animal breeding and holding centres are needed so that all middlemen – the dealers and traders whose only interest in animals is to profit by them – are eliminated. The personnel selected to work in breeding and holding centres would co-ordinate the availability of animals with a much reduced demand from research institutions; they need to be trained for their work, with a suitable background knowledge of animal interests and needs, of laboratory science and of moral principles relating to animal suffering.

To some extent society has lost control of animal experiments.

In such circumstances, should enlightened legislation be taking a lead? We shall leave until the next chapter some of the more fundamental and wider questions relating to society and the law, including the functions of the courts and law enforcement, and confine ourselves at this stage to the inadequacy of current statutes.

The law on animal experiments

It has been common for statutes relating to animal experimentation to be sufficiently imprecise to leave loopholes in the prevention of unnecessary animal suffering. Some of the possible sources of imprecision will become clear in the next chapter when the processes leading to legislation are examined. In this section we shall look particularly at some of the deficiencies of the *Cruelty to Animals Act 1876*, and then at some of the deficiencies in United States legislation.

Apart from the influence of the RSPCA, the *Cruelty to Animals Act 1876* was given impetus by an international congress held in England to discuss, especially, operations on animals for the purpose of instruction in surgery.[65] In its testimony before the Royal Commission which preceded the passing of legislation the RSPCA pointed out that there were many instances in which no anaesthetic was given to animals throughout experiments on them, and in which they suffered extensive pain. Even painless experiments could not be condoned, it was said, 'except under regulations to prevent excesses'.[66] Professors had been using living animals, previously narcotised and operated on, for teaching purposes, and in some instances students had performed secret operations on animals. The leading feature of a bill prepared by the society itself, for the guidance of members of Parliament, was stated bluntly as 'the prohibition of all experiments which cause pain'. Although in a criminal case a judge could give an order for an experiment to be performed on an animal if he considered it necessary, otherwise anyone performing such an operation required a licence from the Secretary of State. Experiments were not to be used merely to illustrate lectures in medical schools or elsewhere, or by persons whose object was not to advance physiological knowledge, or to gain knowledge useful in saving or prolonging life or alleviating suffering. It was necessary to completely anaesthetise the animal during the entire operation and to kill it before recovery from the anaesthetic if in pain or seriously injured. Yet certificates gave experimenters *exemption* from the provisions relating to the use of anaesthetics, the purposes of the experiments and their use in illustrating lectures.[67] When under certain conditions the restrictions of the Act could be relaxed and the onus placed on the experimenter to act in good faith, there was presumably no understanding of the extent to which experimenters' judgements or discretion could be influenced by personal motives and attitudes. It was the research purpose which led to a restrictive interpretation of pain, and the expression 'calculated to cause pain' was used in such a way as to permit various experiments which could lead to animal distress.[68]

An intended amendment of the 1876 Act is The Animals (Scientific Procedures) Bill.[69] At the Committee stage the RSPCA has pressed for a number of amendments to the Bill, to ensure that cruelty to animals is alleviated by insisting that persons handling, caring for and giving anaesthetics and analgesics and euthanasia to animals are competent; that a suitably qualified person is available for advice whenever an animal is in severe pain which cannot be relieved, and a veterinary surgeon or other suitably qualified person is available to give advice on animal health and welfare to those in registered establishments and to those supplying animals; that a licence is required for any experiments which would involve substantially severe pain, and that reference is made to the Animal Procedures Committee of all experiments involving micro-surgery and/or cosmetics; that animals for experiments are used only from designated breeding establishments (dogs and cats included); that in order to ensure that the animal is fully anaesthetised, a qualified anaesthetist is in attendance whenever major surgery is involved, and muscle relaxants are used in it.[70]

Some of the RSPCA's recent recommendations were encompassed within the report of the Littlewood Committee of 1965, such as that, if a veterinary surgeon is not available, only trained anaesthetists should be used, and that curare (a muscle relaxant) should be prohibited except in conjunction with anaesthesia to ensure complete loss of consciousness. But the language continued to be vague, with the use of 'necessary', 'severe' and 'enduring' to apply to pain, each open to subjective interpretation and clouded by obvious indeterminacy.[71]

In the USA there is a similar appearance of humanity in the federal *Animal Welfare Act 1966* (with amendments in 1970, 1976 and 1985), which is the only federal statute relating to animals used in experimentation. The general requirement of 'adequate veterinary care' with an 'appropriate use of anaesthetic, analgesic and tranquillizing drugs' is open to subjective interpretation and variable application. The requirement that each research laboratory keep a record of the numbers of painful experiments and tests conducted without anaesthetics, analgesics and tranquillisers, and give the reason in their annual report, leaves the way open for researchers to make false claims, as some are believed to do, that pain-killing drugs were in fact used and that therefore the animals did not suffer.[72] The researcher is free to decide himself whether pain-relieving drugs are necessary, so that much depends on the attitudes and humane values of the researchers themselves. While the latest amendment to the Act, the *Improved Standards for Laboratory Animals Act 1985*, is designed to improve the conditions of laboratory animals by requiring the training of animal care personnel, requiring animal care committees to include public representation and preventing duplication of experiments, so reducing the demand for laboratory animals, supervision of the Act remains inadequate. Indeed effective care and protection of laboratory animals is a problem throughout the world, exacerbated by inadequate funding even in affluent countries such as the USA. It is sobering to reflect that the situation in the USA, as in the UK, seems to have changed little in a hundred years, with inadequate protection by the law against the infliction of suffering on animals by 'incompetent and irresponsible persons'.[73]

SUMMARY

This chapter has been concerned with the moral debt to animals both in a forward-looking sense, as we consider what we owe to an animal from a moral standpoint when it is about to be subjected to pain or distress of various kinds in biomedical and psychological research, and in a backward-looking sense, when we weigh, ineffectually because it is too late in most cases, what we owe to animals from the knowledge that they have suffered in experiments performed on them. There is indisputable evidence of animal suffering, ranging from aversive procedures which some believe could never have been inflicted by persons of even moderately humane sensibilities, to milder forms of distress from fear or anxiety.

This chapter is a test of the human capacity for impartiality. Only the ideal spectator, non-human and non-animal, rational, knowledgeable, benevolent and capable of complete moral detachment, capable of seeing the world perfectly from the standpoints of the various involved beings, understanding the unity of the animal world through an evolutionary perspective, is able to judge that human interests ought not to override animal interests and that there ought to be an equality of benefits and equality of sacrifices in determining whether animals or humans are to be used as research subjects.

By contrast, the world of practical morality is the world of human imperfection in reason, knowledge, benevolence and especially impartiality, where an individual's motives and attitudes (and perhaps genetic influences as well) interact with his reason, sometimes in support, at other times in opposition, always influencing his thoughts as he makes his moral judgements, decisions or conclusions. Some of these moral judgements relate to the field of animal experimentation. Then it is clear that they come under predisposing influences, especially of motives, attitudes and values.

Motives and attitudes are conspicuous in the case of vested interests, and also in the case of animal abuse in experiments. Those with obvious vested interests include not only commercial enterprises such as drug companies, certain industrial chemists and livestock producers, but also university research departments and defence departments. Abuses of animals refer to all instances of an unnecessary infliction of suffering on them: in futile or redundant experiments, laboratory care, production of redundant drugs, deliberate injuries in military experiments, aversive procedures in psychology.

A wide range of alternative techniques and procedures can contribute to the reduction of the numbers of animals needed in research. Alternatives are not used as widely as they might be, partly through lack of confidence in their use, but largely for reasons of self-interest – on the part of both researchers and politicians. It is scientific opinion that no alternatives are available at present for some biomedical purposes such as the testing of vaccines and new medicines.

The moral conclusion from the ideal spectator standpoint is

unequivocal. The moral conclusion from the standpoint of practical morality is that an absolute minimum of animal experimentation should be permitted, on the advice of a select panel of the most highly qualified and experienced of biomedical researchers, with demonstrated humane values and a thorough knowledge of alternatives to the use of animals. Let us never forget that this is a *human* judgement, the conclusion of practical morality which takes account of all relevant information, with the highest degree of impartiality and benevolence of which a human is capable. It is not trite to observe that if animals could talk, we would find that it would not be *their* judgement. This is a fundamental point for impartiality. If the ideal spectator could give evidence, perfectly detached and disinterested, totally without presumption and capable of complete evenhandedness, it would not be his judgement either. To move as close as we can to the perfect impartiality of the ideal spectator, we can at least conclude that research funds, under the most competent of researchers, should be directed to finding replacements for animals in research as soon as possible. At the present state of biomedical knowledge that will be a daunting task if humans are not to be called on as test subjects for vaccines and new medicines.

The most skilled and knowledgeable of medical researchers have prevented an incalculable amount of suffering among humans and animals. Their use of animals is morally justified only in circumstances at present applying: namely, that many diseases and crippling conditions remain for which prevention or successful treatment has not yet been discovered; and that replacement alternatives to the use of whole animals are not yet available for all research. Suggested conditions for the continuance of animal experimentation have been summarised in the previous section.[74]

In all countries, but notably in the UK and the USA, statutory law designed to protect animals from unnecessary suffering is in need of more regular amendment, and probably too of wide publicity so that some of the motives and attitudes of those influencing legislation are better appreciated by the public. That too is a question to be developed further in the following chapter.

5 The Law, Morality and Education

In this chapter the moral debt to animals will be further developed by considering several relationships: first, between law and morality; second, between law and social values; third, between law and education. The first two of these relationships will be further clarified under the third, from an understanding of both *why* and *how* laws are made.

THE LAW, MORALITY AND THE MORAL DEBT TO ANIMALS

To illustrate the limitations of the law it will be useful to contrast ideal law and ideal morality with the law in practice and practical morality. Again the purpose of the model is to draw attention to the gap between perfection and human performance, and also to emphasise the space between the two as a challenge to human improvement.

Ideal law

Should a person with the powers attributed to the ideal spectator be entrusted with making laws for a community, he would not be swayed by partisan pressure groups regardless of how vocal they were in proclaiming what they perceived to be, and perhaps genuinely believed to be, the 'common interest'. He would go beyond the perceptions of the common interest by different persons or by different groups to something that is in perfect conformity with morality and justice and which might be properly designated the 'common good'.[1] That is not clearly perceptible by imperfect rulers, however benevolent in intent they may be, or by imperfect governments. Even Plato's near-ideal rulers, thoroughly trained in reason, could only glimpse the Form of the good, and Aristotle followed him to the extent of describing laws as just when they serve the common interest

151

(which from a moral standpoint he identified with the common good), not the interests of the rulers.[2] The highest good 'is the political science of which the good is justice' (ch. 12, 1282[b]). Yet this was merely reaching for an ideal; it was not a statement of ideal law made by ideal rulers. Indeed, although he acknowledged, as Plato did, that the *best* men must legislate (ch. 15, 1286[a]), Aristotle was not deluded about human imperfections. It is only in the imaginary situation of perfect law made by perfect legislators that, by definition, the law and morality are one. Then there might be both backward-looking moral debts relating to offences against animals in the past, and forward-looking moral debts relating to what we owe to animals in the future. But in neither case would the law be at fault: its conjunction with morality would not be affected by any human acts.

Another ideal standpoint was Kant's in his view of the uniformity of moral judgements made by all persons of good will, since all rational persons in his view, as we have seen, were obedient to duty as it was commanded by reason. If in fact lawmakers acted entirely on moral duty, obedient always to a rational will, again by definition state laws would be united with moral laws.[3] Only if all citizens too were obedient to a rational will with respect to cruelty to animals would the moral debt to animals in the forward-looking sense be discharged; and in the backward-looking sense there would be no moral debt accumulated. By contrast, the relationship between law and morality in the imperfect world is expectedly different.

The law in practice and practical morality

In legal theory the positivist position is significant for its assertion that the law is law, good or bad, a command of those with power which imposes an obligation to obedience.[4] That does not imply that law-makers are necessarily insensitive to moral issues, such as the issue of cruelty to animals, or that laws are necessarily outside the proper area for moral criticism. On the contrary, moral judgements may be passed on them without in any way affecting their status as laws. One of the more recent positivists, Hans Kelsen, believed that law-makers should impose, with the same obligation to obedience, what the social order considers desirable.[5] That is itself a formidable task, especially in multi-cultural societies, but in so far as the social order's desired objectives are discernible, it is these which the law should express and reflect, and questions of goodness or badness of the laws so derived are not strictly relevant to the position of the laws as such. One of the foremost of contemporary jurists, H. A. L. Hart, sees the *rules* of law as their central characteristic, and an obligation to obey them as dependent on a social acceptance of the rules (that is, an acceptance of the rules as providing suitable standards for members of the society to follow).[6] Although laws have often satisfied the demands of morality, Hart explains that in the legal positivist view 'it is in no sense a necessary truth' that they should do so.[7]

There is much support in practice for the separation of law and morality. As we shall see shortly, the law is often shaped by powerful pressure groups exerting an influence on governments, and when there are opposing forces of approximately equal strength, governments may compromise in their legislation. In such circumstances it would be surprising, if not fortuitous, to find that the legislation satisfied moral principles. But if in practice the moral standing of legislation is either unclear or clouded by political motives, the justification for civil disobedience in some circumstances becomes all the stronger. If social acceptance is to be a criterion for an obligation to obey the law, and there is an established consensus of opinion in the community opposing a particular law, it would seem that civil disobedience may be justified, provided that it is carried through rationally and not impulsively or violently without appropriate discussion, and provided that the objective is the public interest and not sectional interests.[8] Social acceptance does not itself provide a *moral* obligation to obey a law, for there is no contradiction between a wide social acceptance of a law, on the one hand, and on the other hand a law that is immoral, as for example in a disregard for the suffering of animals. Civil disobedience will be considered further in the following section.

As explained in Chapter 2, practical morality is not a perfect match of reason and moral attitudes and values: that may now be applied to law-makers themselves or to those to whom coercive laws are applied. Instead it is a product of reason and the predisposing influences of motives, attitudes and values (and possibly of genetic influences too), some of which may be opposed to both reason and morality, despite a central core of attitudes and values which may be fairly described as moral inasmuch as they are consistent with the fundamental moral principle relating to a consideration of the interests of others. Members of government become legislators without their being selected for qualities of 'best men', as the Greeks thought necessary for the highest position in the land – that of making decisions for the common good. Though in their public appearances they may woo support by frequent references to the 'public interest', their thoughts may be far from the common good, influenced instead by motives of electoral self-preservation. Some may find it politically expedient to support a powerful hunting lobby, for instance, and support the alienation of public forest land for clearing so that it may be used to stock deer for the recreation of a relatively small percentage of the total community. It is not easy to regard such support as contributing to the public interest, and much less to regard it as consistent with moral values relating to the suffering of sentient animals. Unstable political manoeuvring is easiest when the legislators are themselves unclear or confused in their own attitudes and values or share the moral apathy of many others concerning animal suffering. Then they may be subject to the fickle winds of conflicting pressure groups.

References by Kelsen to the significance of the desires of the social order in law-making, and by Hart to the importance of social acceptance in making any law obligatory, lead us now to consider the moral debt to animals as it is reflected in the relationship between the law and social values.

THE LAW, SOCIAL VALUES AND THE MORAL DEBT TO ANIMALS

In considering the variety of possible relationships between the law and social values, it is necessary to distinguish between the 'is' and the 'ought'. For instance, we may ask questions such as these: Does the law *dictate* or *follow* social attitudes and values relating to the treatment of animals? From the fact that in common law countries such as England (and other countries such as the USA and Australia which have been influenced by English common law) statutes have been necessary to protect animals – the common law itself generally not taking account of cruelty to animals – does it follow that statutory law is taking a lead in moulding social attitudes and values?[9] Do inconsistencies in statutes indicate conflicts of values in the community, or compromise by legislators confronted by opposing pressure groups, or even confusion in their minds as they consider Bills before them? When statutes are vague (and judges have the opportunity to interpret them according to their personal values, or according to dominant social values as they perceive them to be) is the vagueness sometimes deliberate, intentionally leaving loopholes for powerful interest groups to exploit? Are animals still seen predominantly in economic terms, without intrinsic value, with an instrumental value only to the owner?

Each of these questions enquires into the existing state of affairs, and might properly be considered a sociological rather than a moral question. Yet the 'is' implies an 'ought', not a necessary one but one which in every case requires justification with reasons. It is not self-evident, for instance, that the law ought to mould social attitudes and values relating to cruelty to animals, for that would require the Greek notion of highly selected 'best men' as rulers and legislators, not those who are commonly strongly influenced by self-interest or whose personal moral values and moral understanding are not usually subjected to careful scrutiny by the electors. It was not difficult to infer the attitudes and values of members of the House of Commons, for instance, who laughed with derision when a Bill was introduced in 1821 to prevent cruelty to asses,[10] and personal attitudes of legislators are not uncommonly exposed today, indicating among some an indifference to animals' interests. The part of the law in moulding social values will now be considered from an 'ought' perspective, along with moral attitudes associated with such values.

The law and the moulding of social values: moral standpoint

Several interrelated questions may be asked which bear on whether the law ought to take a leading or a following role with respect to social values in so far as they affect animal interests. First, ought legislators to take the initiative immediately to prevent conspicuous instances of animal suffering? Second, ought they to concede to social values when those values are unclear, unformed or even acquiescent towards animal suffering as inevitable or unimportant? Third, are there imperative oughts on animal suffering in our contemporary situation, yet overlooked or neglected by legislators? Two further questions have a pragmatic slant, since they refer to the means for achieving a certain end, but the end is immoral in the way it relates to animal suffering. They are: fourth, ought sectional interests to be exposed which promote rather than prevent animal suffering? and fifth, ought national economic or military interests to be exposed which point in the same direction?

There is ample evidence of the conservatism of the law, of a reluctance of legislators to act unless they have the support of public attitudes and values. For this stand there is justification only on grounds of *prudence*: in democracies governments can defend inactivity with the reason, or the rationalisation, that they do not have a mandate from the people, and that if they violate public sympathies they will lose office; from the standpoint of the people, the elected representatives whom they have en-trusted with the power to make laws on their behalf may not have the intellectual and moral insight or courage to act without the people's knowledge and guidance. But in the face of a confused and apathetic public on some questions, it is always possible for governments to become morally enlightened through the efforts of intellectual and moral leaders in the community, and then to advise the people of their proposed Bills before they become enacted. The difficulty in the conser-vatism of the law is that the 'is' has been reinforced with an implied 'ought': that is, there is an implication that the law ought not to lead, but ought always to follow changing social values.

The traditional view was expressed by Henry Salt: 'Legislation is the record, the register, of the moral sense of the community; it follows, not precedes, the development of that moral sense, but nevertheless in its turn reacts on it, strengthens it, and secures it against the danger of retrocession.'[11] Similarly the positivistic viewpoint of Bentham and Austin in the early part of the last century still influences many to the opinion that the law and morality are separate.[12] From the 'is' of this legal–moral separation some have formed the view that the 'ought' follows too: that it is no business of governments to be moral legislators. We shall contend, in opposition to this view, that in some circumstances it is both appropriate for legislators to take a lead in moulding social values (usually in conjunction with other social forces including the influence of intellectual and moral leaders); and that on some issues, such as the prevention of suffering to animals, it is appropriate and necessary for the law and morality to be united.

An exaggerated view of legislators in England at the end of last century was that they withdrew from any humane legislation until the public were well enough educated to accept it, though always ready to make 'cruel and coercive' laws. On the question of the cruel trafficking in birds in London slums it was alleged that when a deputation to the Home Secretary requested that action be taken to prevent the suffering and death of thousands of birds, he replied, in the words of the reporter, 'that it was desirable to do as little as possible in the way of legislation', considering it preferable to wait for 'the gradual education of the people'.[13] There may indeed be many reasons for legislators to do as little as possible on some issues, particularly when action might alienate the sympathies of influential vested interests. In matters pertaining to the preventable suffering of animals, no less than of humans, the moral responsibility of legislators is to act and to educate by their legislative acts. It would be rare indeed for any humane legislation to arouse public antipathy, unless from areas of stubborn self-interest, and also rare in our times for there to be no one to give guidance and support to a government in drafting humane Bills. Therefore the intellectual and moral demands on legislators may be greater in courage than in simple understanding.

Political policies of 'wait and see', or 'do as little as possible', until the electorate are better advised and sympathetic, have been responsible for unnecessary suffering in most countries, even when humane leaders were urging reform, as they did throughout the nineteenth century. Though there was evidence of changing public attitudes to horses by the middle of the century, legislators were dilatory in preventing the animals from being overdriven, overloaded and otherwise abused. Adequate protective legislation was passed in 1911 with the *Protection of Animals Act*[14] which declared a person to be guilty of an offence of cruelty (or 'unnecessary abuse of the animal') if he 'shall cruelly beat, kick, ill-treat, over-ride, over-drive, over-load, torture, infuriate or terrify any animal, . . . or shall, by wantonly or unreasonably doing or omitting to do any act, cause any unnecessary suffering, or, being the owner, permit any unnecessary suffering to be so caused to any animal' (s.1(a)).

One of the foremost illustrations of the failure of some governments to act in our times, when the moral grounds are clear and compelling, is in their failure to prohibit the steel-jaw trap, already described as inflicting protracted suffering as victims sometimes chew off feet to escape, or more commonly die slowly from the effects of gangrene as blood circulation is stopped, or from infection, thirst or starvation. In the USA, for instance, some states have no legal requirements for trappers to check their traps at regular intervals, while in others the law requires checks at intervals of anything from one full day to seven days.[15] Dingo trappers in Australia are not subjected to mandatory trap inspections on a regular basis to prevent unnecessarily prolonged suffering.

There are many such acts of cruelty to animals which should have presented legislators with moral imperatives, but where the ought has been clouded by questions of prudence or expediency, or delayed as secondary to more pressing human problems. Cattle and horses are often terrified by helicopters used in mustering them in some countries, but the practice persists. Aircraft and motor vehicles are sometimes used in hunting animals, either for capture or for killing.[16] It is not that legislators have taken *no* action to prevent cruelty, but rather that it has often been dilatory and has left many other pressing instances without appropriate attention.[17]

The question of whether legislators should concede to social values, when these values do not favour prevention of animal suffering, leads to an equally unequivocal answer. In some third world countries, for instance, animals may be abused for the sake of religious rites, or out of superstition, or simply for popular recreation without thought for animal suffering. It is then that legislators ought to take a moral stand, associated with a programme of mass education in an effort to change the attitudes of people; for legal sanctions on their own, as we shall see shortly, are usually insufficient for the purpose. In advanced multi-cultural societies the problem is much more complex and even more difficult to resolve, for in these it is not always apparent what the social values are. On some issues, indeed, there may be a social, a vocational, or even a geographical or political stratification of values: those of landowners and industrialists, for example; rural dwellers and city dwellers; privileged and underprivileged; well educated and poorly educated; recreational hunters and conservationists; and so forth. In other words there may be difficulty in locating any shared values on the question of animal suffering.

Some social and legal philosophers have gone further, explaining that there may also be an absence of a shared *morality* (or of shared moral values). In such circumstances one philosopher has suggested that when there is no shared morality 'on which to build an acceptable jurisprudence' there must then be compromise, 'from the recognized need – itself a moral reason, of course, to get along together, albeit without a universal conviction that the outcomes are, morally speaking, all that they should be'.[18] With a similar perception of a lack of shared social values (including moral values), though with a different solution, a legal philosopher suggested that the law should make use of sociological evidence on what the diverse values and preferences are in the community, the various wants and claims, and should assume the role of an arbiter in seeing that the various preferences, wants, claims and so forth are harmonised with the least possible friction.[19] The latter of these two viewpoints assumes that the object of legislation is social justice, a justice which excludes animals and a morality of preventing their unnecessary suffering. Indeed the question of animal suffering is irrelevant to this notion of distributive justice, for animals are not included as sharing recipients of social goods. The former of the two viewpoints takes the easy way out of conflict, even though the philosopher acknowledged that in the presence of conflicting values rational viewpoints are still possible. Given these there remains the possibility, as well as the moral need, to foster rational debate on any question relating to animal suffering and to expose – as we shall see shortly – any vested interests which may block or temporarily impede legislation to prevent that suffering. There are still moral obligations on legislators to take a stand, to rise above the expedient course of compromise in the face of conflicting attitudes and values, regardless of how influential some of the defensive interests may be.

We turn now to the third of the interrelated questions, relating to preventable and unnecessary animal suffering in contemporary societies which, though obvious, has escaped the attention of legislators. The steel-jaw trap has been mentioned;

it has been used for a century. The rodeo has also been mentioned, banned in some countries but still flourishing in others such as the USA and Australia. More recently there is the phenomenon of the factory farm which calls for legislation – not a new problem: indeed the situation described over twenty years ago still obtains in the UK, the USA and elsewhere. It has been said that 'The law relating to animals is loose, ill-defined and, moreover, hopelessly out of date.'[20] There is no better example of animal exploitation than the factory farmer's deliberate constriction of the lives and natural instincts of farmed animals for the sake of his personal gain. In the UK ninety per cent of laying hens are still kept in battery cages. Sixty per cent of breeding sows are still confined in cramped stalls, and the farrowing grate is almost universally used. The position with the raising of broiler chickens and turkeys is unchanged: most are crowded together in sheds under artificial light.[21]

Another contemporary problem whose moral demands have not met the attention of legislators is the mass killing of marine animals such as dolphins by the excessively large nets now used in the fishing industry – trawler gillnets, purse-seine and others. The dolphins and seals caught in the nets are also fishing for their natural food. The moral solution confronting legislators is the control of the fishing industry, restricting fishing zones and types of nets used. Politicians tend to serve self-interest by serving their voters' interests, often giving priority to economic rather than to moral values: in such circumstances both a moral and a legal lag may ensue until pressure groups make a stand.

The fourth and fifth questions raised at the commencement of this section refer both to personal or sectional interests, and to national or governmental interests. Ought these to be exposed to public scrutiny whenever they lead to unnecessary animal suffering? In these questions the focus is on the possible means to promoting a moral end, leading – as already indicated – to a more specific consideration of civil disobedience as a means in the next section. If such an exposure is justified as a means of developing moral awareness it falls also under *education*, which will be considered shortly.

The personal and sectional interests to be discussed refer chiefly to property or economic interests, based on material values, and recreational interests – especially in hunting and coursing. Property interests have long been protected in English and United States law, sometimes in ways which do not consider the interests of all animals involved. For instance, the *Animals Act 1971*[22] gives the occupier of land, or the landowner, wide powers in protecting livestock from any dog found on his property, but excessive trust seems to be placed in both his rational powers and the morality of his motives and attitudes. This Act, replacing the common-law rules relating to the protection of livestock against dogs (s.9), requires, to absolve from liability, only that the killing or injuring of a dog found wandering on land and supposedly threatening livestock be notified to the police within two days. The occupier so killing or injuring a dog is said to be acting for the protection of the livestock if either (a) 'the dog is worrying or is about to worry the livestock, and there are no other reasonable means of ending or preventing the worrying; or (b) the dog has been worrying livestock, has not left the vicinity and is not under the control of any person and there are no practicable means of ascertaining to whom it belongs'. The condition of either (a) or (b) is 'deemed to have been satisfied if the defendant believed that it was satisfied and had reasonable ground for that belief' (s.9 (4)). It is noted that under this provision 'the dog need not actually have attacked or worried the livestock or be renewing an attempt'. All the occupier or landowner needs is 'reasonable ground for believing that an attack on the livestock is imminent and no other reasonable means of dealing with the situation is available' (Notes, p. 91). Under this Act a dog would have little chance against a person who believed that all dogs found on properties are marauders, who ruled out the possibility of mistakes of judgement, who was malicious towards a dog known to belong to an unfriendly neighbour and who acted without witnesses. In its protection of property rights the Act leaves open the possibility of an infliction of unnecessary suffering on an animal.

The *Badgers Act 1973* (amended in 1985)[23] makes it an offence to kill, injure or take any badger, or to attempt to do so (s.1 (1)), to have in one's possession a recently killed badger or a pelt from a recently skinned badger (s.1 (2)), to cruelly ill-treat any badger (s.2 (a)), to use badger tongs in killing or taking, or attempting to kill or take, any badger (b), to dig for any badger (c) and so forth. But the exceptions are substantial in the protection of private property. The landowner or occupier (or person authorised by him) needs only the defence that his action in violation of any of these provisions 'was necessary for the purpose of preventing serious damage to land, crops, poultry, or any other form of property or for the purpose of preventing the spread of disease' (s.6 (2)). Again the sectional interests of property owners are protected to the point of excessive reliance on their judgement and testimony, in disregard of such possibilities as personal motives and attitudes, such as prejudices against badgers, and individual incapacity for rational control.

The law gives heavy protection to property and little consideration to birds feeding on or threatening crops. The *Protection of Animals Act 1911*[24] makes it an offence for any person to be knowingly party to the sale or offering or exposing for sale or giving away of any grain or seed 'which has been rendered poisonous except for a bona fide use in agriculture' (s.8 (a)). Thousands of birds may be destroyed each year, sometimes legitimately in the protection of crops, but the means are left to landowners, who are apt to be undiscriminating in choosing between poisons which will inflict suffering (such as arsenic) and others, perhaps more expensive, which will not; or alternatively in choosing entirely different means of control. For centuries landowners in the UK held the view that all birds, regardless of species, were harmful to crops and had to be destroyed.

In both the UK and the USA the law has been strongly protective of recreational interests, especially hunting. Because of traditional values this is an area where legislators may require more than usual courage to prevent unnecessary animal suffering. The provisions intended to prevent cruelty in the *Protection of Animals Act 1911* specifically excluded the coursing or hunting of any captive animal, and gave it little protection from cruelty 'unless such animal is liberated in an injured, mutilated, or exhausted condition' (s.1 (3) (b)). Wild animals were also excluded from the Act. Though coursing of wild animals (chiefly hares) has been outlawed in some countries, it is still permitted in the UK. The animal is eventually caught by pursuing greyhounds and killed.[25] Although in the USA the Supreme Court has repeatedly decreed that wildlife belongs to the people, the hunting lobby has been traditionally influential and the opportunities for hunting and killing animals such as deer are being increasingly extended, with extensive habitat manipulation.

Relevant national or government interests refer mainly to economic and military interests. These are 'national interests' in the minds of governments particularly, and are not to be confused with concepts of the common interest and of the common good. One instance of a government giving precedence to a perceived economic interest is the United States' refusal to join the United Nations Law of the Sea Convention, despite the obvious success of this convention in developing, over more than a decade, a comprehensive series of articles covering many aspects of protection for the seas and the creatures living in them. The need for protection of marine mammals and other animals from unnecessary suffering through recently developed fishing technologies has been noted. But the US Government has been influenced by a commercial lobby which fears that sea-bed mining operations might be affected, to the extent of companies being obliged to share their profits with many other countries.[26] International law relies on the good will of signatory nations in various covenants and conventions. A general indication of unity among nations on some issues can be morally binding in preventing unnecessary suffering to animals. Another instance of a dominant economic interest is in efforts to encourage tourism by attracting hunters from other countries. While pandas are a tourist attraction in China and heavy penalties are imposed for killing them, deer-hunting is seen differently.[27]

Military research is another government interest which overrides moral considerations of the prevention of unnecessary suffering to animals. The cruelty of some experiments has been noted. A major moral obstacle is that governments have it in their power to exempt the Crown from their legislation relating to animal cruelty, on the assumption that the national interest is paramount. The 1876 *Cruelty to Animals Act* is not binding on the Crown. There is no international covenant or convention on the use of animals in military research or in military operations. The moral sensibilities of governments are easily overpowered by perceived threats to national security or by aggressive international rivalry. Whether it is to expose such entrenched attitudes or powerful interests, or for any other reason to increase public awareness of cruelty to animals, one of the means used is civil disobedience.

Civil disobedience

Ought members of the public to break the law in order to increase awareness of cruel practices such as the use of the steel-jaw trap in the fur trade or in protecting livestock against predators? It has become clear that the law is conservative, governments often waiting (partly in their own interests) for firm public guidance on their preferences before attempting to legislate, even when on moral grounds alone imperatives for action may be clear to them. More usually, perhaps, members of governments are as confused as the public generally on what they ought to do, as in the case of appropriate legislation to control frozen embryos used in in vitro fertilisation programmes. Yet in the prevention of cruelty to animals no such complexities or dilemmas arise, and when governments fail to act when on obvious moral grounds they ought, it is usually through moral apathy or through conflicts of values and interests in the community, exacerbated by political motives.

In such circumstances there are times when conscientious citizens lose patience with continued government and public apathy and inactivity. Their moral sensibilities are agitated to the point where they must take the unusual action of breaking the law in order to draw attention to what they regard as a morally untenable situation. In so far as the law-breaking is non-violent, has rational grounds that are explained clearly to governments, to courts or to the media at the time, it may be irreproachable. While the wheels of the law turn slowly animals may find no relief from unnecessary suffering. On the other hand, law-breaking which is violent, as in destroying property, and irrational, as in releasing several thousand mink into the countryside from their captivity in factory farms, is indefensible, for then the animals are used for morally questionable ends.

Whether civil disobedience works is a pragmatic question, though the objective of preventing unnecessary animal suffering is clearly moral. The most peaceful and obviously rational disobedience is frequently the most effective, such as trespassing on university premises as a means of drawing attention to the need for a lay person on an animals care committee or an ethics committee.[28] The positivist principle that the law is law, good or bad, and that it compels obedience must at least allow exceptions on rational and moral grounds, given that the means used are equally rational, benevolent in purpose and non-violent. But sometimes violence has a more fundamental and largely hidden source in social conditions, even though the ostensible motive may be humane in its concern for animal suffering.

The law, social values and social conditions

Outside the context of civil disobedience, social conditions have had a marked impact on social values pertaining to animal cruelty. The historical circumstances discussed in Chapter 1 and elsewhere have indicated the brutality towards animals which was widely accepted in societies in England, the USA and elsewhere even as late as the eighteenth and nineteenth centuries. In the worst years of the industrial revolution human suffering almost matched animal suffering, and preceding mass vaccination against common diseases, when life expectancy was relatively short, human life was cheap and animal life cheaper. If an agricultural worker could be transported for life for stealing a sheep from a wealthy landowner to help ward off starvation in his own family, it was not surprising to many to see a dog or a horse savagely beaten to urge it to greater efforts. Humanitarian leaders came generally from upper or middle classes, those whose own social conditions made it easier for them to espouse the cause of alleviating human and animal suffering. In seriously underprivileged situations today, such as in some Latin American states, human life is still debased: social frustrations are given vent in violence and torture. Laws against cruelty to animals can have little meaning when there is so much human cruelty; and where there are anti-cruelty laws they are usually unenforced, as in Mexico.[29] Social conditions in wartime provide further illustrations of the impact of social conditions on attitudes and values relating to animals, for it is then, in the midst of human cruelty, combined with deprivation and hardship imposed on civilian populations, that the value of life is seen as its lowest and animals usually as the last to be considered for humane attention.

From this historical and sociological evidence the immediate ought implied is to relieve human and animal suffering; but the fundamental ought which facilitates action is to improve human social conditions. It is not too much to say, with cultural preferences excluded such as for hunting, bullfighting or rodeos, that the degree of cruelty to animals which a society tolerates is a reflection of its social conditions. (It may also be a reflection of the quality of its education, as we shall see shortly.) Before there can be effective legislation to prevent unnecessary cruelty to animals, we may have to get our own moral and social house in order. Prevention of unnecessary cruelty to animals must come first, since cruelty is in the mind. Attitudes and values have little prospect of humane reform by education until sharp social inequities are removed and the most acutely impoverished countries given substantial international relief.

Statutory law is coercive, with disobedience countered by legal sanctions, but there is no inbuilt moral obligation to obey. International law *is* morally binding on signatory nations, but it has no external enforceability. Moral obedience to humane statutes can come only when citizens' attitudes and values are informed, and consistent with the purposes of the statutes themselves. This harmony is never universal and seldom very widespread. In situations where governments (if they could be imagined as Platonic in the sense that they were enlightened to a degree beyond the reach of other citizens) attempted to legislate in ways contrary to social values, their legislation would not attract compliance. Questions of the theoretical obligatoriness of the law, enforceability and civil disobedience are interrelated aspects of social and political justice. Just as the law itself has been dilatory in keeping pace with changing social attitudes towards inflicting unnecessary suffering on animals, enforcement of anti-cruelty legislation has often been lax, with insufficient funds allocated for inspection purposes or the courts awarding trivial penalties, both problems reflecting the confusion and apathy in the public mind on this moral question. In 1986 in the USA there was even apprehension in some groups lest *no* funds should be allocated for implementation of the *Animal Welfare Act 1966* as it was amended in 1985,[30] which would have rendered the Act largely ineffectual. When social attitudes and values are changing towards opposition to animal cruelty, costly inspection procedures may be needed to uphold legislation. These are seldom sufficient; surveillance has been carried out largely by voluntary humane societies in the UK, the USA, Australia and elsewhere.[31] It was noted in the *Cockfighting Act 1952*: 'In practice . . . it has proved difficult to obtain sufficient evidence to obtain a conviction either for indulging in cockfighting or keeping a cockpit, because of the secrecy with which these operations are carried out.'[32] When underprivilege is not the root of the problem, how does one account for the persistence of deviant preferences among a minority? One answer may lie in a deficiency in education.

EDUCATION IN RELATION TO THE LAW

The need for better education is not confined to the illiterate, or to those whose formal education has left them with insufficient understanding to be informed and participating citizens or to develop humane values with respect to both people and animals. By community standards biomedical researchers are among the best educated in a specialised sense, yet, as has been noted in Chapter 4, may be no stronger in moral values than are others generally in the community. Education is a universal need, for reasons which become apparent in understanding the concept itself. On the other hand too much can be expected of education, as when we appeal to it for quick and simple solutions to complex social problems. One complaint in 1907 was that children 'are not taught gentleness, kindness, or urbanity. Their head is taught, but not their heart', followed by the pertinent observation that 'the tyranny of teachers to their scholars implants in them a tyranny towards others. There is an enormous amount of cruelty practised upon animals, originating, we believe, in the physical punishment which has been received in the family or in the school.'[33] But violence in the school was itself a reflection of social values outside the school.

Even in such circumstances we may wonder if all people need to *learn* not to be cruel to animals. Are not some compassionate by nature? As for the uncompassionate, what is it that the law teaches them? Fundamentally it is that they will be *punished* if successfully prosecuted for cruelty to animals. Can it teach them the moral principle, with understanding, that they *ought not* to be cruel? Certainly learning morally not to be cruel to animals is more than a matter of learning what the law says. Even if it induced some to comply with the law out of fear of the consequences of breaking the law, that would be to instil a thin-crusted morality, always in danger of collapse from internal and external pressures. As we have seen in Chapter 2, practical morality demands living according to authentic moral attitudes and values, and the knowledge of moral principles that inform them. It is not a matter of following social conventions or of seeking social praise or avoiding social blame. If the nature of morality needs to be understood in questions relating to animal suffering, so too does the nature of education.

Education: its central idea

Education is not merely a process of acquiring knowledge, though acquiring some knowledge, or learning some things, is relevant to becoming *better* educated. If one were to acquire all the knowledge possible about the nature of animals, for instance, or of a particular animal, and all the knowledge possible about ways of treating animals humanely and ways of treating them cruelly, that knowledge would not of itself make one a better educated person, but merely a more knowledgeable person. The kind of education invoked in this context is a *moral* education, an education that will help one to be better in actually treating animals humanely, not merely in knowing how that might be done. Fundamentally it is to have the predisposing attitudes and values which, with reason, will turn the knowledge to good account in a practical situation. All we can do, by various means, is to become better educated than we have been; in other words to improve on an existing or a previous state of affairs. The crux of education is improvement, or 'becoming' in the Aristotelian sense.[34]

Since all humans are characterised by never-ending imperfection, education as a process is always in the direction of improvement, while completion of this process is as impossible of attainment as is perfection itself. When we speak of educating ourselves or others in humane values, we cannot therefore mean that we can grasp these values and consolidate them in a reified sense, so that once we have them there is nothing more to have in this aspect of education. At best we can go on improving, as long as our intellectual powers remain, never on any rectilinear path of progression for long, but undergoing at times lapses of memory, dimming of awareness, expressions of irritation or annoyance, which may affect our relations with others as well as our treatment of animals, however good our intentions. Individual differences among humans imply that the potential for improvement is not unlimited in all conceivable directions, such as in creative imagination or in abstract thought; and that the improvement in moral attitudes and values needs to be kept in the best possible shape by reflection on fresh experiences, new learnings and insights into the necessary consideration of others' (including sentient animals') interests.

In moral education which includes a respect for animals according to *their* natures (without forcing unfavourable comparisons with ourselves) and avoidance of cruelty to them, criteria for what is to count as improvement are clear enough. These criteria may be at odds with social attitudes, in so far as these are discernible, especially (as we have noted) in impoverished or disadvantaged societies; nonetheless in the most general terms the kind of improvement that is to count as educational will be prudently consistent with social values, at least to the extent of not conflicting with those values (values of non-violence or of community co-operation, for instance). The case of seriously impoverished countries, where cruelty to humans and to animals alike appears to be endemic, is one where social and moral values are not clearly formed, though there may be many individual and group values evident. In other cases there may be disintegration of values during civil or international strife; then a gradual re-education of humane values may be necessary.

We shall return to a review of the main objectives and means of education after illustrating the force of these in the context of statutes which, first, reflect a progress in humane attitudes and values concerning animals; and second, illustrate the process of law-making, with particular reference to the UK and the USA. Each of these will demonstrate relationships between law and education, and show how they may be mutually supportive.

Understanding why laws are made

Though laws are coercive, and it is commonly held that ignorance of the law is no excuse for breaking it, it is frequently apparent that laws are insufficiently publicised or that people have never been educated to their meaning and purpose. To understand *why* a law is passed may be halfway to compliance; but if the law appears meaningless, and there is no appreciation of its purpose, failure of education in the law may be halfway to promoting non-compliance. In the second case it may appear to be an *imposed* law, one made by an arbitrary government, and for that reason the failure of understanding may breed resentment or an irrational opposition. These are pragmatic considerations. If a ready acceptance of the law follows from an understanding of purposes, and especially if the law is sympathetic rather than hostile to already held values, it is likely that the understanding will contribute to a further improvement in moral sensitivity in relevant cases, such as laws relating to animal suffering. Even a law which obliges a dog-owner to use a leash outside the home grounds may appear petty and unduly restrictive, until it is understood that such a law protects the dog as well as the public (and indeed the owner against damages).

The *Protection of Animals (Anaesthetics) Act 1954* in the UK stipulated that certain operations on animals 'without the use of an anaesthetic so administered as to prevent any pain during the operation' were deemed to be performed 'without due care and humanity' (s.1(1)).[35] An amendment to this Act in 1964 specified particular minor operations that had been customarily performed without anaesthetics but which were now disallowed, such as the docking of lambs' tails by using a rubber ring and other devices to constrict the flow of blood to the tail (unless performed in the first week of life).[36] A general understanding of the purpose of the Act in terms of the prevention of unnecessary suffering is given depth from the social history of centuries prior to anaesthetics, when physiologists pinned live dogs to tables and operated on them to learn more about anatomy or to demonstrate to students. But the 1964 amendment shows how specific knowledge is needed to understand why the described procedure should not be used in the docking of lambs' tails: the constriction of the blood supply to the tail may cause gangrene and the added suffering associated with it.

Though it is self-evident to most adults, some children may have insufficient knowledge from experience fully to understand the purposes of the *Abandonment of Animals Act 1960*, which declared any person guilty of an offence of cruelty who abandoned an animal 'whether permanently or not, in circumstances likely to cause the animal any unnecessary suffering' (s.1).[37] To encourage the asking of questions of how the animal would get food, water and shelter, or veterinary attention when needed, promotes a better understanding of the many probable sources of suffering for abandoned animals, including distress.

In many instances a background of social history contributes to an understanding of legislation and its purposes, as noted in the case of the Act (with its amendment) on the use of anaesthetics. The *Coal Mines Act 1911*, by which no horse was to be taken underground until it was four years old (1), all horses underground were to be housed in stables with continuous ventilation (2) and (3) and to have a sufficient supply of food and water and medicines (5) and (6), none were allowed to go to work unfit or improperly shod (7) and no blind horses were to be worked (9), reflects the existing conditions which gave purpose to the Act.[38] The purposes of the *Slaughterhouses Act 1974* are informed by the social history of the nineteenth century, when private slaughterhouses conducted their business in secrecy.[39] By this Act, which consolidated a number of previous Acts, slaughterhouses and knackers' yards had to be licensed (s.1). Part II of the Act, s.36, dealt with the methods of slaughter in slaughterhouses and knackers' yards: instantaneously by means of a mechanically operated instrument in proper repair, or by stunning using an electrical instrument or by other means of making the animal 'insensible to pain until death supervenes'.[40] Against the background of the poleaxe, with its dependence on the skill and experience of the operator, the Act's purpose is obvious and its background understanding a means of increasing moral awareness of unnecessary animal suffering and of the dimensions of the moral debt to animals in both the backward-looking and forward-looking senses.

Partly to offset a widespread tendency to evade the law whenever it conflicts with strong self-interest, such as by exploiting loopholes in some of the generalised forms of statutes, there has been a tendency in recent years for legislation to be expressed in a more particularised form. Nowhere has this been more apparent than in the laws enacted in Minnesota, USA. The moral tenor of the *Pet and Companion Animal Welfare Act*[41] is clearly to consider the interests of the animal according to its nature, with an impelling implication of past offences and the threat of recurrence. In other words the law is seen as fulfilling a necessary educational and moral role. To instance some of the relevant detail, equines (horses, ponies, mules and burros) 'must be provided with food of sufficient quantity and quality to allow for normal growth or the maintenance of body weight. Feed standards shall be those recommended by the National Research Council (s.4 (2)). Snow or ice are not to be regarded as an adequate water source (s.4 (3)). Adequate shelter is specified, 'a minimum of free choice protection or man-made shelter from direct rays of the sun when temperatures exceed 95° Fahrenheit, from wind, and from freezing precipitation'. Shelters 'must provide space for the animal to roll with a minimum danger of being cast. Bedding must be provided in all stalls' (s.4 (5)). Equines must have opportunity for regular exercise; if not undertaken voluntarily, 'through a forced work program' (s.4 (6)).

In a Revisor Bill[42] details are provided to protect animals recently clipped or shorn. No person with custody of the animal 'shall cause or permit the animal to stand on a road, street, or other unsheltered place, between November 1 and May 1, within sixty days of the clipping or shearing, unless the animal is blanketed' (346.24). Doghouses have prescribed minimum structural requirements for health and comfort, and must be provided with shade from the direct rays of the sun during the months of June to September. Farm dogs must have access to a barn 'with a sufficient quantity of loose hay or bedding to protect against cold and dampness' (347.23 (3) and (4)). In many different ways these statutes are made specific from past experience of the neglect of animals and their consequent suffering. An obligation is placed on the public to co-operate in preventing animal suffering: 'no person shall allow any maimed, sick, unfirm, or disabled animal to be in any street, road, or other public place for more than three hours after receiving notice of the animal's condition' (346.21 s.2(6)). Minnesota statutes are also specific in their attempts to prevent animal suffering in cockfighting, dogfighting or any other 'violent putting of one domestic animal against another',[43] as well as in prohibiting popular amusements such as greased pig contests and turkey scrambles.[44]

Understanding why laws are made can be equally relevant to practical morality in the provisions of international law, comprising agreements among signatory nations. The articles of the Convention on International Trade in Endangered Species (CITES) include the following: 'Management authorities of the parties shall be satisfied that any living specimen shall be so prepared and shipped as to minimise the risk of injury, damage to health or cruel treatment.' The proposed recipient of a living specimen must be 'suitably equipped to house and care for it'. Research has shown how distinctly necessary such an agreement has been, though international agreements to prevent unnecessary animal suffering are sometimes themselves limited by restricted and even contradictory objectives.[45]

Why are humane laws made? In general terms the reasons are self-evident, providing answers at different levels of understanding for children and adults according to their experiences and their degree of understanding of human and animal natures. Appropriately used, the law in this respect has a significant educational function, quite apart from its pragmatic value in promoting compliance through an understanding of purposes. We turn now to the question of *how* laws are made, for this too may be used as a significant educational instrument, implying also clear moral oughts in preventing animal cruelty.

Understanding how laws are made

Understanding the process of law-making with reference to anti-cruelty legislation involves an understanding of pressure groups. These aim to influence governments, but not to seize power from them or in any way to compete with them for power. If they are moral in purpose they recognise that in most circumstances there are opposing pressure groups equally keen to exert an influence on government. A pressure group working for humane animal laws may be opposed, for instance, by powerful private and corporate economic interests wishing to block legislation that would affect an interest in the fur trade, or the fishing industry, or particular types of agriculture. The strength and influence of pressure groups stems largely from the fact that governments seek and need guidance from the public. Since pressure groups may influence governments even in drafting immoral legislation, in practical morality there is an obligation to act to promote humane animal laws and to prevent inhumane ones. Understanding *how* laws are made is a preparation for fulfilling one's moral obligations in public life to the best of one's ability. Like an understanding of the *why*, it then becomes a moral means, inasmuch as it contributes to moral ends such as the prevention of cruelty to animals.

It has been observed that in advanced contemporary societies it is difficult to tease out a significant area of common values which may be described as 'social values' with the implication that they are widely or generally held in the community. There are different group cultures in most circumstances, some of which conflict in their shared values with those of others. Uniformity of values is much less likely to be encountered than a degree of differentiation, if not of fragmentation, accompanied with widespread vagueness, uncertainty and even confusion. That is why the traditional view of the law, pertaining especially to the early years of this century and to the end of the last, that 'legislation is the record, the register, of the moral sense of the community'[46] (in which 'moral values' may be substituted for 'moral sense') is not strictly tenable. And that is why a more accurate account of the contemporary situation is that 'law is shaped by the values that people have – the values of those who are able to affect the development of the law'.[47] Some of these are influential individual thinkers or community leaders, but on some keenly debated contemporary issues such as the prevention of cruelty to animals, animal welfare, abortion and in vitro fertilisation techniques, the greatest influence on governments and public opinion is usually exerted by pressure groups. If they succeed in affecting the course of legislation, that legislation may then give strength and cohesiveness to a point of view within the community, much in the way that Henry Salt described the earlier traditional view that, once enacted, legislation in its turn reacts on what he called the 'moral sense' and strengthens it. Without further evidence in experience, any suggestion of a uniform effect of such legislation on social values generally remains unconfirmed.

Beginning in 1824, the most influential pressure group working to prevent cruelty to animals in the UK, as well as improvement in animal care generally, has been the RSPCA. It prepared substantial recommendations for the Royal Commission which led to the *Cruelty to Animals Act 1876*. Many of its recommendations were accepted, though in a few respects it was left with some issues unresolved.[48] Thus Royal Commissions provide one opportunity for pressure groups to influence governments. They have the merit of being convened to enquire into particular issues, such as vivisection. The course of events connected with the Animals (Scientific Procedures) Bill illustrates another involvement of pressure groups in the law-making process, again on the subject of animal experimentation, and with the purpose of replacing the now outdated 1876 Act. The recent Bill was introduced as a government measure, supported by a White Paper and a revised White Paper which was published and widely circulated among interested groups for comment. As a pressure group with long experience in influencing governments by the most effective means available to it, the RSPCA decided not to oppose the White Paper, aware that opposition would probably persuade the Home Office to delay translating it into a Bill. A more time-saving strategy was to agree with the White Paper, allow the Bill to be presented to both Houses and lobby for amendments as it progressed through Parliament. The Society's Animal Experimentation Advisory Committee advised the Council of the RSPCA on the revised White Paper and subsequently a detailed list of amendments was drawn up, with an expectation that most of them would be included in the new legislation, especially those relating to improved conditions of laboratory animals and to controls on the licensing of those using animals for research. Amendments were considered by a Parliamentary Committee; in this case the RSPCA placed before it a series of recommendations.[49]

Pressure groups need patience, determination and skill, as well as an understanding of legislative procedure gained from experience, such as that the majority of Bills are introduced by government and that it is governments therefore which need to be lobbied, rather than MPs who wish to introduce Private Members' Bills; that if influence can be exerted prior to the making of the first policy decisions, so much the better, whether or not they are to be conveyed in a White Paper, for an early impact might be made as soon as it is learned that a government is preparing draft legislation; that another sensitive time for a pressure group is the period between a White Paper and the Draft Bill; that members need to be aware of the various readings as the House debates a Bill, of the functions of Standing Committees and other committees, of the Report Stage when further amendments may be made. They need also to be aware of the possibility of the opposition winning a vote of no confidence in the Bill at the third reading, leading to the Bill's rejection.[50]

Knowledge and understanding of a different kind are needed for success against pressure groups *without* humane values and purposes, as well as for influencing Members of Parliament: that is a knowledge with understanding of the nature of motives, attitudes and values, of conflicts of interests and goals, and of the sympathy, sensitiveness and tolerance needed in negotiations without surrendering one's own values and objectives, or the determination to see the matter through. Members of Parliament are *not* uniformly benevolent, or uniformly impartial, or uniformly knowledgeable about animal natures, about human nature or about the nature of practical morality. If they were, there would be no need for protracted debates and negotiations on Bills which clearly have humane ends. From the humane standpoint alone debates about animal cruelty are turned in practice into morally secular debates, very much concerned with worldly matters of imperfect human conflict and often continuing for years against opposition. For some they are political, for others academic, for some no more than further instances of recurring human clashes of interest, but transient, of no great importance because they themselves lack the convictions of clear moral attitudes and values relating to animal suffering. Legislatures are not ideal settings for humane law-making to protect animals.

The legislative process in the USA is little different in kind from that in the UK, with similar reasons for humane pressure groups to understand it when urging measures to reduce animal suffering. Comments are sometimes pertinent: 'Pushing through legislation to ban the steel-jaw, leghold trap seems to be a tougher battle each year.'[51] There are often long delays when Bills are referred to Committees of Congress or Senate, but some humane societies, aware of this, publish regular legislative reports to help educate the public on the current status of various Bills.[52] Lobbying is constant. When acts such as the *Laboratory Animal Welfare Act 1966* are amended (as this was in 1985) pressure groups continue the determined struggle to improve still further on them. To one such group the *Improved Standards for Laboratory Animals Act 1985* still gives animals in the USA less protection than do similar laws in the UK and in most of the North European countries, Congress seemingly moving 'in excruciatingly cautious steps, each meant to prevent a little more suffering'.[53] Another recognised that it was achieved only 'after many years of intense lobbying'.[54] Vested interests circulate literature in attempts to persuade the public of the dangers of following the humane lobby on some matters. Thus the fur industry stresses the dangers of uncontrolled population of fur-bearing animals, which supposedly threaten the spread of diseases such as rabies, and claims that scientists and wildlife managers accept trapping as indispensable to 'responsible wildlife management'.[55] In such cases motives and attitudes are clear. One organisation in the USA devotes its efforts entirely to working for humane legislation, claiming some credit in signifi-cant cases.[56]

Education for humanity to animals: content and means

An understanding of why laws are made and how they are made thus constitutes much knowledge *that* and much know-ledge *about* which are both relevant to a moral education directed specifically at preventing cruelty to animals. But there are two educational requirements: first, that content and means be considered in conjunction; second, that the two be related as closely as possible to the background experiences, the interests and the intellectual capacities of the learners. These require-ments imply that there can be no stipulation of a programme of education in humanity to animals which will suit all learners: both content and means are determinable only by educators with a clear knowledge of educational principles and with experience in applying them.

The subject matter of this and previous chapters is itself such an educational programme, but for some learners it would need to be amplified, for others simplified or adapted according to their needs. What follows therefore on content is no more than a sketch of some educational possibilities, acknowledging the possibility of many other approaches. Preceding chapters have indicated some of the sensitive areas relating to cruelty to animals. For example, from the last chapter it is evident that not only experimenters but also community members generally need knowledge that there are animal abuses both in laborator-ies and in experiments; that there are alternatives available at least to reduce the numbers of animals used; that many experiments are repeated unnecessarily; that animals are used in testing new drugs which may be redundant; that animals suffer unnecessarily in futile or trivial experiments; that govern-ment defence departments use animals in painful experiments;

that experimental psychologists continue to use aversive techniques to little or no purpose; that the continued suffering in both the LD 50 and the Draize tests can no longer be fully supported on scientific or moral grounds. Chapter 3 has indicated that all responsible for animal care in the community generally need to be better informed from relevant studies of animal natures; that modern factory farming methods take insufficient account of the natures of farm animals; that the fur industry accumulates gains at very great cost in animal suffering, especially from the use of steel-jaw traps; that the owners of companion animals need a better knowledge of their natures in some cases to prevent unnecessary suffering. From Chapter 2 it has become clear that the community generally, and in particular those sections of it who make *use* of animals – for gain, for recreation or amusements, for companionship, for food – need a better understanding of the nature of practical morality inasmuch as it is concerned with consideration of the interests of sentient animals; that similarly there is a need for a respect for animals according to their natures; that distinct from moral values, cultural or social values or tendencies are also to be understood, so that when in serious conflict, moral values may be given a proper precedence over them by courageous leaders, pressure groups and eventually legislators; that indeed, since a practical morality is theoretical and inert unless it is practised, every moral agent has a responsibility to act, not to leave moral acts to others. Chapter 1 illustrated the extent of animal suffering both in the past and the present, and the moral debt to animals in a backward-looking sense, with forward-looking moral implications.

The present chapter has shown that everyone needs some knowledge of the law on prevention of cruelty to animals, for reasons that are both moral and pragmatic. From the moral standpoint an understanding of *why* laws are made may shake the apathy of some who have never considered animals to be worth bothering about and sharpen the awareness of others to continuing instances of cruelty to animals in their own environments; an understanding of *how* laws are made increases self-knowledge, bringing to mind that in practical morality there is often a complexity of predisposing tendencies – motives, attitudes and values, dominant self-interests and even the bending of reason at times – to evade moral purposes in efforts to protect cultural habits or practices.

Linking with the law, the activities of humane societies offer suitable content for a curriculum on humanity to animals at particular levels. The activities of the RSPCA in the UK both in the last century and in this, and in the USA the equally effective work of the ASPCA, the Humane Society of the United States, the Animal Protection Institute and the Animal Welfare Institute (to mention only some of the animal welfare societies there), both in animal care and in vigorous political action for legislative change, comprise much sensitive material to be turned to educational advantage. In addition to the activities of such national bodies there is the work of The World Society for the Protection of Animals to be considered, purporting to represent sympathetic world opinion on some issues and attempting to exert this kind of pressure on national governments to change cruel practices.[57]

For those with sufficient educational readiness the content for a curriculum on humanity to animals would certainly benefit from relevant aspects of biology and evolution, and appropriate attention to ourselves as animals also. Certainly scientific knowledge, such as of ethology, to provide a firm foundation of factual evidence to clear away initial misunderstandings is a primary consideration in this context. But despite the best of educational and moral intentions it is appropriate to sound a warning on a possible is–ought gap remaining. No amount or depth of scientific knowledge has any *necessary* connection with a practical morality which aims at preventing cruelty to animals. There is ample evidence of this from the experience of animal experimentation by some biomedical researchers and particularly, perhaps, by some experimental psychologists. Some animal researchers believe it is moral to use animals in situations in which they believe it would be decidedly immoral for people to be used.[58] It is doubtful if researchers could have continued for over ten years conducting experiments in which primates and other animals were inflicted with severe trauma, their heads cemented with dental stone into a device that delivered a planned force to the head, unless their attitude to animal suffering had been quite indifferent and their attitudes to animals completely without respect.[59] It is doubtful too if the observations of an experimental psychologist on infant primates' 'desperate efforts' to contact mothers could have continued except from a similar base of total unconcern for animal suffering, aggravated morally by the fact of little prospect of adding to what was already known from human deprivation studies.[60]

The means for the relevant humane education then will not be an enlargement of scientific knowledge for its own sake: knowledge has to be assimilated by learners in such a way as to change the way they regard animals and the unnecessary suffering humans inflict on them, whatever the reason. It has sometimes been thought that if appropriate attitudes and understandings were to be built on that kindness to animals 'natural to young children', then adult attitudes would also be morally favourable to animals.[61] The assumptions underlying such a claim are unfounded. There is, first, no evidence that in general children are sympathetically disposed towards animals, though *some* are, as some adults are; second, there are ample opportunities for attitudes (and their associated ideas and emotions) to change for the worse as children come under cultural and peer-group influences while maturing to adulthood. The most kindly-disposed child may become a hunter and a killer in adulthood, or a fur-trapper, or a greyhound courser using live animals as lures.

The means sometimes suggested for childhood education in kindness to animals is formal instruction, or 'systematic education', which would leave habits so firmly implanted that they would remain throughout their lives. There is no evidence that such means are successful generally, though they have often been required by state laws.[62] On the contrary, it is because attitudes are characteristically stubborn and resistant to change that bookish and formal methods are usually ineffective. Lively, selected lecturers with authentic values and using a variety of illustrative material have been found to make some impact at primary or secondary school levels, provided that visits are sufficiently frequent. In adolescence intellectual and emotional involvement by means of peer discussion groups is sometimes found to be more penetrating and lasting in attitude modification, when carefully organised, discreetly led and with clear discussion objectives.[63] Other opportunities for personal involvement are in voluntary community projects such as locating and caring temporarily for lost or abandoned animals.

One of the means used by animal welfare societies is to distribute leaflets and brochures. These are apt to be seen as serving propaganda purposes and are often diluted by volume.

A flood of literature has been produced in the USA to gather support for legislation to ban the steel-jaw trap. As a means towards influencing adult attitudes, its effectiveness depends on its use in conjunction with other methods, sometimes dramatic, such as striking displays, street floats and processions and public exhibitions. Similarly the use of the media – press, radio and TV – is effective when the message is repeated sufficiently and when it too is forceful. All the skill of the media advertiser is needed to make the strongest possible impact: repetitions of colourless or merely factual messages may miss the intended mark. Imagination and initiative may, on the other hand, be surprisingly successful. When two researchers from a Canadian university refused to consider the question of the morality of their research using a baboon, an animal welfare organisation decided to bring the matter to public attention in a court hearing. The charge was causing unnecessary suffering to a restrained animal. It was dismissed at the request of the organisation's attorney and the baboon was liberated, in the sense that it was never to be used as an experimental subject again. What was exposed in the trial was the cruelty of a long restraint of experimental animals, in this case of a baboon which suffered when its spine was held in a completely abnormal vertical position.[64]

No single campaign to influence adult attitudes significantly and durably is likely to be successful. It is rather multiple and varied approaches that are needed, conducted with forethought, skill and subtlety, before legislative reforms to reduce animal cruelty have a chance of being influenced by adult education. Apart from publishing booklets and leaflets, preparing teaching packs, producing new videos and various displays and exhibitions, for instance, the RSPCA has encouraged personal involvement in establishing a Wildlife Treatment Unit and Animal Welfare Field Centre near Hastings.[65]

The means used in the successful modification of attitudes are often all the more effective if they are novel, non-aggressive, discreet in the perception of when to stop or reduce the presentation when there are signs of public satiation, boredom, irritation, anger or strong disapproval. Part of the mind's resistance to attitude change is expressed in resentment when the change is too sharp or clumsy; part of its readiness to accept change may be gauged from its acceptance of a quiet invitation to consider another point of view. Bernard Shaw's rapier-like weaponry appealed to the converted. Tolerance, sympathy and patience are more successful educational approaches than his cutting thrusts at the general blindness of recreational hunters, the 'silly imitative sheep', stupid rather than cruel, acting out of habit without realising what they are doing, so dull as to find the destruction of life a source of amusement.[66]

Miseducation is as obvious as inept education in the changing of attitudes, for miseducation may simply strengthen unfavourable attitudes already entrenched or develop afresh unfavourable attitudes in the young. Science Fairs in the USA encourage schoolchildren to experiment with animals: in one instance a tenth grade student administered a potent drug to mice by adding it to drinking water for over three weeks; almost half the animals died.[67] Teachers' attitudes to animal suffering may influence students, either favourably or unfavourably; especially harmful may be teachers' indifference, callousness or cynicism, even to the extent of ridiculing students who recoil from performing classroom biology experiments and are not offered a preferred alternative.[68]

SUMMARY

Both the law in practice and practical morality are distinct from ideal law and ideal morality, when the law and morality are one. The view of legal positivism that the law and morality are distinct does not imply that the law is unconcerned about moral questions, or that it does not sometimes accord with moral principles. Similarly social acceptance of the law as a necessary institution does not provide a moral obligation to obey it.

Despite the conservatism of the law, on some questions such as cruelty to animals it is morally incumbent on legislators, guided by enlightened community leaders and pressure groups, to take a more positive part in moulding social attitudes and values, attempting to bring the law and morality together, and acting when necessary with both moral and political courage, especially against powerful interest groups such as recreational hunters. Legislators might be persuaded by moral and rational leaders and pressure groups to reconsider military experiments on animals and any refusal to sign animal-protective international conventions for economic reasons. Civil disobedience is morally justified when it is supported on rational grounds, is non-violent and is used to arouse public awareness of unnecessary animal suffering when both governments and a large proportion of the public show apathy.

Social conditions influence attitudes towards animals. Cruelty to animals in impoverished countries, or in areas of underprivilege in affluent countries, is likely to remain until social justice is more widespread. The central notion of education as an improving process may be applied to a moral education directed specifically towards the humane treatment of animals, involving a respect for animals according to their natures and a readiness to avoid or prevent cruelty to them. Understanding *why* humane laws are made with respect to animals, and *how* they are made, both contribute to moral understanding and may serve useful educational functions. In humane education certain knowledge and understanding may contribute to the changing of minds, but the fundamental educational tasks are to change the predisposing tendencies of attitudes and values, and to provide practice in the application of reason. Methods need to be varied, adapted to age, experience, amenability or intractability of the subjects, sometimes quietly persuasive, at other times dramatic and demonstrative, at all times subtly directed by skilled strategists sensitive to changing attitudes and to stubborn resistances, knowledgeable about individual and social psychology and the significance of personal involvement, aware when one strategy is reaching its mark or glancing off, prepared to change direction when repetition has led to signs of satiation, always imaginative and constructive, and sensitive to individual and group differences which mean that what is successful in one area may fail in another. Team work and ample resources are needed, with educational campaign directors keenly aware of contrary pressures.

REVIEW AND GENERAL CONCLUSIONS

Review

Chapter 1 showed that cruelty to animals bridges the centuries. Practical morality must ask, Why does cruelty persist? Why do we think of animals with widespread unconcern for their suffering – except in our devotion to companion animals or pets? Some of the answers may lie in a failure of moral education, some – perhaps more fundamental – in social conditions, some in the nature of man. Is human aggression genetically determined, as some ethologists have speculated?

Chapter 2 offered three approaches to practical morality: first, the 'disinterested and benevolent spectator' stance of Mill which has a chance of removing much of human presumption and partiality; second, the intuitive stance of Kant by which we respond to duty (in his interpretation according to a rational will, but in ours according to moral dispositions, especially attitudes and values); third, the utilitarian stance which is influenced by the sheer weight of suffering in the world, human and animal, and by the fact that sentient animals have interests which we ought to consider. Respect for animals according to their natures is also a moral standpoint, prompted by impartiality and benevolence. The moral debt to animals is simply what we have owed to them in the past, and what we owe to them now and in the future. It does not refer necessarily, or only, to a wrong committed against animals, though in the backward-looking sense we do apply it usually to the unnecessary suffering we have inflicted on them. In the forward-looking sense the moral debt is the duty we owe, as moral agents, to other sentient animals, to those incapable of reciprocating or acting as moral agents themselves. The justification for ascribing rights to animals is political, *not* philosophical, yet the pragmatic value of the first needs to be acknowledged, especially when rights language is used by animal welfare groups for influencing legislation.[69] In this case the means arguably justifies the end, for the means – even if it does rest on conceptual confusion – is not itself immoral.

Chapter 3 justifies the notion of a moral respect for animals by referring to their natures, acknowledging that they do have interests and needs to be considered by us. This involves not only the prevention or avoidance of unnecessary animal suffering, but also the promotion of their wellbeing, inasmuch as this is practicable in a world of conflicting interests, so that mammals in particular, with wider awareness than some other vertebrates and the capacity to experience emotions of affection, protectiveness and so forth, and not merely of fear, anxiety or frustration, may be helped to live out their lives with a measure of satisfaction according to their natures. Although sufficient is known at present to promote this principle, much has yet to be learned about the natures of particular species and of individual differences within species. The speculations of early ethology and sociobiology have assisted little in furthering moral directions in our understanding of animals, and behavioural emphases on what is clinically measurable also have limited application to morality. But the total fabric of knowledge is complex, and even these may have more to add to a knowledge of animal natures than is apparent at present. When genetic assumptions linking animals to man are relaxed by those ethologists who take a more open view of their subject as the study of human behaviour, relying not merely on specific measurements of small units of behaviour but rather on close observations of whole animals under natural conditions, still using rigorous observational methods to avoid unwarranted inferences, understanding of animals and their natures tends to increase rather more quickly. The early ethologists' preoccupation with instinctual or hereditary traits or tendencies was too narrow a focus, influenced too much by historical convictions that animals ran on predetermined rails, or were completely 'immutable beings', as Voltaire saw them, which 'have never varied'.[70]

Chapter 4 is concerned with one of the most contentious social and moral questions for more than a century, the justification of animal experimentation. There are two areas of suffering to be considered: the suffering of experimental subjects – mostly animals; and the suffering of humans, and of animals as well, from the many diseases to which they are prone, some with the capacity to cripple for life, some to sharply restrict life expectancy. In the backward-looking sense we owe an immense debt to suffering animals whose subjection to human will (rather than any voluntary sacrifice) has alleviated human suffering on a very large scale: that debt can never be discharged to animals of the past. In the forward-looking sense we have a moral duty to accelerate research on alternatives to animals in research. It will probably always be impracticable to quantify pain, or distress, even if one could justify a utilitarian sum of advantages or benefits to humans to set against a sum of animal suffering. No one can say how much suffering is morally enough, beyond which there shall be no more, regardless of the benefits to human and animal health in the future. Cost-benefit judgements are useful only in the broadest sense of the 'general impression' favoured by Preference Utilitarians. In practice the motives and attitudes of researchers and of vested interests such as drug companies and agriculturists may influence judgements of what experiments are to be conducted, without fundamental moral perspectives. Several qualifications need to be made in fairness to biomedical researchers who use animals: first, they do have their own ethical guidelines laid down usually by their respective national research councils, offering a self-imposed discipline by members; second, the worst abuses against animals have been committed by a minority and therefore charges of cruelty against *all* researchers are unjustified; third, governments are often responsible for providing inadequate funds for proper laboratory accommodation and care of animals; fifth, from a human standpoint, the benefits of biomedical research are far-reaching, touching almost every family (except in underprivileged countries) at some point in their lives.

General conclusions

The extent of the moral debt to animals is substantially unchanged in human history, though *forms* of cruelty have varied. There has always been some compassion, some understanding of sentience and of animal natures, and some understanding of a moral debt to animals, but none of these has been widely diffused through human populations. The contemporary moral debt, in a backward-looking sense, stems in part from ignorance of animals' natures, including ignorance of present relevant knowledge; second, from indifference to that knowledge when it conflicts with self-interest; third, from a continuing presumption of superiority over animals amounting to a right simply to *use* them for human advantage.

On the question of human superiority there is no point in comparing ourselves with other animals except in particular dimensions, such as intellectual capacity. In this respect (but not in some others) even the disabled, it is sometimes observed, such as those with Down's syndrome, have powers exceeding those of the higher apes. But in his presumptuous comparisons with animals man needs humility. There is much to be said for animals' limited powers of hate and destruction. They do not make wars, nuclear or biological weapons, intercontinental ballistic missiles or long-range bombers. There is not much in our means of killing one another 'to be wished for by the beasts'.[71] They do not destroy vast expanses of forest where thousands of other animals may live, or shoot at other animals for sport, or cruelly trap some for their furs, or hold them captive for life in zoos or in cramped cages for public exhibition. They do not inflict torture. Their life satisfactions are usually related to freedom, but man has either deprived them of it or progressively narrowed its bounds. Indeed they are entirely at the mercy of man, who has tied their future, and that of all other life on earth, to his precarious own. In what ways are animals inferior? It would be contradictory to consider man as also a *moral* master of all life on earth, for his treatment of animals and of other humans shows plainly that he is not. There is simply no evidence that cruelty to animals is decreasing and that moral sensitivity to animal suffering is becoming more diffused. Much has been written recently about animal awareness: exceptional persons aside, the most pressing moral need is to appreciate the shallowness of *human* awareness.

The three approaches to morality outlined in Chapter 2 seem not to have impressed themselves generally on human perceptions of cruelty to animals. Mill's detached moral stance is sometimes disregarded even by scientists, who respect objectivity perhaps more than most.[72] Except among the highly dedicated few, committed even at personal sacrifice to preventing human and animal suffering in the future, there is little general evidence that scientists in animal experiments respond to imperatives of moral duty rather than to the commands of self-interest. As for the third moral approach, the utilitarian, there is little evidence that scientists, any more than the general public, pause to weigh the total animal suffering throughout the world from animal experimentation, to say nothing of the volume of suffering that is unnecessary. This is ironic in view of the presumption that they understand, better than most in the community, the physiology of pain in vertebrate animals. With notable exceptions they conform to the social values of their own communities, neither debasing them nor elevating them.

The most conspicuous moral failure of our times relates to the first approach. That is why a moral philosopher may be misunderstood by preoccupied biomedical researchers, or others, whenever he casts off all committed viewpoints with their

predisposing tendencies and pushes *impartiality* to the conceptual limit.[73] There *is* a suggestion of detachment in the biological
perception of the unity of life on earth. In itself that is a scientific
perception, based on biology and the evidence of evolution.
That and other relevant knowledge may contribute to a moral
perception of all sentient life, in particular vertebrates, as having
similar interests to be considered by us as moral agents. But such
a perception has no necessary connection with a consideration of
their interests. It does not follow that because there is (factually)
a unity of life on earth we *ought* to treat all life as one, all living
things alike – animals and plants, earthworms and sponges,
lichens and humans – as creatures with survival interests. It is
much clearer that we ought to consider the interests of living
things which are capable of suffering; and further, that we
ought to consider the interests of living things, mammals in
particular, which are capable of pleasure as well. The reason in
each case is that they have *interests*, not that there is a unity of all
life on earth, or that we should adopt a 'bioethic' as a kind of
fellow-creature religion.

In the second case, or when we refer to promoting animal
wellbeing beyond preventing unnecessary suffering, our practical morality is much more circumscribed. It is much easier to
know what to do in ceasing to use a dog, horse or donkey as a
whipping-post for aggression or frustration than it is to know
what to do in promoting its wellbeing: it is not always clear in any
detail what that wellbeing is. Horses and donkeys may benefit
from freedom; domestic dogs may not. But within limits the
wellbeing of animals can often be promoted. One of the major
difficulties is that humans as well as animals have interests: we
too are part of a competitive struggle for survival. In day-to-day
practical morality we have to consider our own interests along
with those of animals, and whenever we face a conflict of
interests, as the only rational beings on earth we need to be clear
on the reasons for the moral decisions which we make. That too
is bordering on the simplistic, for our practical morality is not
generally of that uniformly rational kind, even with the best of
intentions. Moral judgements are influenced by relatively settled
moral convictions, our individual moral attitudes and values.
With respect to our relations with animals, we alone can resolve
conflicts, so that the supposedly rational resolution of conflict is
ever in danger of being slanted in our favour. With respect to

our relations with other humans, we can at least enter into rational discussion with them whenever we face conflicts of interest, and the resolution of these conflicts may *require* the giving of reasons by each side. Bentham was inclined to dismiss as a non-question the fact that animals cannot talk, but if they could it is possible that they would help us to understand ourselves better, in particular the limits of our reason and the limits of our sensibilities when we are cruel to them.

At times we may wonder if humans can be fairly described as rational beings. 'The great Principle and Foundation of all Virtue and Worth is plac'd in this,' said Locke: 'That a Man is able to *deny himself* his own Desires, cross his own Inclinations, and purely follow what Reason directs as best, tho' the Appetite lean the other Way.'[74] Regrettably, for the sake of animals and for our own sakes, Locke's rational ideal does not present things as they are in the interaction between imperfect reason and imperfect moral attitudes and values. But in doing the best we can with our limitations, our moral debt to animals, in the forward-looking sense and in the most general terms, is our moral duty to them, what we owe to them by considering their interests without unreasonably subtracting from our own. The moral initiative and responsibility which are ours alone is an even heavier moral responsibility than to consider the interests of other humans, for they are able to understand their interests, to stand up for them, to enter into negotiations with us should there be a conflict of interests. It is the moral custodianship which puts us most to the test. Can we trust ourselves to assume Mill's moral stance of disinterested detachment, significantly improving on our historical failures? Can we ever be *impartial enough*?

By combining the first and the second of the three moral approaches we may ask, What are the moral imperatives of our time? What duty do we owe to animals to reduce the dimensions of the moral debt in the future, taking as benevolent and as impartial a stance as we can? Certain prohibitions are demanded. There is, first, no moral justification for trapping or farming animals for furs. Second, there is no moral justification for using animals to test cosmetics for toxicity, or household or agricultural products or new drugs which are similar to products already marketed and necessary for no better reason than to keep the economy going. There is no moral justification for using animals in research whenever effective alternative techniques are available. There is no moral justification for aversion techniques practised by behavioural psychologists, or for biomedical research which cannot be justified by representative panels as 'absolutely necessary', to use the terms of the *Cruelty to Animals Act 1876* (an expression which regrettably has remained loose in its application, with insufficiently precise criteria for its determination). There is no moral justification for factory farming.

Animal experimentation is one of the most conspicuous moral and social issues of our time. It is also complex, but that does not indicate the need for *compromise*, even for supposedly moral reasons as suggested by some. The give and take of discussion is merely the means for members of representative panels to see and to weigh points of view that are novel to them, or which they have not considered seriously before. It does not imply that solutions, to be fair to all, must include something from each of the major contributions. If economic or political interests were represented, for instance, collective discussions would not imply any moral necessity for conceding even a modicum to such interests. The best moral solution to social problems is necessarily a moral solution, not an eclecticism as an expedient way of getting things moving. But in discussions on the morality of animal experimentation, when considerations of *human* suffering are involved as well as the suffering of animal subjects, it is not always possible for participants to discuss on equal terms. Animal welfare representatives, moral philosophers and laymen are usually inadequately informed on scientific matters, and it is necessary to accept the opinions and judgements of biomedical researchers and veterinarians. Scientific representatives can readily adduce evidence on the very extensive human suffering which has been prevented by animal experimentation on life-saving surgery; on the need for 'whole body' testing of drugs rather than using in vitro or test-tube methods; and on the need for continued animal experimentation if the end is the relief from suffering of millions of human beings in the future.[75] In terms of the prevention and successful treatment of human suffering, the success of biomedical researchers justifies profound human respect. The non-scientific layman must accept the scientific judgement, based on compelling evidence, that at present there is no way of dispensing entirely with animals in research.

From a scientific standpoint, then, the moral debt to animals is *necessary*, to prevent much greater and continuing human and animal suffering in the future. From a human standpoint it is a reasonable cost-benefit judgement. Practical morality's only answer in these circumstances is to insist on an urgently necessary concentration of research efforts on finding replacement alternatives to animals in research, and on a modification of research techniques and procedures to reduce pain and distress to the lowest possible limit: a requirement that anyone experimenting with animals undergo extensive training to develop skills; that there be training in anaesthesia as well as in surgery; that there be strict national controls on research departments in universities and elsewhere so that the numbers of researchers and of animals are reduced to an essential minimum, and not determined locally where personal and institutional interests are likely to prevail. In these respects we recognise that practical morality is not a morality of total impartiality in which there is an equal consideration of the interests of animals and humans alike. When we are able to dispense entirely with animals in research, practical morality in this respect will move a little closer towards the ideal benevolent impartiality which only an external, non-human and non-animal observer could attain.

We conclude with three distinct points of view in order to highlight a moral perspective as distinct from a combined scientific and pragmatic one. The first is a return to the ideal spectator's point of view. The judgement of such a being is likely to be that humans have been exploitative in *using* animals to serve their purposes: for food and clothing, draught work on farms and elsewhere, research to treat and prevent diseases, recreation and conspicuously for commercial profit as in factory farming and so forth. From his uninvolved perspective, though there are undoubted benefits to animals in veterinary research, the benefits to humans from biomedical research far outweigh them; although a scientist may be acclaimed courageous in acting as a human experimental subject, the number of animal subjects in experiments far outweighs the number of human subjects. Whatever we have done *for* animals, what we have done *to* them for our own advantage weighs far more heavily.

The second viewpoint is one which we shall call a combined moral and pragmatic one, putting biomedical research on animals within the context of the complexity of social problems of which it is one. It is this which is the best moral viewpoint under existing circumstances where we face conflicts of values (moral, political, economic, military and so forth) and which is at the same time *workable*. For instance, most humans agree from their anthropocentric perspective that in view of the frightening consequences of viral diseases such as AIDS and hepatitis non-A and non-B it is important to get results quickly, to use animals in research because techniques and procedures relating to their use are known to be workable, rather than to press ahead with an effort to find alternatives to animals altogether. So in the first place this viewpoint is both biased towards ourselves and pragmatic.

But no such simple explanations can account for the complexity of the total situation: for our attitudes to animals themselves, our belief that they are inferior and expendable in ways in which no humans are and in some cases our religious beliefs are related to the complexity of our social circumstances. Attitudes to animals may be influenced by social injustices, economic maladjustments leading to unemployment, violence of wars, the failure of political and economic systems to curb excessive wealth and to prevent excessive poverty, expanding human populations and entrenched cultural values such as those in the UK and the USA which support hunting and killing in the name of 'sport'.[76] In these circumstances of conflicting social attitudes, pressures and anxieties, with a great deal of unclarity on the larger moral questions and much preoccupation with self-interest, it is unlikely that the interests of animals will always be considered with due moral concern and understanding.

Therefore we move to the third viewpoint, one which takes the moral problem out of the normal hurly-burly of conflicting values, demands for quick solutions and the complex social situation where the moral apathy of the people is at least a convenient protection from serious moral challenge. This is the Platonic viewpoint which leaves decision-making on some issues to persons carefully selected from among the best each nation has to offer – best both rationally and morally, with a demonstrated concern for others' interests and an unconcern for money-making; without, indeed, any value preferences inclining them towards material gain.[77]

Such persons would not be value-free, but they would *not* be persons of strong political alignment. Rather they would be conspicuous for open-mindedness, for a judicious examination of issues as they arise, for fairness and selflessness, and for a ready co-operativeness with others. They would be less perfect than Plato's rulers and therefore, rather than making decisions alone, they would engage with others similarly selected to concentrate all their efforts towards reaching decisions on the issues which political leaders, acting often superficially and in a piecemeal fashion, leave unresolved with at best pragmatic and short-term solutions. Such questions are animal experimentation, conservation and the nuclear threat, factory farming, human population growth, the distribution of social goods including educational opportunities, underprivilege both nationally and internationally. All of these in some way affect the moral debt to animals, as well as to people. These selected decision-makers would require an executive capacity given them by the people – something that would probably require in turn a distinctly higher rational and moral understanding among the people of the world than obtains at present, though constitutional reform of present political systems might in the first instance be appreciated by them. On some issues, such as conservation and animal wellbeing, which may cross political and geographical boundaries, they would need to meet with their counterparts from other nations.

In principle it *is* possible to select the rational and moral best from the societies of the world. Though perfect decisions would be beyond them, they would reach towards the detachment of the rational-moral ideal of the external spectator. They would be concerned with the 'practical guidance of men in the business of the world', as the function of practical morality itself has been described, with the high degree of detachment which permits them to see contradictions, as Sidgwick saw them, in physiologists being 'allowed to torture innocent animals', a contradiction similar to that of a general in war hanging enemy spies but using spies of his own.[78]

The best decisions would probably involve some material sacrifices, especially among citizens of affluent nations, but when minds are prepared by modified attitudes and values, sensitive to cruelty and to all forms of suffering among people and animals alike, such sacrifices would be appreciated by most as long as privileges are removed and the sacrifices fairly distributed. The moral debt to animals will remain as long as there is a moral debt to people. We must never forget that the English gin-trap (or steel-jaw trap) was first used by humans on humans; that brutality to convicts in Australia two hundred years ago gave little reason to treat animals otherwise; that the torture of people today is almost as common, in some countries, as the torture of animals.

How can people be persuaded to accept the decisions of the nation's rational and moral best? While we may agree with Locke that 'the faults to be amended lie in the mind' and that 'force and violence' corrupt it, his inference that 'Cruelty comes not from Nature but from Habit' is uncertain. The ethologists' concern for aggression in man in their comparisons of animals leads some to attribute it to genetic tendencies: that is, to heredity or to 'nature'. From evidence of human improvability through education it is unlikely to be nature alone which is responsible for cruelty, for cruelty is learned from experiences of violence, as Locke knew through his observations of child-rearing practices in eighteenth-century England. Indeed Locke's conjecture was that nine-tenths of the making of any man comes from his education.[79] Therefore to reduce the moral debt to animals to its absolute human limit there is a threefold requirement: first for social justice, including equal opportunities for education everywhere; second for greatly improved moral education, with suitable education of attitudes and values to include compassion and relevant knowledge of animals' natures; and third, lest there be genetic impulses remaining in some which harden the more sympathetic tendencies, stronger law enforcement to cope with the ingenious and crafty evasiveness of those whose morality is a matter of convenience in clutching at self-interest in every opportunity. 'There is little doubt', said Samuel Butler in his satirical *Erewhon*, that those living under a vegetarian law who bred dogs especially for killing other animals 'were deliberately evading the law; but whether this was so or no they sold or ate everything their dogs had killed'.[80]

Butler's satire, with its mildly cynical view of human improvability, leaves a false emphasis in practical morality. Evasiveness is the trademark of the morally uneducated, the individual who remains cunningly determined to find gaps in moral and legal fences or to be cruel when no one is looking. It is also the trademark of the morally lazy, of individuals who blame human cruelty to animals on human nature, on 'simply the way we all are', without the will to change habits, to learn different values, to become morally better than they have been. When legislation is left to those most able of all humans to be fair-minded between humans and sentient animals, the law and morality will be brought together as effectively as is humanly possible. Following that, when there is mass education in humane values, including perhaps much of the content of these pages, and with the informal and varied skills of the enterprising marketplace rather than the formal instruction of the pedagogue, the moral debt to animals, though ineffaceable retrospectively, will be reduced in future in proportion to individual human improvability.

Two ideals have helped to convey the central importance of impartiality in our moral relations with animals. First, the ideal spectator is guaranteed impartiality both by his rational-moral perfection and by his elevation above human and animal kind. Second, Pan is impartial inasmuch as he is both human and animal. Since scientific knowledge has replaced mythological explanations, we no longer need horns on the head to destroy our lofty presumptions, or to realise our kinship with other animals, or to develop the attitudes of compassion and care which characterised Pan's perception. Our uniquely human attribute is the potential to live a practical morality, armed not only with appropriate knowledge, understanding, attitudes and values, but also with the will to rectify uninformed and thoughtless perspectives on animals and to rid ourselves resolutely of every manifestation of cruelty to them.

Notes

CHAPTER 1

1 J. Swain, *Brutes and Beasts* (London: Noel Douglas, 1933) p. 10.
2 L. Gompertz, *Moral Enquiries on the Situation of Man and of Brute*, 1829. Cited in Charles D. Niven, *History of the Humane Movement* (New York: Transatlantic Arts, 1967) p. 70.
3 *The Animal World*, RSPCA, vol. 3, no. 25 (2 Oct. 1871) p. 1. (The RSPCA now publishes a magazine of the same name, but specifically for children.)
4 E. G. Fairholme and W. Paine, *A Century of Work for Animals: The History of the RSPCA 1824–1924* (London: John Murray, 1924) p. 12. This offence occurred in 1790, when the driver was prosecuted. He was acquitted because there was no proof of 'malice'. *The Animal World*, vol. 13, no. 148 (2 Jan. 1882) p. 23, records a visit to the ASPCA in New York, where a horse's tongue was preserved in alcohol. The driver had tied a strong cord around it and attached the cord to a wagon. When the wagon was pulled along the horse's tongue was torn out, as punishment for being 'balky'.
5 Ibid., p. 87.
6 These practices were exposed from time to time in *The Animal World*.
7 At the time of writing over 60 countries have outlawed the trap, but the USA, Canada, the USSR, Finland, Australia and many other countries have not. The steel-jaw trap was even used in medieval times to catch poachers.
8 Karakul sheep are originally from the Bukhara region in central Asia, and were introduced into Afghanistan. Pregnant ewes are sometimes beaten with rods to induce premature births. Then the 'broadtail' is obtained from newly-born lambs, with the unique softness of the skin and tightness of the tiny curls. At other times the lamb is killed a few days after birth. The usual method of obtaining 'broadtail' nowadays is to kill a pregnant ewe, then withdraw the foetus and skin it. See G. Nilsson et al., *Facts About Furs*, 3rd edn (Washington: Animal Welfare Institute, 1980) pp. 82–3.
9 One account of this practice is given in *Animal Liberation*, no. 18 (July–Sept. 1986) p. 11. Official Philippines Government confirmation is given in *Animal Liberation*, no. 20 (Jan.–March 1987) p. 2.
10 Attempts at differentiation sometimes lead to confusion, as in the University of South California Code of Ethics, para. 6: 'In no case should pain and distress result in suffering, i.e., that degree of pain which causes significant behavioral distress or change in the animal.' *Animal Welfare Institute Quarterly*, vol. 35, no. 1 (Spring 1986) p. 4. Pain and distress themselves constitute suffering.
11 A. W. Moss notes that this sport dates at least from the 14th century, when Chaucer referred to it. See *The History of the RSPCA* (London: Cassell, 1961) p. 131.
12 G. Carson, *Men, Beasts and Gods* (New York: Charles Scribner's Sons, 1972) p. 64. In California in 1868 cockfights and dogfights were daily occur-

rences. See F. M. Hubbard, *Prevention of Cruelty to Animals in the States of Illinois, Colorado and California* (New York: Columbia University Press, 1916) p. 70.

13 *The Animal World*, vol. 19, no. 229 (1 Oct. 1888) p. 35. In England cockfighting had been banned for a time at the end of the 14th century. It was banned again in 1849.

14 'Solicitor' [pseudonym], *The Citizen and the Law* (London: Routledge and Sons, 1934) p. 201.

15 Charles D. Niven, *History of the Humane Movement*, p. 571. See note 2 above.

16 J. Swain, *Brutes and Beasts*, p. 59. Elizabeth I relished bear-baiting and bear-beating.

17 F. M. Hubbard, *Prevention of Cruelty to Animals...*, p. 70. See note 12 above.

18 G. Carson, *Men, Beasts and Gods*, pp. 67–8.

19 'Ouida' [pseudonym], in *Critical Studies* (London: T. Fisher Unwin, 1900) p. 245. 'Ouida' was the English novelist Marie Louise de la Ramée, who knew how to appeal to the emotions of uncritical readers. Her impressions need to be read with caution, but in this case the condition of travelling animals is confirmed in a number of contemporary accounts.

20 L. Gompertz, *Moral Enquiries on the Situation of Man and of Brute*, cited in Charles D. Niven, *History of the Humane Movement*, p. 69.

21 B. Richardson, MD, FRS in *The Animal World*, vol. 3, no. 28 (1 Jan. 1872). Richardson's letter was a plea to use, in killing animals for food, the same means as we use 'to save our own bodies from pain of operation'.

22 *Report of the Committee on Humane Slaughtering of Animals*, presented to both Houses of Parliament, 1904 (London: HMSO). See p. 157 for the reference to the number of blows required in killing, and p. 173 for the reference to animals' terror in smelling blood.

23 *The Animal World*, vol. 9, no. 103 (1 April 1878) pp. 50–1.

24 Ibid., vol. 9., no. 105 (1 June 1878) pp. 83–4.

25 So called from 'poll' (head) and 'axe' (hammer with a sharp edge). The early form of the English poleaxe had a blade like a butcher's chopper. The head of the poleaxe was a punch-bolt. A punch was a hollow tube used for cutting, with a sharp, circular edge. By 1878 the chopper had been replaced by a hook, useful in pulling the animal's head aside by hooking onto its horns. See *The Animal World*, vol. 9, no. 108 (2 Sept. 1878) p. 147.

26 'Ouida' in *Critical Studies*, pp. 259–60. Astrakhan fleeces, from Astrakhan in Russia, were similar to the Karakul fleeces.

27 Ibid., pp. 252–3.

28 *The Animal World*, vol. 5, no. 56 (1 May 1874) p. 76.

29 Ibid., vol. 13, no. 148 (2 Jan. 1882) p. 23.

30 E. G. Fairholme and W. Paine, *A Century of Work for Animals*, p. 128.

31 *The Animal World*, vol. 3, no. 34 (1 July 1872) p. 160.

32 E. G. Fairholme and W. Paine, *A Century of Work for Animals*, p. 87.

33 *The Animal World*, vol. 13, no. 148 (2 Jan. 1882) p. 23. In one case a pair of mules had been beaten by a driver with a whip made of chain from a chain pump, with a sharp-edged circular plate at the end. When apprehended, the driver was striking the animal so viciously as to drive the edges of the iron into the flesh.

34 Ibid., vol. 9, no. 100 (1 Jan. 1878) p. 6.

35 One such case was of a dog made to pull a 500 lb load at a rate of 12 mph. Cited by Charles D. Niven in *History of the Humane Movement*, p. 71.
36 This account was given by the Rev. Henry Crowe in 1822 and cited by E. G. Fairholme and W. Paine in *A Century of Work for Animals*, p. 107.
37 One such case was at the Nottingham Cattle Market, reported in 1871. *The Animal World*, vol. 3, no. 27 (1 Dec. 1871) p. 35.
38 Many animals and birds were caught other than dingoes.
39 One instance was the cruel punishment of animals in the code of the Zendavesta, influenced by magical ideas. See L. T. Hobhouse, *Morals in Evolution: A Comparative Study of Ethics* (London: Chapman and Hall, 1906) bk 1, ch. 3, p. 95.
40 For an account of court procedure see E. G. Fairholme and W. Paine, *A Century of Work for Animals*, p. 141. In 1404 a pig was sentenced for killing a child. In 1497 a sow was condemned to be beaten to death for mutilating the face of a child. The ecclesiastical courts usually tried groups of animals, the lay courts individual animals, prosecuting for causing bodily harm to a human. Formal court procedure was followed, the result a foregone conclusion. See J. Swain, *Brutes and Beasts*, p. 91. In 1692 in the USA 19 men and women and 2 dogs were hanged for refusing to answer charges of witchcraft. See G. Carson, *Men, Beasts and Gods*, p. 72.
41 'Solicitor', *The Citizen and the Law*, pp. 200–1. Two traditions may have been caught up in this practice: first, the relatively recent anti-popery fervour; second, the belief in the evil powers of cats, especially black ones, which was as old as the Middle Ages.
42 A practice brought frequently to the attention of the RSPCA. In 1829 Lewis Gompertz wrote of the continual sound of whipping and beating. See Charles D. Niven, *History of the Humane Movement*, p. 70. Common mutilations in England, even after the *Cruelty to Animals Act 1876*, were docking of horses' tails, dehorning of cattle too close to the head, cutting ears of sheep for identification, cutting off the ears of dogs, sometimes for punishment, and cutting off the combs of cocks (termed 'dubbing' cocks).
43 W. K. C. Guthrie, *A History of Greek Philosophy* (Cambridge University Press, 1962) vol. 1, p. 186. It is noteworthy that Pythagoras did not insist on banning the eating of flesh (p. 191).
44 An abridged edition was published in 1831 with the title *The Duty of Humanity to Inferior Creatures: Deduced from Reason and Scripture* (London: J. Nisbett, 1831). A copy of the original edition of 1776 is held by the British Library, London. Page numbers refer to the abridged edition.
45 J. Bentham, *An Introduction to the Principles of Morals and Legislation*, ch. 19, section 1, p. 143. From *Works*, vol. 1. (Edinburgh: William Tait, 1843). The first edition of *An Introduction to the Principles of Morals and Legislation* was printed in 1780, four years after Primatt's book first appeared, but Bentham's work was not published until 1789 (see Preface to above, p. i). The credit sometimes given to Bentham for providing the impetus for much of early 19th-century awareness of animal suffering is due rather to Primatt.
46 See E. G. Fairholme and W. Paine, *A Century of Work for Animals*, p. 14. Young's essay was published in 1798.
47 These explanations were offered in *The Animal World*, vol. 5, no. 56 (1 May

1874) p. 76.
48 RSPCA, *162nd Annual Report*, 1985, p. 21.
49 Bulldogs kept as pets have been reported stolen in one Australian state recently, to be used for dogfighting. Cockfighting and dogfighting were both discovered at a remote farm in England in 1985. See RSPCA, *162nd Annual Report*, 1985, p. 19. Similar incidents have occurred in 1987, both in England and in the USA.
50 See S. Smiles, *Duty* (London: John Murray, 1907) p. 391. There has been isolated resistance to the sport for more than a century.
51 It is recorded that in 1970 over 40 million spectators in the USA paid to see one or more rodeos. See Gerald Carson, *Men, Beasts and Gods*, p. 156. The sport originated in the 19th century when cattle drovers found recreation in competing in the breaking of wild horses. The rodeo is outlawed in the UK but still permitted in the USA, Australia and some other countries.
52 Ibid., p. 64. Only a few states now permit live bird shoots for recreational sport. In one town in Pennsylvania there has been a live pigeon shoot on each Labour Day since 1934; thousands of birds are killed on each occasion. Birds that are wounded are killed by boys who collect them when they fall. Reported by the International Society for Animal Rights, Clarks Summit, Pa, *Report*, Nov. 1986, p. 1.
53 S. Smiles, *Duty*, p. 392.
54 A decision by Congress in 1949. The opening of refuges for hunting is escalating, with many thousands of animals killed on them each year. In each of 1985 and 1986 at least 7 additional refuges were opened for hunting.
55 The first hunting trip from the USA to China was organised in 1984, with 13 people visiting the Taoshan hunting range to hunt red deer. *China Reconstructs*, vol. 34, no. 3 (March 1985) pp. 31–2.
56 These and other powerful game fish may die in the encounter, or they may be hauled aside and released for another day of 'sport'. Their spectacular leaps in the air are frantic efforts to be free of the angler's torment.
57 *Report of the Committee on Cruelty to Wild Animals* (London: HMSO, June 1951).
58 See J. Swain, *Brutes and Beasts*, for an account of fox-hunting (p. 99) and of otter-hunting (pp. 129–30) which leaves a very different impression of animal suffering in prolonged distress from the pursuit and the eventual exhaustion and submission to being killed.
59 *Report of the Committee on Humane Slaughtering of Animals* (London: HMSO, 1904). Its terms of reference were 'to ascertain the most humane and practicable methods of slaughtering animals for human food, and to investigate and report upon the existing slaughter-house system' (p. 217).
60 More humane situations are to be found in some slaughterhouses, and some of the private killing on farms by skilled shooting is swift and unanticipated. For an account of the distress of cattle facing electrocution in an Australian abattoir, see C. Townend, *In Defence of Living Things* (Sydney: Wentworth Books, 1980) p. 17. This subjective impression is confirmed by other accounts.
61 S. Smiles, *Duty*, p. 393. The extent of the trade in feathers is indicated by one dealer's single consignment of 32 000 dead hummingbirds, 80 000

aquatic birds and 800 000 pairs of wings. Aquatic birds suffered heavily. See the account (p. 398) of the slaughter of solan geese in the Firth of Forth.

62 The *Animal Welfare Institute Quarterly*, vol. 35, no. 1 (Washington, DC: Spring 1986) p. 12, refers to a report in the Spring 1986 issue of *The Voice of The Trapper*. Here it is explained that smooth or padded jaws would only squeeze together material such as frozen soil, leaves and ice, allowing the animal to strip its foot clear and to escape.

63 Ibid. Illustrations of 1985 and 1885 traps are given on p. 12. See also note 38 above.

64 In 1933, 50 000 horses, ponies and mules were reported to be used in England's mines. The only time they were brought to the surface was during a strike. See J. Swain, *Brutes and Beasts*, pp. 247–9.

65 Roswell C. McCrea, *The Humane Movement* (New York: Columbia University Press, 1910) p. 61. Earlier in the century, when the common pastures in the public ranges of the USA became overcrowded, stockmen sometimes fenced in watering holes to keep out competitors' stock.

66 Some farmers in Australia have been persuaded to cover sheep with nylon coats, but the first consideration is economic gain from the reduction in sheep losses. By 1915 the Humane Society of New York had demonstrated and made available a canvas blanket for horses. See F. Morse Hubbard, *Prevention of Cruelty to Animals in New York State* (New York: Columbia University Press, 1915) p. 18.

67 G. Carson, *Men, Beasts and Gods*, p. 175. Blistering agents known as 'creeping cream' (oxide of mercury) and 'scootin juice' (oil of mustard) cause blisters to the pastern area. The names are self-revealing. Soring of horses was banned by federal legislation in 1970.

68 The capacities of particular breeds differ. In some cases capacity is prodigious in relation to the size of the animal (as in the case of the small horses used in China).

69 A. Brown, *Who Cares for Animals?* (London: Heinemann, 1974) pp. 129–36. In some cases airlines themselves are responsible: crates of animals have been accepted without any consignee's address. Ironically drug companies demand better care in crating animals, because any arriving in poor health are unsuitable for experimental purposes.

70 See especially Ruth Harrison, *Animal Machines: The New Factory Farming Industry* (London: Vincent Stuart, 1964): foreword by Rachel Carson. Since this book was written factory farming has been extended not only to mink, foxes and rabbits, but also to a variety of birds such as turkeys, ducks, geese, partridges and quail.

71 Ibid., pp. 66–7. Ruth Harrison likened the second situation to a row of stocks. The small pens, 22 inches wide by 4–5 feet deep, with calves yoked in the manner described, the sides of the pen slatted as well as the floor, was the pattern recommended by agricultural experts. Each pen was open at the back for cleaning. In the front was a fixed bucket-holder for feeding purposes. For graphic photographs of animals on factory farms see ibid., pp. 98ff. (For veal calves see fig. 15.)

72 *Report of the Technical Committee to Enquire into the Welfare of Animals Kept under Intensive Livestock Husbandry Systems* (London: HMSO, 1965) para. 37.

(Widely known as the Brambell Report after the chairman.) Recent information on the changing methods in the intensive farming of veal calves has been confirmed from a variety of sources.

73 The skim milk has additives to promote growth, including fats, starch and sugar, vitamins and antibiotics. For illustrations of veal calves in confined stalls see Jim Mason and Peter Singer, *Animal Factories* (New York: Crown Publishers, 1980) pp. 14, 126. See also Peter Singer, *Animal Liberation* (London etc.: Granada Publishing, 1977) ch. 3, plate 6. The standard pens in the USA are similar in size to those described earlier, or if anything rather smaller. Conditions are also similar.

74 See Ruth Harrison, *Animal Machines*, pp. 94–8 (and the plates following p. 98) on the unhealthy 'sweat-boxes' for pigs in England. Feral pigs are found in many parts of the world, usually close to water. The pigs' inability to cope with high temperatures is aggravated by insufficient sweat glands. Diseases among animals in factory farms are combated with disinfectants, antibiotics and pesticides, with doubtful effects on the animals' health.

75 See P. H. J. H. Gosden, *How They Were Taught* (Oxford: Basil Blackwell, 1969) pp. 1–8, for an account of the monitor system in practice. In the case of pigs in the factory farm, a 1:1000 ratio was reported in Ruth Harrison, *Animal Machines*, p. 96.

76 Illustrations of the confinement pens are available in a variety of books, journals and farming magazines published in the USA. See, for example, Jim Mason and Peter Singer, *Animal Factories*, pp. 1 (oppos.), 31, 46, 62, 87, 104.

77 See ibid., pp. 30–1, for a fuller account.

78 Sometimes agribusiness companies process animal waste and sell it as 'feed supplement'. More repugnant cases are cited: one farmer let his pregnant sows eat up the excreta in pits below their pens, claiming that this avoided feeding them for 90 days and saved him $9300 each year as a result. Ibid., p. 48: the authors refer to an article in *Hog Farm Management*, April 1978.

79 A. Brown, *Who Cares for Animals?*, p. 146.

80 Again there are clear photographs available in published material to show conditions in broiler factory farms. See, for example, *Mainstream*, vol. 17, no. 1 (Winter 1986) p. 20.

81 In the USA furs are now marketed for dinner suits, dresses, trousers, children's wear, even for dolls and Christmas tree ornaments. The fur industry is expanding since factory methods were introduced.

82 The wound is about the size of a saucer. The operation is named after Mules, an Australian farmer who practised the technique without anaesthetic 60 years ago. Now the operation is carried out in a variety of ways. Some veterinarians believe that the operation should be performed only when no alternatives exist, and only on sheep which have wrinkled breeches which predispose them to blowfly strike. *Animal Liberation*, no. 20 (Jan.–March 1987) p. 21.

83 From Minutes of Evidence, *Report of the Committee on Humane Slaughtering of Animals* (London: HMSO, 1904) p. 157. For an explanation of dishorning and disbudding see J. O. L. King, 'Dairy Cattle', in the *UFAW Handbook on the Care and Management of Farm Animals* (Edinburgh and London: Churchill Livingstone, 1971) p. 21. Disbudding refers to the removal of the

horn bud in young calves. In the response quoted, the assessment of 'harmlessness' as unconnected with animal suffering was clearly defensive. Now the law requires the disbudding of calves after the first week of life to be performed with an anaesthetic. Dishorning of dairy cows is recommended to avoid injuries to udders and flanks.

84 In May 1986 the Australian Government prohibited fishing with gillnets longer than 2½ kilometres. Taiwanese fishermen had been responsible for drowning thousands of dolphins in nets 20 kilometres (12½ miles) long as they fished off the northern coast.

85 For a fuller account see L. T. Hobhouse, *Morals in Evolution*, pp. 95–6.

86 *Animal Liberation*, no. 18 (July–Sept. 1986) p. 12.

87 In accordance with the beliefs of Shamanism, the Daur people of China sacrifice sheep and cattle to their gods of heaven, earth, mountain and river. *Beijing Review*, vol. 30, no. 21 (May 1987) pp. 32–3.

CHAPTER 2

1 This and other page references are to the edition by J. B. Schneewind of Mill's *Ethical Writings* (New York: Collier Books; London: Collier-Macmillan, 1965).

2 Kant, *Fundamental Principles of the Metaphysic of Morals*, in *Critique of Practical Reason and Other Works on the Theory of Ethics*, trans. T. K. Abbott, 6th edn (London: Longmans, 1909) p. 47.

3 J. Bentham, *An Introduction to the Principles of Morals and Legislation*, in *Works*, vol. 1, ch. 19, section 2, p. 142.

4 R. M. Hare, *Moral Thinking: Its Levels, Method and Point* (Oxford: Clarendon Press, 1981) p. 228.

5 G. E. Moore, *Principia Ethica* (Cambridge University Press, 1962) p. 106. First edition published in 1903.

6 M. de Montaigne, *Works*, trans. William Hazlitt (London: C. Templeman, 1865) ch. 12, 'Apology for Raimond Sebond', pp. 206–7.

7 Richard Dean, *An Essay on the Future Life of Brute Creatures*, cited by E. G. Fairholme and W. Paine in *A Century of Work for Animals*, p. 6.

8 H. Primatt, *The Duty of Humanity to Inferior Creatures*. See Chapter 1, note 44. Broome amended Primatt's original title in the 1776 edition.

9 Ibid., pp. 10–11.

10 Bentham's words are quoted in Chapter 1. On the printing and publication dates of *An Introduction to the Principles of Morals and Legislation* see Chapter 1, note 45.

11 J. Bentham, *Works*, vol. 10, Bentham's correspondence, p. 549.

12 J. Beattie, *Elements of Moral Science* (Edinburgh: Constable, 1817) p. 471. Beattie was a Professor of Moral Philosophy and Logic, University of Aberdeen. In context his remarks seem to refer to sentience as well as emotions.

13 H. Calderwood, *Handbook of Moral Philosophy*, 6th edn (London: Macmillan, 1879) p. 132. First edn 1872. Calderwood was a Professor of Moral Philosophy at the University of Edinburgh.

14 J.-J. Rousseau, *A Discourse on the Origin of Inequality*, Preface. Various editions, e.g. 'Great Books of the Western World', ed. R. M. Hutchins, vol. 38 (Chicago: William Benton, 1952) p. 331.

15 See also W. D. M. Paton, *Man and Mouse: Animals in Medical Research* (Oxford University Press, 1984) p. 98.

16 See ibid., p. 11: 'The parallels in bodily physiology, in the nervous pathways transmitting signals from damaged tissues, and in the behaviour in response to such signals, make it improbable that man is grossly more sensitive to "pain" than other warm-blooded vertebrates.'

17 See J. Bentham, *An Introduction to the Principles of Morals and Legislation*, in *Works*, vol. 1, ch. 4, section 2, p. 16: 'To a person considered *by himself*, the value of pleasure or pain considered *by itself*, will be greater or less according to the four following circumstances: its *intensity*, its *duration*, its certainty or uncertainty, its propinquity or remoteness.' (For a number of persons, to these criteria he added its fecundity, its purity and its extent.)

18 See J. Bentham, *Codification Proposal*, in *Works*, vol. 4, part 1, section 3, p. 540. Bentham instructed the reader to give a numerical weight to intensity, multiplying it by another number 'expressive of the moments of time contained in its duration'.

19 J. Bentham, *An Introduction to the Principles of Morals and Legislation*, in *Works*, vol. 1, ch. 1, section 5, p. 2.

20 For instance, the *Protection of Animals (Amendment) Act 1980*, Victoria, Australia, states that 'animal' means a member of any species of the sub-phylum *vertebrate* except a fish, human being or venomous reptile. Acts of Parliament, 1980, p. 246.

21 I. Kant, *Lectures on Ethics*, trans. L. Infield (London: Methuen, 1930) p. 239.

22 For a fuller discussion of 'person' from a moral standpoint, see the author's *Justice, Morality and Education* (London: Macmillan, 1985) pp. 37–8.

23 M. de Montaigne, 'Apology for Raymond Sebond', in *Works*, pp. 206–7.

24 See *Justice, Morality and Education*, ch. 2 and ch. 8, for a fuller discussion of morality; also the author's *Conservation and Practical Morality* (London: Macmillan, 1987) ch. 1.

25 See J. Beattie, *Elements of Moral Science*, ch. 3, p. 383; and H. Calderwood, *Handbook of Moral Philosophy*, ch. 5, p. 93.

26 T. Fowler, *Progressive Morality: An Essay in Ethics* (London and New York: Macmillan, 1895) pp. 185–6. Fowler had been Professor of Logic in the University of Oxford.

27 G. Chaucer, 'The Franklin's Tale', lines 1194–5, in *The Canterbury Tales* (London: Macmillan, 1928) ed. A. W. Pollard et al., p. 234.

28 In Kant's *Introduction to the Metaphysic of Morals* in *Critique of Practical Reason and Other Works on the Theory of Ethics*, p. 279, he asserted that '*duty* is the action to which a person is bound'.

29 See W. D. Ross, *The Right and the Good* (Oxford University Press, 1930) for a discussion of *prima facie* duties as a way of relaxing the notion of duties as unconditional.

30 D. Hume, *Enquiries Concerning Human Understanding and Concerning the Principles of Morals*, 3rd edn (Oxford: Clarendon Press, 1975) pp. 172–3. Reprinted from the posthumous edition of 1777 and edited by L. A. Selby-Bigge.

31 See the author's *Justice, Morality and Education*, pp. 122–6, 174–6; and *Conservation and Practical Morality*, pp. 35–7.

32 World Society for the Prevention of Cruelty to Animals, *Annual Report*, June 1984–May 1985 (London: 1985) p. 13. That our immediate responses in such situations are largely a matter of personal attitudes and values is supported by many similar comments, such as Bentham's when protesting his inability to 'understand how some see it as a matter of amusement to see a horse or a dog suffer'. *Principles of the Penal Law*, in *Works*, vol. 1, p. 550.

33 From 'Angell's Lessons on Kindness to Animals II', in *The Animal World*, vol. 13, no. 148 (2 Jan. 1882) p. 71.

34 From an article in *The Animal World*, vol. 1, no. 5 (1 Feb. 1870) p. 88.

35 This expression was used in 'Angell's Lessons on Kindness to Animals IV', with reference to the horse. *The Animal World*, vol. 13, no. 148 (2 Jan. 1882) p. 131.

36 In *Animals and Why They Matter* (Harmondsworth: Penguin Books, 1983) p. 63, Mary Midgley commented: 'to say that "animals do not have rights" does not sound like a remark about the meaning of the word *rights* but one about animals – namely, the remark that one need not really consider them'.

37 Henry S. Salt (ed.), *The New Charter* (London and New York: G. Bell, 1896) Introduction, p. x. Salt was to write a book which he called *Animal Rights* (London: G. Bell, revised edn 1922).

38 F. H. Bradley, *Ethical Studies*, 2nd edn (London: Oxford University Press, 1927) pp. 208–9. (First edn 1876.)

39 A familiar view in some religions, and also among some scientists with humane values. The scientific view expressed by a member of the Humanitarian League in 1896 was that 'there was a true brotherhood of all that lives'. J. Oldfield, 'The Scientific View', in Henry Salt (ed.), *The New Charter*, p. 82. Another stated as part of the ethical view that the highest 'brutes' are 'our fellow-beings'. F. Harrison, 'The Ethical View', ibid., p. 98.

40 T. Fowler, *Progressive Morality*, p. 186. Fowler's attitude was condescending, without an ability to accord animal interests equal consideration with human; he was 'considering their place in the economy of nature' (pp. 185–6), and in the 'scale of being' they were viewed clearly as inferior. Fowler was ambivalent, doing his utmost to show that moral values were changing, emphasising that 'recent researches, and still more, recent speculations, have tended to impress us with the nearness of our kinship to other animals', conceding that 'our sympathies with them and our interest in their welfare have been sensibly quickened', but still insufficiently impartial to perceive the moral position of an equal consideration of interests (p. 189).

41 Richard Whately (ed.), *Paley's Moral Philosophy* (London: Parker, 1859) p. 96.

42 J. Bentham, *An Introduction to the Principles of Morals and Legislation*, in *Works*, vol. 1, ch. 19, section 1, pp. 142–3, fn.

43 These rationalisations of the hunter in the USA have been exposed by animal welfare organisations. Wildlife management is particularly susceptible to criticism when it attempts to make compromises between conserva-

tion and hunting interests. The rationalisations of the hunters are more transparent still.

44 See D. Hume, *A Treatise of Human Nature*, ed. L. A. Selby-Bigge (Oxford: Clarendon Press, 1888) bk 3, part 2, section 2, pp. 493–6. Hume's *Treatise* was first published in London in 1739.

45 For Plato's theory of Forms, see *The Republic*, various editions, such as Everyman's, trans. A. D. Lindsay (London: J. M. Dent, 1935) bks 6 and 7, especially p. 203.

46 See the author's *Conservation and Practical Morality*, ch. 3, p. 91.

47 From a utilitarian stance Peter Singer argues that 'like suffering' of beings is to be regarded as equal: 'There can be no moral justification for . . . refusing to count it equally with the like suffering of any other being', *Animal Liberation* (London: Granada Publishing, 1977) p. 175. Whenever the aggregate of pain is considered morally important, some attempt at the quantification of the suffering is implied. But alternatively, comparisons of the suffering of animals and humans may be made on general impressions.

48 The Ewenki people, who live in the Heilongjiang province in North-East China, were almost entirely dependent on reindeer for food and other necessities prior to 1949. The reindeer provided meat and milk, clothes from their hides, fuel from their droppings, and traditional medicines from their antlers, bone muscle and heart. *China Reconstructs*, vol. 33, no. 4 (April 1984) p. 27.

49 For example, in some countries the poleaxe is still used, with its possibilities for bungling; in Asian and Latin American countries knives and lances are used to sever the neck vertebrae as a means of preventing movement during slaughter; Moslems and Jews still slaughter by cutting the throats of conscious animals.

50 In Australia there are economic drives to satisfy overseas markets for venison, goat, suckling lamb, pheasant, guinea fowl, crocodile, buffalo, horse and feral pig. Deer are killed also for the export of velvet, the newly-formed soft antler of the buck, in heavy demand for Asian medicine. *Animal Liberation*, no. 19 (Oct.–Dec. 1986) pp. 4–6.

51 In recreational hunting, for example, marksmanship is not usually skilled, and as a result a high proportion of animals are not killed instantly; many animals not wanted by human sportsmen perish in habitat manipulation to suit deer and other game shooters; trapping inflicts suffering not only on wanted species of animals, but also on many others 'accidentally' trapped. See *Ecos*, no. 38 (Summer 1983–4) p. 29 for an account of 8 different species of domestic dogs caught in dingo traps in Gippsland, Victoria.

52 Modifications of the bullfight are practised in Latin America and in China. In Costa Rica the killing of the bull is banned, but the animal is tormented by spectators, suffering from distress more than from physical injury. See J. Praded, *WSPA in Latin America* (Jamaica Plain: World Society for the Protection of Animals, no date) p. 18. Among the Miao and Dong people of China bulls are encouraged to rush at each other, lock horns and fight, but injuries are minor. *China Reconstructs*, vol. 35, no. 8 (August 1986) p. 67.

53 See *Animal Liberation*, no. 19 (Oct.–Dec. 1986) pp. 14–17 for an account of monkeys in concrete compounds without trees to climb and baboons in

individual cages little larger than the animals themselves.

54 From the standpoint of implementation, vast social changes would be needed, especially in impoverished countries; as would a modification of attitudes towards animals through education; a development of rational powers far above the general level now apparent. Vegetarianism is supported also on scientific and economic grounds: various scientists have explained that it is more efficient to obtain proteins from soya beans than to feed them to cattle and then to eat the meat. Efficiency in food production will become an urgent problem as attempts are made in future to feed an increasing human population. On moral grounds the solution ought not to be higher levels of factory farming.

55 Marine animals such as porpoises and dolphins are regarded by professional fishermen as their competitive enemies. Some are allowed to drown in nets; others are shot. Attempts to produce an improved net to facilitate the release of animals have failed to solve the problem: they are renetted soon after release and eventually killed. On the size of the nets see Chapter 1 above, note 88.

56 J. Bentham, *An Introduction to the Principles of Morals and Legislation*, in *Works*, vol. 1, ch. 19, section 1, p. 142.

57 P. H. Holbach, *The System of Nature, or The Laws of the Moral and Physical World*, 3rd edn (London: Sherwood, Neeby and Jones, 1817). See vol. 1, ch. 17, p. 534: 'The true function of all morals' is that 'merit and virtue are founded upon the nature of man', and p. 619: 'What benefit has the human race, hitherto drawn from those sublime, those supernatural notions, with which superstition has fed mortals during so many ages?'

CHAPTER 3

1 D. Hume, *A Treatise of Human Nature*, bk 3, part 2, section 2, pp. 494–5. See Chapter 2 above, note 44.

2 W. Fleming, *A Manual of Moral Philosophy* (London: John Murray, 1867) bk 2, part 1, p. 261. Fleming was formerly Professor of Moral Philosophy at Glasgow.

3 *The Animal Welfare Institute Quarterly*, vol. 33, no. 2 (Summer 1984) p. 6. From 'Notes on Hearings on H.R. 1797 to end use of steel-jaw traps': 'Until the animal can talk to me in our language', one witness said, 'I don't believe we can say he feels pain.'

4 I. Kant, *The Analytic of Pure Practical Reason*, in *Critique of Practical Reason and Other Works on the Theory of Ethics*, pp. 131–2.

5 I. Kant, *Fundamental Principles of the Metaphysic of Morals*, in ibid., p. 31. See also Chapter 2, note 2.

6 For a fuller account of the interaction of reason and dispositions (in the sense of a predispositional complex) see the author's *Justice, Morality and Education*, pp. 114–37; and *Conservation and Practical Morality*, pp. 152–4.

7 Cf. S. I. Benn, 'Persons and Values: Reasons in Conflict and Moral Disagreement', in *Ethics*, vol. 95, no. 1 (Oct. 1984) p. 36: 'Within the modern consciousness, practical reason is located, in the first instance, not in the mustering of knockdown arguments to persuade or to justify oneself

to others but in the process of individual choice and judgement.'
8 *Report of the Committee on Cruelty to Wild Animals*, p. 42, para. 144. See also Chapter 1 above, note 57.
9 In *Moral Thinking: Its Levels, Method and Point* (Oxford: Clarendon Press, 1981) ch. 2, R. M. Hare does not make it clear that reason and intuition, which he sees as the two levels of moral thinking, are concurrent as moral judgements are being made. Instead of his 'intuitions' we have offered a more explicit account of predisposing tendencies, particularly attitudes and values which are expressed as moral convictions.
10 J. Huxley, *Man in the Modern World* (London: Chatto and Windus, 1947) p. 1.
11 T. Hobbes, *Leviathan* (Harmondsworth: Penguin Books, 1968) ch. 28, p. 353. (First published 1651.)
12 N. Tinbergen, *The Animal and its World*, 2 vols (London: Allen and Unwin, 1973) vol. 2, p. 162: 'No informed person can doubt any more that Man has evolved.'
13 The point is illustrated in the case of the horse named 'clever Hans' for purportedly understanding arithmetic and language. Careful investigation showed that the owner was unwittingly transmitting his own body signs to the horse as cues to correct answers.
14 Welfare organisations in the USA have estimated that there alone each year 25 million puppies and kittens are born to die from abandonment, starvation or destruction. The USA has an estimated total of over 50 million companion dogs and about the same number of cats. In countries with large numbers of companion animals which are overbreeding, there is a moral debt on a national scale, as animal welfare organisations repeat.
15 D. Hume, *Enquiries Concerning Human Understanding and Concerning the Principles of Morals*, p. 105 (See Chapter 2, note 30). Hume explained that in these inferences animals are like children, and indeed like 'the generality of mankind, in their ordinary actions and conclusions', since they too make inferences of this kind without reasoning (p. 105).
16 See A. F. Fraser, *Farm Animal Behaviour* (University of Edinburgh, 1974) pp. 42–3. When a horse rolls itself when grooming, it pauses briefly with feet in the air. A fatal gut twist can be caused when a horse is rolled quickly, especially with full intestines (p. 43).
17 R. P. Evans, 'The Effects of Social Behaviour on Production in Dairy Cows', in the *Veterinary Annual*, Eighteenth Issue (Bristol: John Wright, 1978) p. 67. Intensive farming of dairy cows has been criticised for inducing physical suffering from farm diseases as well. See M. W. Fox, 'Moving Nature off its Course', in the *Humane Society News* (Spring 1986), pp. 12–13.
18 M. W. Fox, 'Veterinarians and Animal Rights', in *California Veterinarian*, 1, 1983, p. 16. Acknowledgement is here given to E. Carpenter, *Animals and Ethics* (London: Watkins, 1980) and to animal protection legislation in West Germany.
19 Published in *The Animal World*, vol. 8, no. 89 (1 Feb. 1877) p. 20.
20 This recent report on roadside zoos refers to 120 in the state of Florida. The conditions described are usually in violation of laws protecting captive wildlife, but law enforcement is inadequate, as is often the case elsewhere.

J. Roush, 'Life in Florida's Concrete Jungles' (Washington, DC: Humane Society of the USA, 1986). Similar conditions have been found in Australia. See Chapter 2, note 53.

21 A. Brown, *Who Cares for Animals?* (London: Heinemann, 1974) pp. 139–40. To simulate natural conditions for large animals such as elephants and giraffes would be almost impracticable: elephants are destructive of vegetation and regeneration areas to provide alternative feeding would generally need to be prohibitively large.

22 Some of the stereotypes have been observed by D. Morris in *The Naked Ape* (London: Granada Publishing, 1977) pp. 126–7.

23 'Learned helplessness', used in experimental psychology, is induced in animals such as dogs. They may be first subjected to aversive stimulation (such as electric shocks) until they learn certain procedures to obtain food and to avoid suffering. But when the experimenters change the procedure and give further aversive shocks, eventually the animals surrender all attempts to avoid them, seeing that the situation is hopeless. (The expression is credited to M. E. P. Seligman: see for example his 'Chronic Fear Produced by Unpredictable Shock', in *Journal of Comparative and Physiological Psychology*, vol. 66 (1968) pp. 402–11.

24 In the early part of this century the Bronx Zoo exhibited a human pygmy from the Congo in the same cage as an orang-utan. No one could appreciate his thoughts and feelings because of the language barrier. He is reported to have committed suicide, something animals can achieve only by surrendering the will to live and starving.

25 Present conditions in the shipment of captive animals are summarised in a report by J. Brookland et al., *Injury, Damage to Health and Cruel Treatment: Present Conditions in the Shipment of Live Fauna* (London: Environmental Investigation Agency, 1985). Primates reaching zoos are only a small proportion of those captured. One trader in Indonesia admitted that 60–70% of macaques trapped in Indonesia die prior to shipment (p. 6). When 10 howler monkeys had been crated for 84 hours without attention, as they were shipped from Paraguay to London via Lima and Paris, all died in quarantine from privations (p. 11). When primates eventually reach their country of destination up to 50% of them die in quarantine in the UK and in the USA (p. 6). Animals need to be 'acclimatised to captivity' (p. 32) before shipment; trappers, exporters and importers all need knowledge of wildlife (p. 33).

26 Though countries in which live lures are used have humane laws banning the practice, law enforcement is difficult and usually left to humane societies. In the USA greyhound racing is legal in some states, not in others; there are pressures from gambling interests to have the sport extended.

27 Aristotle, *History of Animals*, trans. D'Arcy Wentworth Thompson, bk 8, ch. 1, 588ª.

28 An appraisal of Lorenz by Sir Julian Huxley in the Foreword to Lorenz's *On Aggression* (London: Methuen, 1973) p. vii. First published in Vienna in 1963. Huxley described modern ethology as 'that rapidly growing branch of science which is destined to provide a strong foundation for the science of human behaviour and psychology'. The *idea* of a science of animal behaviour had been proposed by a French naturalist more than a century

earlier.

29 N. Tinbergen, *The Animal and its World* (London: Allen and Unwin, 1973) vol. 2, p. 130.

30 K. Lorenz, *Studies in Animal and Human Behaviour*, trans. R. Martin (London: Methuen, 1970) vol. 1, p. xvi.

31 I. Eibl-Eibesfeldt, *Ethology: The Biology of Behaviour*, trans. E. Klinghammer (New York: Holt, Rinehart & Winston, 1970) Preface, p. viii.

32 The author uses a different example: that of the Yucca moth which responds to an innate mechanism whereby it collects pollen and rubs it into the stigma of the Yucca flowers *before* it lays its eggs. The larvae depend for food on the seeds which develop from the flowers.

33 I. Eibl-Eibesfeldt, *Love and Hate*, trans. G. Strachan (London: Methuen, 1971) pp. 3, 4, 101.

34 A Russian physiologist, Pavlov had found that dogs will salivate not only on the appearance of food, but also by learning that an entirely different stimulus, such as the sound of a metronome, may be associated with food. The discovery of this 'conditioned reflex' led him to make generalisations such as that the habits of all learned behaviour are no more than a chain of conditioned reflexes.

35 E. L. Thorndike formulated his 'law of effect': 'behaviour changes because of its consequences'. See 'The Psychology of Learning', in *Educational Psychology*, vol. 2 (New York: Teachers' College, Columbia University, 1913).

36 B. F. Skinner's animals were found to work harder when the food rewards were increased in quantity, delivered less frequently than originally. Skinner's view of the environment as offering a total explanation of behaviour was modified after World War II. See *The Behavior of Organisms* (New York: Appleton-Century, 1938; and *Walden Two* (New York: Macmillan, 1948). In contrast with the ethologists' close observation of animals, Skinner was satisfied to leave animals to themselves as they pressed levers in the Skinner Box, were rewarded, and their activities recorded on tickertape for analysis.

37 Roughly since World War II neither ethologists nor experimental psychologists have generally supported one-sided genetic or one-sided environmental interpretations of animal behaviour. William Thorpe showed that chaffinches acquire the rudiments of their song by instinct, but need to learn the greater part of it by listening to adults. In experimental psychology Harlow and others have shown that instinct and the environment need to interact in the rearing of young rhesus monkeys.

38 For a variety of viewpoints on such inferences see M. Von Cranach, *Methods of Inference from Animal to Human Behaviour* (The Hague: Mouton, 1976); in particular, K. Foppa, 'Comparative Implications of Learning Psychology', pp. 343–4, on the statistical difficulties of making generalisations from rats, mice and pigeons.

39 J. L. Gould, *Ethology: the Mechanisms and Evolution of Behaviour* (London: Norton, 1982) p. 541. For a criticism of Gould for his 'instinct-spotting' and a challenge to his oversimplifications, see T. J. Roper's review in *Animal Behaviour*, vol. 31, no. 3 (August 1983) p. 960.

40 See R. Descartes, *Philosophical Writings*, trans. E. Anscombe and P. Geach

(Sunbury-on-Thames: Nelson, 1970) p. 276. From 'Letters: Soul and Body'. To Descartes only humans had souls: being without souls, animals had no reason.

41 See note 15 above.

42 T. Hancock, *Essay on Instinct and its Physical and Moral Relations* (London: Phillips, 1824) p. 1.

43 C. Darwin, *The Descent of Man* (London: Watts, 1930) p. 85. Darwin was reporting the observation of Westropp, whom he called 'a well-known ethologist'. This view attracted much attention in the last century. See *The Animal World*, vol. 19, no. 220 (1 Jan. 1888).

44 L. T. Hobhouse, *Morals in Evolution: A Comparative Study of Ethics* (London: Chapman and Hall, 1906) p. 261.

45 J. Huxley, *Man in the Modern World*, p. 18.

46 See, for example, W. H. Thorpe, *Animal Nature and Human Nature* (London: Methuen, 1974) p. 301, with particular reference to communication, but applying also to 'many other instances'.

47 Instincts have a variable 'openness'. See M. Midgley, 'The Concept of Beastliness', in *Philosophy*, vol. 48, no. 184 (April 1973) p. 125.

48 R. Lewin, 'D.N.A. Reveals Surprises in Human Family Tree', in *Science*, no. 226 (1984) pp. 1179–83.

49 From the 'Second Meditation: Mind and Body', in *Philosophical Writings*, p. 69. Descartes was clearly not thinking of the comatose, who do not actively experience; or of the severely intellectually-handicapped, who may be totally unaware of their surroundings. For his ideas on the soul and consciousness, with perceptions of the intellect and inclinations of the will, see p. 276.

50 N. Tinbergen, *Animal Behaviour* (Amsterdam: Time-Life International, 1960) p. 14. See also I. Eibl-Eibesfeldt, *Love and Hate*, p. 6, where the author claims that statements about the emotions referring to either individual or social bonds between or among animals are 'fundamentally impossible for epistemological reasons'.

51 K. Lorenz in the Preface to C. Darwin, *The Expression of the Emotions in Man and Animals* (Chicago and London: University of Chicago Press, 1965) pp. xi–xii. For expressions supposedly showing our animal descent, see Darwin in ibid., pp. 237, 251.

52 C. Darwin, *The Descent of Man*, pp. 77–8.

53 E. C. Tolman, *Purposive Behavior in Animals and Man* (New York: Century, 1932) p. 217.

54 Voltaire, *Philosophical Dictionary*, selected and translated by H. T. Woolf (London: George Allen and Unwin, no date) p. 22. The reference is to 'Animals'. The original work is very long; 'Animals' is not always included in the various selections.

55 C. Darwin, *The Expression of the Emotions in Man and Animals*, p. 356. Descartes had no such doubts in his explanation of cognition and volition. See *Philosophical Writings*, p. 187.

56 W. D. M. Paton, *Man and Mouse*, pp. 17–18.

57 For a discussion of the concept of 'intention' see the author's *Justice, Morality and Education*, ch. 4, pp. 117–22. D. R. Griffin in *The Question of Animal Awareness* (New York: Rockefeller University Press, 1976) p. 44 refers to

ethologists' use of 'intention movements' in animals which give information about their probable future behaviour to other animals. See also Griffin's *Animal Thinking* (Cambridge, Mass.: Harvard University Press, 1984).

58 Aristotle, *History of Animals*, bk 8, 588ᵃ. Some psychologists have discerned a 'psychological continuity', e.g. J. L. Mackie, 'The Law of the Jungle', in *Philosophy*, vol. 53, no. 206 (Oct. 1978) p. 440. Mackie refers to an article on this subject by D. O. Hebb in *Psychological Review*, vol. 53 (1946) p. 104.

59 R. Seyforth, 'Vervet Monkey Alarm Calls: Semantic Communication in a Free-ranging Primate', in *Animal Behaviour*, vol. 28 (1980) p. 1070. The natural habitat was in the foothills of Mt Kilimanjaro, Kenya.

60 T. A. Sebeok (ed.), *How Animals Communicate* (Bloomington and London: Indiana University Press, 1977). On the possible hereditary basis of language see P. Lieberman, 'The Phylogeny of Language', in the above.

61 For recent research evidence see M. M. Bryden and R. J. Harrison (eds), *Research on Dolphins* (Oxford: Clarendon Press, 1986). Following Lilly, who believed that dolphins were as intelligent as humans, others made enthusiastic claims for the possibility of dolphins learning to talk. See W. F. Evans, *Communication in the Animal World* (New York: Crowell, 1968) p. 171.

62 See Carolyn Ristau and D. Robbins, 'Language in the Great Apes: A Critical Review', in *Advances in the Study of Behavior*, vol. 12 (1982) pp. 141–255. The authors refer to disagreements in the definition of language, 'although the capacity for a generative grammar and the meaning of a word and an utterance remain as central issues in most discussions' (p. 154). Animals may know *how* without knowing *that*.

63 For a review of recent research on play, see Paul Martin and T. M. Caro, 'Play in Behavioural Development', in *Advances in the Study of Behavior*, vol. 15 (1985) pp. 59–103.

64 Some of the more open studies in ethology stress the importance of long-term studies of social behaviour and organisation, and in natural habitats. See for example T. T. Struhsaker and L. Leland, 'Socioecology of Five Sympatric Monkey Species in the Kibale Forest, Uganda', in *Advances in the Study of Behavior*, vol. 9 (1979) pp. 166, 177.

65 Samuel Johnson, *The Idler and the Adventurer*, ed. W. J. Bate et al. (New Haven and London: Yale University Press, 1963) p. 75. From *The Idler*, no. 24 (30 Sept. 1758).

66 E. O. Wilson, *Sociobiology: The New Synthesis* (Cambridge, Mass., and London: Harvard University Press, 1975) p. 4. Wilson saw some hope for sociology and the other social sciences, as well as the humanities, for they are simply 'the last branches of biology to be included in the modern synthesis'.

67 For this and other experiments in infant deprivation with rhesus monkeys see H. F. Harlow, *Learning to Love* (New York: Ballantine Books, 1971).

68 See E. O. Wilson, *Sociobiology: The New Synthesis*, p. 562, for one such confusion.

69 It has had a fascination too for some philosophers. Michael Ruse, in *Sociobiology: Sense or Nonsense?* (Dordrecht, Boston and London: R. Reidel, 1979) p. 162, asserts his belief that sociobiology should be taken seriously because of evidence that 'some important social attitudes may well have significant genetic backing'. Peter Singer, in *The Expanding Circle: Ethics and*

Sociobiology (Oxford University Press, 1981) p. 81, believes too that 'the sociobiological explanation of the origin and development of ethics may well be right'.

70 The Preface to the first number of *Advances in the Study of Behavior* (1965), p. vii, indicated the diversity of research: 'descriptive and experimental studies of behavior under natural conditions, laboratory studies of the organization of behavior, analyses of neural and hormonal mechanisms of behavior, and studies of the development, genetics, and evolution of behavior . . .'. *Animal Behaviour* (formerly the *British Journal of Animal Behaviour*) also illustrates the wide-ranging studies of behaviour undertaken, from goal-specific and particularised stimulus-response measurements to broad observational studies of behaviour in social organisations. Some of the studies are ill-planned and lead to trivial or foregone conclusions, such as the effect of shade in summer on the behaviour of pigs (vol. X, no. 1, 1962, pp. 15–19); others emphasise clinical measurement such as that of heart rates (ibid., pp. 168–70).

CHAPTER 4

1 From Frances Power Cobbe, *The Modern Rack* (London: Swan Sonnenschein, 1889) p. 19. See p. 191 for illustration of a dog and a pig each firmly tied to a table (taken from Bernard's *Physiologie Opératoire*).

2 Rutherford's own account of his experiments is given in *British Medical Journal* (14 Dec. 1878) p. 861. Reported in *The Animal World*, vol. 11, no. 127 (1 April 1880) p. 63. Curare is a plant-derived paralytic drug used by South American Indians in blowpipes.

3 See *The RSPCA and the Royal Commission* (London: Smith, Elder, 1876) for accounts of such painful experiments: a dog starved for 72 hours (pp. 57–95); cats injected with arsenic (p. 64); a dog, injected with rabbit's blood to cause bloody urine, wasting to death (p. 65); rabbits starved and diabetes induced in them (p. 77); bone curvature induced in rabbits (p. 77). A 'Handbook for the Physiological Laboratory' was mentioned, designed for beginners, with elaborate instructions for conducting about 100 experiments.

4 Experiments reported in various biomedical, pharmacological and psychological journals. For references see J. Diner, *Test Tubes with Whiskers* (Chicago: National Anti-Vivisection Society, 1986) pp. 36–9.

5 At the Sleep Research Laboratory, University of Chicago, rats were put on a rotating disk over water. Those remaining on the disk suffered a 90% loss of sleep for up to 33 days. Rats either died during the experiment or were killed afterwards because of their condition. Autopsies showed stomach ulcers, internal bleeding, enlarged bladders, collapsed lungs etc. Reported in *Science*, no. 221 (1983) pp. 182–4.

6 Experiment at Head Injury Clinic Laboratory, University of Pennsylvania.

7 Recorded in *The Case Book of Experiments with Living Animals* (Jenkintown, Pa: American Anti-Vivisection Society, no date) pp. 19–20. The Noble-Collip drum has been in use for over 40 years. For the report of the

invention see R. L. Noble and J. B. Collip in *Quarterly Journal of Experimental Psychology*, vol. 31, no. 187 (1942).

8 Ibid., pp. 22–3. Reported by H. C. Brandt et al., *American Journal of Orthodontics*, vol. 75, no. 301 (1979).

9 M. L. Stephens, *Maternal Deprivation Experiments in Psychology: A Critique of Animal Models* (Jenkintown, Pa: American Anti-Vivisection Society, 1986) pp. 46–8. The description of the separation and its effects on mother and infant is from G. D. Jensen and C. W. Tolman, 'Mother-infant Relationship in the Monkey . . .', in *Journal of Comparative Physiology and Psychology*, vol. 55, pp. 131–6.

10 M. L. Stephens, ibid., pp. 48–9. On p. 84 references are given to Harlow and Suomi, who used the vertical chambers extensively.

11 See W. M. S. Russell and R. L. Burch, *The Principles of Humane Experimental Technique* (London: Methuen, 1959) pp. 18–24. Pain is described as one source of *distress*, which to physiologists is the inclusive term. The degree of distress of pain is 'a matter of central nervous analysis' (p. 19), carried to the brain by sensory nerve endings in the skin. The other main sources of distress in experiments are fear and conflict. Except in special conditions of primate societies, conflict states are believed never to persist in nature, when 'automatic mechanisms' operate. Under experimental conditions these natural mechanisms cannot function, so both fear and conflict are experienced. (For various interpretations of 'pain' and 'distress' see the Preface above.)

12 Two only of many experiments in electric shock avoidance and 'punishment'. From a submission to the United States Department of Agriculture on *Pain and Anesthesia: With Reference to the Improved Standards for Laboratory Animals Act of 1985* by the Animal Legal Defense Fund: see Part 3 of bibliography for journal references. See also Chapter 3, note 23.

13 See Part 2 of ibid. for references for the burn experiments and Part 4 for the acceleration experiment reference.

14 The 6 viewpoints are summarised in *The RSPCA and the Royal Commission*, Introduction, p. 1, as those of members of the society, all of whom were committed to the prevention of cruelty to animals 'and nothing else' (p. 1). Yet even among these there were signs of value conflict and doubt.

15 J. Bentham, *Works*, vol. 10, Correspondence, p. 549. From a letter to the *Morning Chronicle*, 4 March 1825.

16 Evidence by Sir Thomas Watson MD to the Royal Commission on Vivisection: 'Evidence of Witnesses', pp. 153–90. Published also in *Nature* (13 August 1875).

17 From Roswell C. McCrea, *The Humane Movement* (1910) pp. 125–6.

18 *The RSPCA and the Royal Commission*, p. 144.

19 Psychologists for the Ethical Treatment of Animals, *Position Papers by the Dozen* (Lewiston: 1985) p. 6. The group responsible for this publication comprises 'some 300 psychologists who share a common concern that psychology reexamine its treatment of research animals'. But there remain 'significantly divergent' views on the use of animals in research (Preface).

20 W. D. M. Paton, 'Animal Experiment and Medical Research: a Study in Evolution', in *Conquest*, no. 169 (Feb. 1979) pp. 3–6. *Conquest* is the journal of the Research Defence Society in the UK.

21 G. Lapage, *Achievement: Some Contributions of Animal Experiments to the Conquest of Disease* (Cambridge: W. Heffer, 1960) pp. 35, 37. The curare experiment is reported in *Anaesthesiology*, vol. 8, pp. 1–14.

22 W. W. Keen, *Animal Experimentation and Medical Progress* (Boston and New York: Houghton Mifflin, 1914) p. 3. In 1914 Keen was enthusiastic about Koller's discovery of cocaine, our nearest approach, he thought, 'to the ideal anaesthetic' (p. 10).

23 One of the sensitive areas exposed by the Medical Research Modernization Committee (MRMC) of the United States. See *Responding to the Media: Medical Research Question and Answer Handbook* (New York: no date) p. 6.

24 Ibid., p. 8. Different animal species may react differently to a specific drug, as they do in the case of thalidomide. Rats and mice are normally resistant to this drug, but in some pregnant animals the effects are teratogenic (literally 'monster producing').

25 A. Rowan, in *Of Mice, Models and Men* (Albany: State University of New York Press, 1984) p. 139, refers to 'the psychological paradox': 'the more suitable the animal is as a model of the human psyche, the greater should be the attention to the ethical issues relating to the research. The paradox boils down to this – the better the animal is as model of the human psyche, the more restricted its use should be.'

26 From an article by Robert Sharpe (former senior research fellow at the Royal Postgraduate Medical School in England) first published in the *Guardian*, 5 August 1982.

27 Ibid. Reference is made to R. W. Smithell: 'The extensive animal reproductive studies to which all new drugs are now subjected are more in the nature of a public relations exercise than a serious contribution to drug safety.'

28 For a criticism of the futility of some cancer research using animal models see Brandon Reines, *Cancer Research on Animals: Impact and Alternatives* (Chicago: National Anti-Vivisection Society, 1986) summarised in the Conclusion, pp. 103ff.

29 From a critique of animal models in cardiovascular research by Brandon Reines, *Heart Research on Animals* (Jenkintown, Pa: The American Anti-Vivisection Society, no date) p. 71. Each of the studies is appropriately documented.

30 For *motives* as part of a predispositional complex see the author's *Justice, Morality and Education*, pp. 115–22.

31 For example, cosmetics such as lipsticks, hair dyes and face powder may be tested by force feeding, using a tube into the stomach. Internal organs may be blocked or ruptured. In other cases the dose may be given by injections, application to the skin or inhalation. Test subjects are usually rats, mice, birds, rabbits or guinea pigs. Indications of suffering as the animals are poisoned are a variety of calls such as sharp screaming, tears, diarrhoea, convulsions, bleeding from the eyes or mouth, hunching of the back, shivering. The LD 50 test is now regarded by scientists as unreliable: results of tests may vary between species and according to many other test variables. Often they give little indication of the likely effect of the substance on a human being. The LD 50 test is one examined by A. Rowan in *Of Mice, Models and Men* (1984).

32 See A. Rowan, *The Draize Test – A Critique and Proposals for Alternatives* (Washington, DC: Humane Society of the US, 1980); and D. H. Smyth, *Alternatives to Animal Experiments* (London: Scolar Press, 1978) pp. 68ff.

33 *The RSPCA and the Royal Commission*, Introduction, p. viii.

34 Roswell C. McCrea, *The Humane Movement*, p. 123. Though a staunch supporter of the use of animals in research, D. H. Smyth, in *Alternatives to Animal Experiments*, noted the 'ingrained resistance of the majority of scientists to use alternative methods or even to allow them to become better known' (p. 151). In England the Research Defence Society (founded in 1908) aims to emphasise the importance of animal experiments to the welfare of mankind and 'to defend research workers in the medical, veterinary and biological sciences against attacks by anti-vivisectionists'. See Sir Henry Dale, *Humanity's Rising Debt to Medical Research* (London: Research Defence Society, 1955) p. 19.

35 Understandably the Taub case in the USA led a number of fellow researchers to react defensively. Taub was found guilty under the Maryland anti-cruelty statute of not giving adequate veterinary care to 6 of 17 monkeys he was using to study the effects of deafferentation. It was the first time a biomedical researcher had been prosecuted for cruelty to experimental animals. (Taub appealed twice before all convictions were finally overturned.)

36 In 1982 one large animal-breeding company in the USA returned a profit of $41 million from the sale of animals for research.

37 Investigators of the Humane Society of the United States discovered in one dealer's kennel (in 1984) decaying bodies of 37 dogs and cats that had died of starvation. Another 87 were barely alive. The dealer saw no reason for the commotion: the victims, he said, were 'just animals'. See *The Animal Slave Trade: Brutality on the Road to Research* (Washington, DC: The Humane Society of the United States, 1985).

38 The American Anti-Vivisection Society, *The Case Book of Experiments with Living Animals*, p. 35. Tasks performed by the primates were to simulate those of a pilot of a strategic bomber and in an environment similar to that of an operational mission. See pp. 35–7 for other experiments at an airforce base in the USA.

39 'Programme for Action', in *Mobilisation for Laboratory Animals* (London: no date). Reported from I. V. Allen et al., in *Acta Neuropathologica*, vol. 59 (1983) pp. 277–82. *Mobilisation* was formed recently to oppose the British Government's White Paper proposals 'Scientific Procedures on Living Animals', intended as a basis for amending the 1876 Cruelty to Animals Act.

40 For 'intentions' see the author's *Justice, Morality and Education*, pp. 117–22.

41 From data collected by Psychologists for the Ethical Treatment of Animals in *Position Papers . . .*, p. 22. Deprivation studies with infant primates were initiated by H. Harlow.

42 For a discussion of the repetition and futility of deprivation studies with infant primates, see M. L. Stephens, *Maternal Deprivation Experiments in Psychology: a Critique of Animal Models*, pp. 38–9.

43 Ibid., pp. 39–40. Over 1300 animals (mostly primates) had been used in deprivation experiments up to this time in the USA. Most suffered long-

term psychological disturbances. Some suffered physical injuries and some were killed (p. 40).

44 Medical Research Modernization Committee, *Responding to the Media*, p. 4. Similarly there were found to have been 500 studies of the effects of cocaine on animals and 38 000 experiments on radiation-induced cancer, when substantial data existed already from human studies.

45 *The RSPCA and the Royal Commission*, Introduction, p. xvi. It was claimed about the same time that researchers should be prosecuted 'if it can be shown that their experiments are carried on for the mere purpose of demonstrating over again what has been sufficiently demonstrated already . . .' *The Animal World*, vol. 5, no. 56 (1 May 1874) p. 76.

46 J. Swain, *Brutes and Beasts*, p. 214.

47 Robert Sharpe, article first published in the *Guardian*, 7 August 1980. The author's opinion is that there is no suitable animal model for testing weak carcinogens. In testing for teratogenicity (capacity to produce malformations in offspring) the indifference of scientists to the suffering of animals is aggravated by politicians' insistence that tests be conducted on animals to allay the fears of the public. Sharpe points out that there seems to be no reliable way to predict whether a new drug, tested on animals, will cause foetal malformations in human offspring (p. 3). See notes 24 and 27 above.

48 For documented instances of such experiments, see Animal Legal Defense Fund, Submission to the US Department of Agriculture, p. 12 for deceleration experiments; pp. 30–3 and 98 for burns; p. 43 for sleep deprivation; p. 98 for effects of addictive drugs.

49 M. A. Giannelli, 'Three Blind Mice, See How They Run: a Critique of Behavioral Research With Animals', in *Advances in Animal Welfare Science*, 1985–6, eds M. W. Fox and L. D. Mickley (Washington, DC: The Humane Society of the United States, 1986) p. 135.

50 H. Harlow is reported as confessing that his only interest in experimenting with animals was to use them as a means to getting something published, adding his dislike of animals including cats, dogs and monkeys. Ibid., p. 134. Quoted by Giannelli from D.Pratt, *Painful Experiments on Animals* (New York: Argus Archives, 1976) p. 164. It is simply not known what proportion of researchers share Harlow's attitude to animals; his unguarded comment was at least candid.

51 In the UK it has been estimated that about 18 000 licensed medicinal products were marketed in 1980, containing 3000 active ingredients; most are not necessary for health. (The WHO estimate of the number of drugs essential for health is about 200.) See 'Programme for Action', in *Mobilisation for Laboratory Animals*, last page (unnumbered).

52 For a vigorous condemnation of behavioural psychologists for their use of negative reinforcement, see B. E. Rollin, *Animal Rights and Human Morality* (New York: Prometheus Books, 1981) p. 126.

53 This three-sided interpretation of alternatives is influenced by W. M. S. Russell and R. L. Burch, *The Principles of Humane Experimental Technique* (London: Methuen, 1959). Their '3Rs' refer first to the *replacement* of living higher animals with insentient material (pp. 69–104); second to the *reduction* in numbers of animals used (pp. 105–33); third to *refinement* of procedures to decrease inhumanity to animals (pp. 134–53). The first of

the three is influenced by D. H. Smyth in *Alternatives to Animal Experiments*, p. 165, in which he illustrates 'true' alternatives and distinguishes them from others which merely provide supplementary information.

54 D. H. Smyth, ibid., p. 166. From a scientific standpoint tissue cultures are most advantageous for some purposes such as vaccine production because of the standardisation of the test material and the relatively short time needed.

55 For example, from foetuses following therapeutic abortions; from stillborn infants or those dying soon after birth; from individual cancer patients for the testing of drugs likely to be individually effective in treatment. Organ cultures may be grown from heart tissue obtainable from heart transplant patients; tumour tissue from lung, skin or intestine. For an explanation of tissue cultures derived from the kidneys of monkeys (necessitating their death), see D. Pratt, *Alternatives to Pain in Experiments on Animals*, pp. 192–4.

56 The Ames test is one of the most extensively used of the in vitro methods, to test for carcinogenicity in chemicals as well as for structural genetic effects in the tissue material.

57 For example, the CAT scan quickly projects on a computer screen small slices of the brain or other organs and is able to detect tiny lesions. The PET scan is useful mainly in research: it too projects onto a computer screen small slices of the brain, using isotypes, showing biochemical changes occurring during brain activity. The NMR scan uses a magnetic field to generate images which are projected onto a screen with the aid of a computer: it is used to detect stroke in humans and disorders such as metabolic diseases, scanning for hydrogen in the body. A further development of the NMR can detect sodium, whose presence can indicate dead tissue.

58 Epidemiology grew out of large-scale studies of infectious diseases. It was applied first to the study of epidemics, but has now been extended to diseases such as cancer which do not involve infection, as well as other diseases and conditions such as malnutrition.

59 Judgements of experts are sometimes biased towards techniques of known effectiveness, with respect to some other biomedical purposes.

60 'Programme for Action', in *Mobilisation for Laboratory Animals*. The authors refer to several relevant articles, such as to the proceedings of the Draize Test Workshop in Zurich, April 1984, published in *Food and Chemical Technology*, vol. 23, no. 2 (1985).

61 G. Zbinden and M. Flury-Roversi, 'Significance of the LD 50 Test for the Toxicological Evaluation of Chemical Substances', in *Archives of Toxicology*, vol. 47 (Springer-Verlag, 1981) pp. 77–99.

62 Some believe that instruction of students in experimental procedures causing animal suffering may dull their sensibilities in future research. See J. A. Kelly, 'Alternatives to Aversive Procedures With Animals in the Psychology Teaching Setting', from M. W. Fox and L. D. Mickley (eds), *Advances in Animal Welfare Science, 1985–6*, pp. 167–8.

63 There are already a number of data banks, especially in the USA, such as MEDLARS, AGRIS, BIOSIS, TOXLINE, CAIN. France has PASCAL and the UK has CAB.

64 By contrast, D. H. Smyth's approach is one-sidedly scientific: 'The deciding

factor in every case will be the scientific demonstration that the alternative method is better for the particular problem than the animal method.' *Alternatives to Animal Experiments*, p. 166.

65 The international congress was held at the Crystal Palace in 1863 to discuss cruelty to animals in general, but with the specific purpose as stated.

66 These and other points are made in *The RSPCA and the Royal Commission*, Introduction. p. xvi. They constituted articles of a proposed Bill.

67 For example, Certificate B gave the experimenter the right to defer killing an animal before it recovers from an anaesthetic if he certified that by so doing the object of the experiment would be frustrated.

68 The injection of sterile water into a mouse to demonstrate a technique to students is held as not 'calculated to cause pain' and so to be permissible. On the other hand, the inoculation of guinea pigs with material that may be tuberculous *is* calculated to cause pain because it may interfere with the animal's health; therefore it comes within the Act. See the Research Defence Society, *Notes on the Law on Animals in Great Britain (The Act of 1876)*, 2nd edn (London: no date) p. 4.

69 At the time of writing before both Houses of Parliament, the Bill was introduced in November 1985.

70 RSPCA, *162nd Annual Report* (Horsham: 1986) p. 43.

71 For example, para. 298 of the Littlewood Report states, 'we suggested that the Act should be based on the concept of preventing unnecessary suffering' and that effective precautions should be taken 'to prevent or reduce to a minimum any pain or other distress or discomfort in the animals used'. But what is 'unnecessary suffering' and what is a 'minimum'? At what point can an experimenter perceive that pain is 'enduring' if he were to follow the precept that 'in no case shall any animal be subjected to severe pain which endures or is likely to endure'? The Littlewood Report lapsed, without government attention. A similar fate had been the Royal Commission's of 1906, set up to review criticism of the 1876 Act. The 1876 Act has remained unamended to the time of writing (see note 69 above).

72 This criticism is widely levelled at the 1966 Act. See Christine Stevens, 'Mistreatment of Laboratory Animals Endangers Biomedical Research', in *Nature*, vol. 311 (27 Sept. 1984).

73 In 1882 the President of the American Society for the Prevention of Cruelty to Animals wrote that 'probably thousands, and possibly tens of thousands of dogs and other animals are now being subjected to experiments; and there are no laws in this country which can effectively prevent incompetent and irresponsible persons from thus inflicting upon as many of these creatures as they can obtain useless suffering and torture'. *The Animal World*, vol. 13, no. 148 (2 Jan. 1882) p. 7.

74 Biomedical researchers have themselves set up their own codes of practice which acknowledge most of the objections raised to the use of animals. In Australia there is the National Health and Medical Research Council code, known in combined form as the NH & MRC/CSIRO/AAC Code of Practice. In addition there is an active Committee of the Australian Biomedical Societies on Animal Experimentation, which comprises a membership of 10 separate societies.

CHAPTER 5

1 For the distinction between the common interest and the common good see the author's *Conservation and Practical Morality*, ch. 1, pp. 16–18.
2 Aristotle, *Politics*, trans. Benjamin Jowett, bk 3, ch. 6, 1279ᵃ. See the *Republic* for Plato's views.
3 See I. Kant, *The Analytic of Pure Practical Reason*, in *Critique of Practical Reason and Other Works on the Theory of Ethics*, pp. 131–2. With a 'supersensible nature' rational beings obey laws 'which are independent on every empirical condition, and therefore belong to the *autonomy* of pure reason' (p. 132). See chapter 2 above, note 2.
4 See, for instance, J. Austin, *The Province of Jurisprudence Determined*, ed. H. A. L. Hart (London: Weidenfeld and Nicolson, 1954) p. 126. (First published 1832.)
5 H. Kelsen, *General Theory of Law and State* (Cambridge, Mass.: Harvard University Press, 1946) p. 18.
6 H. A. L. Hart, *The Concept of Law* (Oxford: Clarendon Press, 1961) pp. 80–8.
7 Ibid., pp. 181–2.
8 In *A Theory of Justice* (Oxford University Press, 1972) p. 364, John Rawls defines civil disobedience as 'a public, non-violent, conscientious yet political act contrary to law usually done with the aim of bringing about a change in the law or policies of the government'.
9 Statutes are the enactments of legislatures (or other law-making bodies). Though 'common law' is now used variously, its usual sense is of law derived from custom and tradition – 'unwritten law' in contrast with the 'written law' of statutes. 'The law' is used here and in other contexts to refer to statutes, unless common law is specified.
10 C. D. Niven, *History of the Humane Movement*, p. 61. Despite the derision, Martin's anti-cruelty Bill passed the Lords in 1822.
11 H. Salt, *Animals' Rights Considered in Relation to Social Progress*, revised edn (London: G. Bell, 1922) p. 90.
12 Although Bentham affirmed that whether the law is good or bad it has to be obeyed, he still believed that legislators should take a moral stand on some issues such as animal suffering. In *Principles of Penal Law*, pt 3, ch. 17, he asked, 'Why should the law refuse its protection to any sensitive being?' *Works*, vol. 1, p. 562.
13 'Ouida', *Critical Studies* (1900) p. 253.
14 *The Public General Acts etc.* (London: HMSO, 1911) ch. 27, *Protection of Animals Act*. The Act protected animals in other ways, such as by prohibiting the fighting or baiting of animals (s.1). The Act of 1835 had already protected dogs and outlawed bear-baiting, badger-hunting, bull-baiting, dogfights and cockfights, but enforcement was difficult. The 1835 Act gave dogs protection from wanton and cruel beating, but they were used as draught animals until the practice was banned by the *Protection of Animals Act 1911* (s.9).
15 The Humane Society of the United States estimated that in 1984 in the USA alone 22 million animals were trapped, mostly in the steel-jaw trap.

Nevada requires traps to be inspected only once in 7 days; some states set a period of 3 days or 72 hours. The *Protection of Animals Act 1911* stated that traps for rabbits or hares had to be inspected at least once a day, between sunrise and sunset (s.10).

16 Helicopters are used in some countries for killing deer. The US Congress has prohibited the use of aircraft or motor vehicles 'to hunt, for the purpose of capturing or killing, any wild unbranded horse, mare, colt, or burro running at large on any of the public lands or ranges . . .' (8 Sep. 1959, 73, Stat. 70) US Code, 1976 edn, vol. 4, title 18, ch. 3, p. 1018. Yet the government funds projects to round up wild horses and burros by helicopter in the Nevada desert and elsewhere. *Mainstream*, vol. 18, no. 1 (Winter 1987) p. 132.

17 In 1903 California banned the 'bristle bur' or 'tack bur' implanted under a horse's hoof to make it lift its legs high. (See Roswell C. McCrea, *The Humane Movement*, p. 234.) More recently other means have been used in the training of performing horses such as the Tennessee Walking Horses, though banned by federal law in 1970.

18 S. I. Benn, 'Persons and Values: Reasons in Conflict and Moral Disagreement', in *Ethics*, vol. 95, no. 1 (Oct. 1984) p. 37. (The author was not considering cruelty to animals.) See also Chapter 3 above, note 7.

19 R. Pound, *Social Control Through Law* (New Haven: Yale University Press, 1942) pp. 64–5.

20 Ruth Harrison, *Animal Machines: The New Factory Farming Industry*, p. 3.

21 By 1986–7 the only significant improvement in factory farming in the UK has been that veal calves are now mostly raised in straw-bedded housing instead of the individual veal crates. Only 10% of producers now use the individual veal crate. (Compassion in World Farming, Petersfield, Hampshire.)

22 Halsbury's *Statutes of England* (London: Butterworths) vol. 41, pp. 84ff.

23 Ibid., vol. 43: continuation volume 1973 (London: Butterworths, 1974). The *Wildlife and Countryside (Amendment) Act 1985* makes it more difficult for an offender to escape prosecution if he is found attempting to dig or to take badgers, but the landowner is still protected. See continuation binder 1985, vol. 2, p. 167.

24 *The Public General Acts etc. 1911*.

25 Australian states have generally legislated against live animal coursing. See *The Statutes of Western Australia*, vol. 2 (Perth: 1976) p. 790, referring to Act no. 84 amending the *Prevention of Cruelty to Animals Act 1920*.

26 By 1984 the United Nations Law of the Sea Convention (UNCLOS) had 134 signatories; leadership by the USA might have led to more effective prevention of unnecessary suffering to sea mammals and birds.

27 See *China Reconstructs*, vol. 33, no. 1 (Jan. 1984) p. 3 for tourists hunting in China. See also Chapter 1 above, note 55.

28 Five persons were arrested for trespassing at the University of Arizona recently; their purpose was to make the public more aware of the suffering of laboratory animals prior to and during experiments. University administrators who had refused to have a lay person on the Animal Care Committee changed their minds and appointed the director of the local humane society to the committee. Reported in *Peta News* (Washington, DC: People for the Ethical Treatment of Animals, no date) pp. 7–8.

29 For the current situation in Mexico see J. Praded, *WSPA in Latin America* (Jamaica Plain: World Society for the Protection of Animals, 1985) p. 20. See also pp. 18–19 for the situation in Colombia.

30 *ASPCA Report* vol. 6, no. 2 (New York: The American Society for the Prevention of Cruelty to Animals, 1986) pp. 2, 15.

31 In the USA raids on cockfighting premises are made by the ASPCA and other bodies; see ibid., p. 11. The *162nd Annual Report* of the RSPCA, 1985, reported a case of organised dogfighting in England (p. 16) and also cockfighting and dogfighting at a remote farm (p. 19). A number of dogfight rings have been exposed by the Humane Society of the United States. Since 1975, 29 states have legislated to declare dogfighting a felony offence. The Humane Society of the United States, *Close-up Report: Dog-fighters on the Run* (1986). In 1987 there were reports of illegal dogfighting and cockfighting in the UK, as well as of pitting dogs against badgers.

32 Halsbury's *Statutes of England*, vol. 2, p. 257.

33 S. Smiles, *Duty*, pp. 401, 404–5. Smiles reflected: 'How much time is spent in cramming children with useless knowledge, and how little is spent in teaching them useful humanity.'

34 See the author's *Justice, Morality and Education* for the formal notion of education, pp. 3–7, 295–300; and *Conservation and Practical Morality*, pp. 146–8. The viewpoint is based on Aristotle's notion of 'becoming' (*Politics*, trans. B. Jowett, bk 8, ch. 1, 1342^b).

35 Halsbury's *Statutes of England*, vol. 2, p. 260. Does not apply to Northern Ireland.

36 Ibid., p. 274. Other minor operations listed are the castration of a male animal, the dehorning of cattle and the disbudding of calves (except by means of chemical cauterisation within the first week of life).

37 Ibid., p. 267. Does not apply to Northern Ireland.

38 *The Public General Acts etc. 1911*, Ch. 50: *Coal Mines Act*, Third Schedule, p. 309. This schedule amplifies sections 86 and 109. The Act refers mainly to the protection of miners; animals are relegated to an appendage – hence the numbering of items.

39 The RSPCA suspected that brutal methods of slaughtering were often used. *The Animal World*, vol. 18 (1887), Report of the Annual Meeting, p. 124.

40 Halsbury's *Statutes of England*, vol. 44, continuation volume 1974 (London: Butterworths, 1975) pt 2, p. 255. the Act does not apply to slaughtering according to Jewish or Moslem practices.

41 *Laws of Minnesota*, vols 1 and 2 (1983). Illustrations from vol. 2, ch. 358 – S.F. no. 682.

42 The Act defined 'abuse' as 'intentionally causing unnecessary pain, suffering, or unjustifiable injury or death' (s.2(3)); and 'neglect' as 'failure to provide the minimum care required for the health and well-being' of the animal (s.2(5)). *Laws of Minnesota*, 1981. The Revisor Bill amended certain sections of Minnesota Statutes, 1980.

43 *Laws of Minnesota*, 1981, ch. 22, S.F. no. 345.

44 *Laws of Minnesota*, 1981, Revisor Bill. See 346.34 for specification of greasing or oiling of pigs and the throwing of chickens or turkeys in the air for capture.

45 See J. Brookland et al., *Injury, Damage to Health and Cruel Treatment*, for

cruelties which have made this agreement necessary. Ironically the Interim Convention on the Conservation of North Pacific Fur Seals has led to serious reduction in numbers: whereas the USA agrees to conduct the seal killing on the Pribilof Islands, distributing the pelts between itself, Canada and Japan, Russia agrees to control a similar killing programme in its territory and distributes the pelts similarly.

46 See note 11 above.

47 D. Lyons, *Ethics and the Rule of Law* (Cambridge University Press, 1984) p. 61.

48 See *The RSPCA and the Royal Commission* and Chapter 4, notes 3, 14, 33, 45. Also *The Animal World*, vol. 5, no. 56 (1 May 1874).

49 Some of the major recommendations have been reported in Chapter 4 above.

50 For an instance of instruction of group members in legislative strategy, see J. Beggs, 'Taking Sides: Westminster Unravelled, A Brief Guide to the Passage of a Bill Through Parliament', in *Liberator* (British Union for the Abolition of Vivisection) Dec. 1984–Jan. 1985, p. 11.

51 *Mainstream*, vol. 17, no. 1 (Winter 1986) p. 23.

52 See the Legislative Report in ibid., pp. 14–15, and in vol. 17, no. 2 (Spring 1986) pp. 17–18. On p. 18 a Legislative Worksheet shows at a glance what legislation is finally enacted and what is still in Committees.

53 Expression used by The American Fund for Alternatives to Animal Research in *News Abstracts*, Spring 1986, p. 4.

54 *ASPCA Report*, Summer 1986, p. 3. The Act required that an information service be set up partly to prevent duplication of experiments; that there be public representation on animal care committees; and that animal care personnel be trained. The information service (established in the National Agricultural Library in co-operation with the National Library of Medicine) is also to provide information on alternatives to laboratory animals and information for the instruction of scientists and other personnel in humane practices now required by law.

55 From *Fur Age Weekly*, 11 June 1984 (Society for Animal Protective Legislation) in C. Stevens, 'Statement in Support of H.R. 1797 To End The Use of the Steel-jaw Leghold Trap Before the Subcommittee on Health and the Environment', p. 3.

56 The Society for Animal Protective Legislation has lobbied for the *Humane Slaughter Act 1958* referring to anaesthetisation, mechanical or electrical instant stunning prior to slaughter; the *Wild Horse Act 1959* prohibiting poisoning of waterholes used for drinking by wild horses and burros; the *Laboratory Animal Welfare Act 1966* setting minimum standards of care and housing of dogs, cats, primates and other animals; the *Animal Welfare Act 1970* prohibiting the soring of Tennessee Walking Horses for show purposes; the *Animal Welfare Act 1976* requiring carriers, intermediate handlers and animal brokers to adhere to humane standards; and the previously mentioned *Improved Standards for Laboratory Animals Act 1985*.

57 This world society has made a submission to the Royal Commission on Sealing in Toronto, Canada, and has continued to lobby members of the European Parliament in denouncing bullfighting.

58 See M. A. Giannelli, 'Three Blind Mice, See How They Run: a Critique of

Behavioral Research with Animals', in *Advances in Animal Welfare Science, 1985–6*, p. 148.

59 Experiments conducted in the Head Injury Clinical Research Laboratory at the medical school of the University of Pennsylvania. In a tape produced from the medical school's own videotapes, which had been stolen, researchers' attitudes to animal suffering were exposed as boyish, flippant, totally unconcerned (*Animal Law Reporter*, Winter 1984–5). Confirmation has been obtained from other sources giving the author excerpts from the tape. The University of Pennsylvania suspended its long-running research into the nature of severe and often irreversible brain damage in Sept. 1985 and reprimanded the researchers.

60 See M. L. Stephens, *Maternal Deprivation Experiments in Psychology: A Critique of Animal Models*, p. 21, for reference to an article by H. F. Harlow in B. M. Foss (ed.), *The Determinants of Infant Behavior* (New York: Wiley, 1963) pp. 3–33.

61 W. Fleming, in *A Manual of Moral Philosophy* (London: John Murray, 1867) p. 75, argued that 'children always passionately interest themselves on that side where kindness and humanity are found; and detest the cruel, the covetous, the selfish, or the treacherous'. But the effects of habitual cruelty gave concern to one writer in *The Animal World*, vol. 15, no. 183 (1 Dec. 1884) p. 178; and another observed, p. 40: 'Children laugh at the miseries they inflict on unfortunate animals. All savages are ingenious in contriving, and happy in executing most exquisite tortures.'

62 E. G. Fairholme and W. Paine, in *A Century of Work for Animals*, p. 159, claimed success in the RSPCA's educational work and noted that, by 1924, 28 of the states of the USA had passed laws for the regular teaching of kindness to animals. The RSPCA had supplementary methods, such as lectures, prizes, nature books and lantern lectures. A children's group was formed called the Band of Mercy. The USA formed a similar group in 1882. At this time humanitarian leaders believed that education is 'the indispensable condition of humanitarian progress' (H. Salt, *Animals' Rights Considered in Relation to Social Progress*, pp. 82, 86). In the first number of *The Animal World* (1 Oct. 1869) the RSPCA expressed its aims as: 'to protect animals from torture and to ameliorate their condition, and to awaken in the minds of men a proper sense of the claims of creatures under their dominion', p. 8. It had confidence especially in its *own* lecturers. In New York State, early in this century, compulsory humane education in schools was not considered effective: 'it is thought that many of the teachers have no particular training or interest and it is feared that any work done would be entirely perfunctory' (F. Morse Hubbard, *Prevention of Cruelty to Animals in New York State*, p. 29).

63 See the author's *Justice, Morality and Education*, pp. 137–40, 181–2.

64 The case is reported in The Anti-Vivisection Society *Bulletin*, Fall–Winter 1985, pp. 12–14.

65 RSPCA, *162nd Annual Report*, pp. 39–40. In 1985, 4600 people attended Mallydams or heard talks. The centre treated 400 animals in a single year, including oiled seabirds, injured badgers and foxes. Most importantly it invited the public to an Open Day. The ASPCA (USA) similarly provides school programmes with lectures, discussions, films and other visual aids,

visits with animals. It coordinates workshops on issues such as factory farming, animal experimentation, trapping.

66 *Prefaces by Bernard Shaw* (London: Constable, 1934). See 'Killing for Sport', 1914, pp. 139–48.

67 The *Animal Welfare Institute Quarterly*, vol. 34, no. 3 (Fall 1985) reported widespread improper use of animals in elementary, junior and high school competitions. In 1984–5 there were 14 local, regional and national science fairs, and deficiencies in humane standards were found in each. Some allegedly disregard the humane rules laid down by the National Science Teachers Association and endorsed by the National Academy of Sciences.

68 One such case is reported in the National Anti-Vivisection Society *Bulletin*, Fall–Winter 1985, p. 9.

69 As a campaign weapon 'animal rights' language is likely to be much more effective than 'moral duty' or 'moral debt'. 'Animal rights' fits politically into a framework of other rights demands; it is a successful pragmatic tool.

70 See Voltaire, *Philosophical Dictionary*, under 'Contradictions', p. 83: 'I know only two kinds of immutable beings on the earth, mathematicians and animals; they are led by two invariable rules, demonstration and instinct: and even the mathematicians have had some disputes, but the animals have never varied.'

71 M. de Montaigne, *A Book of Good Faith*, selections from the *Works* by Gerald Bullett (London: Watts, 1938) p. 55.

72 W. D. M. Paton, *Man and Mouse*, p. 134. The evidence adduced in Chapter 4 above does not convincingly support the claim that severe pain is 'very rare, partly because scientists are as humane as anyone else'. Some scientists are concerned about reducing pain in particular situations lest it should 'destroy the effectiveness of the experiment'.

73 See Peter Singer, in *In Defence of Animals* (Oxford: Basil Blackwell, 1985) p. 8. When a philosopher himself has a committed viewpoint, or a committed scientist attempts to explain a philosophical position, the limited impartiality is sometimes apparent. For example, C. Cohen, 'The Case for the Use of Animals in Biomedical Research', in *The New England Journal of Medicine*, no. 14, vol. 315 (2 Oct. 1986) p. 867, in the assertion of the superior moral standing of humans; and J. A. Stone, 'Man and Other Animals', in *Proceedings of the Australian Physiological and Pharmacological Society*, vol. 16, no. 2 (1985) pp. 56–7, in an apparent misunderstanding of impartiality in Peter Singer's illustration.

74 J. Locke, *Some Thoughts Concerning Education*, ed. R. H. Quick (Cambridge University Press, 1898) sect. 33, p. 21. (First published 1693.)

75 Successful vaccines from animal experiments include those for prevention of poliomyelitis, which had killed or crippled many thousands before the vaccine's development in the 1950s; rubella; hepatitis B; diphtheria; tuberculosis; measles; yellow fever; tetanus and smallpox. Significant antibiotics have been discovered, such as penicillin. Snake and spider antivenes have been prepared, drugs for the treatment of ulcers, high blood pressure, asthma and cancer in some of its forms. Anaesthetics have been developed and insulin for the treatment of diabetes. Animal experimentation has led to organ transplants such as the kidney, and to dialysis for kidney failure; to open heart surgery and artificial pacemakers

for hearts; to micro-surgery used to restore severed limbs and fingers; to various emergency techniques used in hospitals for treatment of casualty patients and those in intensive care and coronary care. Because of the complexity of living organisms, scientific problems cannot always be solved in isolated parts (Paton, *Man and Mouse*, pp. 87–8). Relevant factors are the complicated nature of the blood itself, the fact that some tissues undergo biochemical transformations affecting the whole body, the body's power of adaptation. 'It is the whole body that gives us our greatest chance of seeing the unexpected' (p. 88). Paton sees the need for continued animal experimentation to prevent suffering from 'chronic neurological illnesses, schizophrenia, senile dementia, most forms of cancer, congenital deformity, deafness, blindness, arthritis, and anti-immune diseases . . .' (p. 71). AIDS and hepatitis non-A and non-B pose threats in many countries. Certain drugs used in human and veterinary medicine require improvement, and new drugs are needed for particular problems. (It was not until the drug cyclosporin was developed and tested on animals that programmes of heart and liver transplants could be resumed with confidence.) New drugs are needed when bacteria are found to become resistant to existing antibiotics. Animals are still needed for the testing of chemicals for toxicity, unless humans are to be put at high risk.

76 RSPCA, *162nd Annual Report*, p. 42. Badgers were in fact given better protection. For the relevant Bill see note 23 above. At the Report Stage there was discussion among various groups in order to give badgers greater protection in their setts without interfering with the interests of 'field sportsmen', which were considered legitimate.

77 For an account of the qualities and responsibilities of such persons, see the author's *Conservation and Practical Morality*, pp. 159–64, in reference to national commissions.

78 H. Sidgwick, *Practical Ethics: A Collection of Addresses and Essays* (London: Swan Sonnenschein, 1898) p. 19.

79 J. Locke, *Some Thoughts Concerning Education* (Cambridge University Press, 1898) section 37, p. 23; sections 116 and 117, pp. 101–2: 'Children should from the beginning be bred up in an Abhorrence of *killing* or tormenting any living Creature'. As for men, he noted in section 1 that 'nine parts of ten are what they are, good or evil, useful or not, by their education'.

80 Samuel Butler, *Erewhon*, revised edn 1901 (London: Dent, 1932 & 1959) ch. 26: 'The Views of an Erewhonian Prophet Concerning the Rights of Animals', p. 166.

Select Bibliography

BOOKS AND COLLECTED WORKS

Aristotle, *History of Animals*, trans. D'Arcy Wentworth Thompson.

Aristotle, *Politics*, trans. B. Jowett.

Austin, J., *The Province of Jurisprudence Determined*, ed. A. L. Hart (London: Weidenfeld and Nicolson, 1954).

Beattie, J., *Elements of Moral Science* (Edinburgh: Constable, 1817).

Bentham, J., *Works* (Edinburgh: William Tait, 1843).

Bradley, F. H., *Ethical Studies*, 2nd edn (London: Oxford University Press, 1927).

Brown, A., *Who Cares for Animals?* (London: Heinemann, 1974).

Brown, L. M., *Justice, Morality and Education* (London: Macmillan, 1985).

Brown, L. M., *Conservation and Practical Morality* (London: Macmillan, 1987).

Bryden, M. M., and R. J. Harrison (eds), *Research on Dolphins* (Oxford: Clarendon Press, 1986).

Calderwood, H., *Handbook of Moral Philosophy*, 6th edn (London: Macmillan, 1879).

Carson, G., *Men, Beasts and Gods* (New York: Charles Scribner's Sons, 1972).

Dale, H., *Humanity's Rising Debt to Medical Research* (London: Research Defence Society, 1955).

Darwin, C., *The Descent of Man* (London: Watts, 1930).

Darwin, C., *The Expression of the Emotions in Man and Animals* (Chicago and London: University of Chicago Press, 1965).

Descartes, R., *Philosophical Writings*, trans. E. Anscombe and P. Geach (Sunbury-on-Thames: Nelson, 1970).

Eibl-Eibesfeldt, I., *Ethology: The Biology of Behaviour*, trans. E. Klinghammer (New York: Holt, Rinehart & Winston, 1970).

Eibl-Eibesfeldt, I., *Love and Hate*, trans. G. Strachan (London: Methuen, 1971).

Fairholme, E. G., and W. Paine, *A Century of Work for Animals: The History of the RSPCA 1824–1924* (London: John Murray, 1924).

Fleming, W., *A Manual of Moral Philosophy* (London: John Murray, 1867).

Fowler, T., *Progressive Morality: An Essay in Ethics* (London and New York: Macmillan, 1895).

Fox, M. W., and L. D. Mickley (eds), *Advances in Animal Welfare Science, 1985–6* (Washington, DC: The Humane Society of the United States, 1986).

Fraser, A. F., *Farm Animal Behaviour* (University of Edinburgh, 1974).

Gould, J. L., *Ethology: the Mechanisms and Evolution of Behaviour* (London: Norton, 1982).

Griffin, D. R., *The Question of Animal Awareness* (New York: Rockefeller University Press, 1976).

Guthrie, W. K. C., *A History of Greek Philosophy* (Cambridge University Press, 1962).

Hancock, T., *Essay on Instinct and its Physical and Moral Relations* (London: Phillips, 1824).

Hare, R. M., *Moral Thinking: Its Levels, Method and Point* (Oxford: Clarendon Press, 1981).

Harlow, H. F., *Learning to Love* (New York: Ballantine Books, 1971).

Harrison, R., *Animal Machines: The New Factory Farming Industry* (London: Vincent Stuart, 1964).

Hart, H. A. L., *The Concept of Law* (Oxford: Clarendon Press, 1961).

Hobbes, T., *Leviathan* (Harmondsworth: Penguin Books, 1968.)

Hobhouse, L. T., *Morals in Evolution: A Comparative Study of Ethics* (London: Chapman and Hall, 1906).

Holbach, P. H., *The System of Nature, or The Laws of the Moral and Physical World*, 3rd edn (London: Sherwood, Neeby and Jones, 1817).

Hubbard, F. M., *Prevention of Cruelty to Animals in the States of Illinois, Colorado and California* (New York: Columbia University, 1916).

Hubbard, F. M., *Prevention of Cruelty to Animals in New York State* (New York: Columbia University, 1915).

Hume, D. A., *A Treatise of Human Nature*, ed. L. A. Selby-Bigge (Oxford: Clarendon Press, 1888).

Hume, D. A., *Enquiries Concerning Human Understanding and Concerning the Principles of Morals*, 3rd edn, ed. L. A. Selby-Bigge (Oxford University Press, 1975).

Huxley, J., *Man in the Modern World* (London: Chatto and Windus, 1947).

Johnson, Samuel, *The Idler and the Adventurer*, ed. W. J. Bate et al. (New Haven and London: Yale University Press, 1963).

Kant, I., *Critique of Practical Reason and Other Works on the Theory of Ethics*, trans. T. K. Abbott, 6th edn (London: Longmans, 1909).

Kant, I., *Lectures on Ethics*, trans. L. Infield (London: Methuen, 1930).

Keen, W. W., *Animal Experimentation and Medical Progress* (Boston and New York: Houghton Mifflin, 1914).

Kelsen, H., *General Theory of Law and State* (Cambridge, Mass.: Harvard University Press, 1946).

Lapage, G., *Achievement: Some Contributions of Animal Experiments to the Conquest of Disease* (Cambridge: W. Heffer, 1960).

Locke, J., *Some Thoughts Concerning Education*, ed. R. H. Quick (Cambridge University Press, 1898).

Lorenz, K., *On Aggression* (London: Methuen, 1973).

Lorenz, K., *Studies in Animal and Human Behaviour*, trans. R. Martin (London: Methuen, 1970).

Lyons, D., *Ethics and the Rule of Law* (Cambridge University Press, 1984).

Mason, J., and P. Singer, *Animal Factories* (New York: Crown Publishers, 1980).

McCrea, R. C., *The Humane Movement* (New York: Columbia University Press, 1910).

Midgley, M., *Animals and Why They Matter* (Harmondsworth: Penguin Books, 1983).

Mill, J. S., *Ethical Writings*, ed. J. B. Schneewind (New York: Collier Books; London: Collier-Macmillan, 1965).

Montaigne, M. de., *Works*, trans. W. Hazlitt (London: C. Templeman, 1965).

Montaigne, M. de., *A Book of Good Faith*, selections from the *Works* by Gerald Bullett (London: Watts, 1938).

Moore, G. E., *Principia Ethica* (Cambridge University Press, 1962).

Morris, D., *The Naked Ape* (London: Granada Publishing, 1977).

Moss, A. W., *The History of the RSPCA* (London: Cassell, 1961).

Nilsson, G., et al., *Facts About Furs*, 3rd edn (Washington: Animal Welfare Institute, 1980).

Niven, C. D., *History of the Humane Movement* (New York: Transatlantic Arts, 1967).

'Ouida' [pseudonym] *Critical Studies* (London: T. Fisher Unwin, 1900).

Paton, W. D. M., *Man and Mouse: Animals in Medical Research* (Oxford University Press, 1984).

Plato, *The Republic*, trans. A. D. Lindsay (London: J. M. Dent, 1935).

Pound, R., *Social Control Through Law* (New Haven: Yale University Press, 1942).

Primatt, H., *The Duty of Humanity to Inferior Creatures: Deduced from Reason and Scripture* (London: J. Nisbett, 1831).
(Abridged from *A Dissertation on the Duty of Mercy and Sin of Cruelty to Brute Animals*, London: 1776.)

Rawls, J., *A Theory of Justice* (Oxford University Press, 1972).

Reines, B., *Cancer Research on Animals: Impact and Alternatives* (Chicago: National Anti-Vivisection Society, 1986).

Reines, B., *Heart Research on Animals* (Jenkintown, Pa: The American Anti-Vivisection Society, no date).

Rollin, B. E., *Animal Rights and Human Morality* (New York: Prometheus Books, 1981).

Ross, W. D., *The Right and the Good* (Oxford University Press, 1930).

Rousseau, J.-J., *A Discourse on the Origin of Equality*, Preface. Reprinted in various editions (such as 'Great Books of the Western World', ed. R. M. Hutchins, vol. 38, Chicago: William Benton, 1952).

Rowan, A., *Of Mice, Models and Men* (Albany: State University of New York Press, 1984).

Rowan, A., *The Draize Test — A Critique and Proposals for Alternatives* (Washington, DC: Humane Society of the United States, 1980).

RSPCA and the Royal Commission, The (London: Smith, Elder, 1876).

Russell, W. M. S., and R. L. Burch, *The Principles of Humane Experimental Technique* (London: Methuen, 1959).

Salt, H. S., *Animals' Rights Considered in Relation to Social Progress* (London: G. Bell, 1922). Revised edn.

Salt, H. S. (ed.), *The New Charter* (London and New York: G. Bell, 1896).

Sebeok, T. A. (ed.), *How Animals Communicate* (Bloomington and London: Indiana University Press, 1977).

Shaw, George Bernard, *Prefaces* (London: Constable, 1934).

Sidgwick, H., *Practical Ethics: A Collection of Addresses and Essays* (London: Swan Sonnenschein, 1898).

Singer, P., *Animal Liberation* (London: Granada Publishing, 1977).

Singer, P., *The Expanding Circle: Ethics and Sociobiology* (Oxford University Press, 1981).

Singer, P., *In Defence of Animals* (Oxford: Basil Blackwell, 1985).

Skinner, B. F., *The Behavior of Organisms* (New York: Appleton-Century, 1938).

Skinner, B. F., *Walden Two* (New York: Macmillan, 1948).

Smiles, S., *Duty* (London: John Murray, 1907).

Smyth, D. H., *Alternatives to Animal Experiments* (London: Scolar Press, 1978).
'Solicitor' [pseudonym] *The Citizen and the Law* (London: Routledge and Sons, 1934).
Stephens, M. L., *Maternal Deprivation Experiments in Psychology: A Critique of Animal Models* (Jenkintown, Pa: American Anti-Vivisection Society, 1986).
Swain, J., *Brutes and Beasts* (London: Noel Douglas, 1933).
Thorpe, W. H., *Animal Nature and Human Nature* (London: Methuen, 1974).
Tinbergen, N., *Animal Behaviour* (Amsterdam: Time-Life International, 1960).
Tinbergen, N., *The Animal and its World*, 2 vols (London: Allen and Unwin, 1973).
Tolman, E. C., *Purposive Behavior in Animals and Man* (New York: Century, 1932).
Voltaire, *Philosophical Dictionary*, selected and translated by H. T. Woolf (London: George Allen and Unwin, no date).
Whateley, R. (ed.), *Paley's Moral Philosophy* (London: Parker, 1859).
Wilson, E. O., *Sociobiology: The New Synthesis* (Cambridge, Mass., and London: Harvard University Press, 1975).

JOURNALS, PERIODICALS AND REPORTS

Advances in the Study of Behavior.
American Anti-Vivisection Society, Jenkintown, Pa, *The Case Book of Experiments With Living Animals.*
American Fund for Alternatives to Animal Research, *News Abstracts.*
American Journal of Orthodontics, vol. 75, no. 301 (1979).
Animal Behaviour (formerly *British Journal of Animal Behaviour*).
Animal Liberation (Australia).
Animals International (World Society for the Protection of Animals).
Animal Welfare Institute, *Beyond the Laboratory Door* (1985).
Animal Welfare Institute Quarterly (Washington, DC).
ASPCA Reports (New York: The American Society for the Prevention of Cruelty to Animals).
ATLA (Alternatives to Laboratory Animals), Nottingham, England.
California Veterinarian, 1, 1983.
China Reconstructs, vols 33, 34, 35.
Environmental Investigation Agency, London, *Injury, Damage to Health and Cruel Treatment: Present Conditions in the Shipment of Live Fauna* (J. Brookland et al., 1985).
Ethics, vol. 95, no. 1 (Oct. 1984).
Journal of Comparative and Physiological Psychology, vols 55 and 66.
Halsbury's *Statutes of England* (London: Butterworths).
Humane Society of the United States, *Reports.*
International Society for Animal Rights, Clarks Summit, Pa, *Reports.*
Laws of Minnesota.
Mainstream (Animal Protection Institute of America).
Medical Research Modernization Committee (MRMC), USA, *Responding to the Media: Medical Research Question and Answer Handbook.*

National Anti-Vivisection Society, Chicago, *Test Tubes with Whiskers* (J. Diner, 1986).

Peta News (People for the Ethical Treatment of Animals, Washington, DC).

Philosophy, vols 48 and 53.

Psychologists for the Ethical Treatment of Animals (PsyETA), USA, *Position Papers by the Dozen* (Lewiston: 1985).

Report of the Committee on Cruelty to Wild Animals (London: HMSO, 1951).

Report of the Committee on Humane Slaughtering of Animals (London: HMSO, 1904).

Report of the Technical Committee to Enquire into the Welfare of Animals Kept under Intensive Livestock Husbandry Systems (London: HMSO, 1965).

Research Defence Society, *Notes on the Law on Animals in Great Britain (The Act of 1876)*, 2nd edn (London: no date).

RSPCA, *162nd Annual Report, 1985* (Horsham: 1986).

The Animal World, 1869 to end 19th cent. (RSPCA: London).

The Public General Acts etc. (London: HMSO, 1911).

UFAW Handbook on the Care and Management of Farm Animals (Edinburgh and London: Churchill Livingstone, 1971).

Veterinary Annual, Eighteenth Issue (Bristol: John Wright, 1978).

Subject index

Author index

237